12ω

D1525414

BOLLINGEN SERIES LXXXV

Selected Works of Miguel de Unamuno

Volume 2

Selected Works of Miguel de Unamuno

Miguel de Unamuno

The Private World

Selections from the Diario Íntimo
and Selected Letters 1890–1936

*Translated by Anthony Kerrigan, Allen Lacy,
and Martin Nozick*

*Annotated by Martin Nozick with Allen Lacy,
with an Introduction by Allen Lacy*

Bollingen Series LXXXV · 2
Princeton University Press

THIS IS VOLUME TWO OF THE
SELECTED WORKS OF MIGUEL DE UNAMUNO
CONSTITUTING NUMBER LXXXV IN
BOLLINGEN SERIES
SPONSORED BY BOLLINGEN FOUNDATION.
IT IS THE SEVENTH AND LAST VOLUME OF THE
SELECTED WORKS TO APPEAR

Printed in the United States of America by
Princeton University Press
Princeton, N.J.

Table of Contents

Illustrations

(between pages 82 and 83)

Portrait of Unamuno by Ignacio Zuloaga y Zamora. Courtesy of the Hispanic Society of America

Introduction

"IN MOST OF the histories of philosophy that I know," Miguel de Unamuno remarks in the opening pages of *The Tragic Sense of Life in Men and Nations* (1913), the book that brought him the international recognition for which he had ardently thirsted since his youth, "philosophic systems are presented to us as if growing out of one another spontaneously, and their authors, the philosophers, appear as mere pretexts. The inner biography of the philosophers, of the men who philosophized, is assigned a secondary place. And yet it is precisely that inner biography which can mean most to us."

In thus describing the biographical questions which frame the history of philosophy, Unamuno warns his readers that if they, men of flesh and bone like himself, expect to understand his thought they must also explore the inner biography of one who passionately refused to be the mere "pretext" of his ideas. *Thinking* and *being* are inextricably linked to one another in such tight connection that anyone who attempts to separate them not only falsifies both but also denies his own humanity as "the man of flesh and blood, the man who is born, suffers, and dies—above all, who dies; the man who eats and drinks and plays and sleeps and thinks and loves; the man who is seen and heard; one's brother, the real brother." It is Unamuno's insistence on this point that places him solidly in the company of St. Augustine, Pascal, Hamann, Kierkegaard, and other thinkers who have argued, with passion equal to his, for the primacy of concrete human existence over any abstract system of ideas.

It sometimes happens that when the private papers of notable persons are published, they occasion great surprise and astonishment. The well-known diplomat and man of action turns out to have been a mystic. The great spiritual leader indulged himself without apology in the grossest sensual excesses. The world-famous authority on sexuality lived in impotence and died a virgin. The author of a sensitive book on love and friendship ruined his children's lives and was a beast to all who knew him.

Such cases are not unknown, but *The Private World*, this selection of letters and diaries of Miguel de Una-muno, will reveal no astonishing surprises to readers who are familiar with his published work—even though many of the materials presented here deal with an agonizing spiritual crisis he experienced in 1897, a crisis which received no attention from scholars until 1950.

The crisis burst on Unamuno in the spring of 1897 like an explosion, but it is deeply rooted in his personal history, from childhood on. Born in 1864 to a devoutly religious and politically conservative family, he was raised a Roman Catholic. As a youth in Bilbao, in Spain's Basque country, he grew up in a pious at-mosphere in which the great iconographic scenes and personages of the New Testament were incarnate in the rhythms of cultural life. In the town of his birth the dramas of salvation were played out in the midst of common life. During Holy Week, street and church were held together in ancient and predetermined movement. Time was marked by fast and feast, and Christ was crucified anew each spring.

In his adolescence, Unamuno belonged to the Congregación de San Luis Gonzaga, a group of religious
young people who met Sunday mornings to hear Mass
and Sunday evenings for meditations under the direction of a spiritual guide who, Unamuno writes in his
Recuerdos de niñez y de mocedad (*Memoirs of Childhood
and Youth*), "called us sheep times without number
and spoke to us of spiritual pastures." During these
meditations, he dreamed of becoming a saint. But he
also, at the age of fourteen, began to read philosophical
works, immersing himself in such books as the *Filosofía fundamental* of the Catholic apologist Jaime
Balmes, whom he later sharply criticized for his intellectual shallowness and narrow dogmatism. The effect of his reading was to plunge him into the world
of philosophy. With friends he walked along the banks
of the Nervión River in Bilbao, ardently discussing
"the first cause and the ultimate meaning of everything." Of these fledgling efforts at philosophizing, he
later wrote: "I bought a cheap notebook and began to
develop in it a *new* philosophical system, very sym-
metrical, bristling with formulas, and as labyrinthine
as I could possibly make it."

When Unamuno left Bilbao for the University of
Madrid in 1880, two things characterized him: an
unquestioning piety, somewhat tinged with mystical
romanticism derived from his extensive readings of
such curious authors as Ossian, and a deep thirst for
knowledge. His piety soon departed: not long after
arriving in Madrid, he ceased attending Mass. But his
thirst for knowledge sharpened. He became an avid
reader, with special taste for positivistic philosophy,
physiological psychology, and Italian and British poetry. He taught himself German in order to read Hegel
and English in order to read Spencer and Carlyle (both

of whom he subsequently translated), just as two decades later he taught himself Danish in order to read Kierkegaard, becoming one of the first persons outside of Denmark to fathom the extraordinary significance of that solitary Dane. He soon became part of the circle of students and writers who frequented the Ateneo de Madrid, which one of his teachers, Ortí y Lara, once called "the little blasphemy shop on Montera Street." Above all, he read: Krause, Hegel, Kant, Spencer, Schopenhauer, everything he could get his hands on.

In 1884 Unamuno finished his studies at Madrid, presenting a doctoral thesis on the problem of the origin and history of the Basque people. The thesis shows his determination to use scientific method in dealing with this question, and it rejects almost everything that had previously been written about the Basques for failure to formulate the critical problems with sufficient clarity. It also gives evidence of the author's formidable intellectual development: at the age of twenty Unamuno knew eleven languages—Castilian, Basque, Greek, Sanskrit, Latin, Hebrew, Arabic, German, French, Italian, and English—with varying degrees of proficiency, and he had mastered the discipline of philology, a course of study not then offered at the University of Madrid.

After graduating from Madrid, Unamuno returned to Bilbao, where he spent six years in rather precarious economic circumstances, eking out a living by private tutoring, meanwhile writing newspaper articles against those of his fellow Basques who espoused separatism and the replacement of Castilian in their provinces by the Basque language, and making several unsuccessful attempts to gain a teaching appointment in a university. It is clear that during this period, Unamuno was wholly antipathetic toward religion. His own com-

mitments were to materialistic monism, to science, and
to positivism. In a fragment of manuscript written
somewhat prior to 1886, he wrote, "Seek the kingdom
of science and its righteousness, and all the rest will
be added unto you."

But Unamuno's views were not cast in concrete,
and in the late 1880s they became more fluid. He was
engaged to marry his childhood sweetheart, Concepción Lizárraga, as soon as his future became more
secure, and in a letter to her, written sometime before
1890, he reported a disturbing and strangely prescient
dream:

> One night there lowered into my mind one of those dark,
> sad, and mournful dreams which I cannot banish from my
> thoughts, even during moments of happiness during the
> day. I dreamed that I was married, that I had a child, that
> this child died, and that over its body, which seemed to
> be made of wax, I said to my wife: "Behold our love!
> Shortly it will decay: this is the way everything ends."

The significance of the dream is that it raises a profoundly unsettling question for someone committed to
a belief in salvation through positivistic science: how
do you speak of the death of a person, a loved one, in
the language of science? What are the "facts"—stories
about the cessation of movement, the halting of bodily
processes, embalment, entombment, chemical changes,
microbiological events? And what "laws" emerge from
the contemplation of these facts in a detached and ob-
jective manner? The very question is an obscenity, and
it underlines the necessity for some kind of personal,
perhaps even religious, vocabulary for talking about
love and death.

In 1891, Unamuno married Concepción and se-
cured an appointment to the faculty of the University
of Salamanca as a teacher of Greek. He continued to

write newspaper articles, worked assiduously on his novel *Peace in War*, and carried out philological research on the language of ordinary people in their daily lives. Two sons were soon born to the young couple, and then, on January 7th, 1896, a third, Raimundo Jenaro ("Raimundín"), whose tragic illness precipitated Unamuno's intense religious crisis of 1897.

In November 1896 Raimundo contracted a severe case of meningitis which left him hydrocephalic and partially paralyzed, and doomed him to an unconscious existence that lasted until his death in 1902. Unamuno felt on the verge of paralysis himself, was preoccupied with worries over the state of his own heart, and fell into a deep depression, until one night in March 1897, when his wife awoke to find him weeping, and uttered two words—"My child!"—which altered forever the horizons of his life. Writing during his exile in 1925 about his episode, he remarked that in a sense his Concha, the mother of his eight children, was

> my own true mother as well. In a moment of supreme, of abysmal anguish, wracked with superhuman weeping, when she saw me in the claws of the Angel of Nothingness, she cried out to me from the depths of her maternal being, superhuman and divine: "My child!" I discovered then all that God had done for me in this woman, the mother of my children, my own virgin mother, . . . my mirror of holy, divine unconsciousness and eternity.

The words spoken by his wife on that spring night, which in some inexpressible way he saw as the answer to his own "abysmal anguish," his tormented anxiety over the sense of nothingness and meaninglessness provoked in him by his son's condition, were forever engraved on Unamuno's mind. In a letter of January 11th, 1901, to Pedro Corominas, he wrote: "I will never forget the tone with which on a certain occasion

xiv*

Introduction

. . . , on hearing me weep, she exclaimed, 'My child!'
She called me *child*, and it is true: I own that I am her
child, her spiritual child, in not a little of the good that
I have today." These words are enigmatic, but at least
a part of their meaning is that what Concepción said
to him on that night in March 1897 brought Unamuno
to some kind of feeling of his *sonship* before God the
Father, providing him a single paradigmatic moment
to which he could relate many of the traditional con-
ceptions of Christianity, but in a uniquely personal and
private way. The diary which Unamuno kept during
the outworking of his crisis returns again and again
to deep meditation upon the words "Padre nuestro"—
"Our Father."

Unamuno's first impulse was to return by force to
the faith of his childhood. He wrote the rector of the
Congregación de San Luis in Bilbao, Father Juan José
Lecanda, asking for his spiritual guidance and indi-
cating his desire to spend Holy Week in his company.
Lecanda wrote back, advising him to avoid solitude
and inviting him to come to Alcalá de Henares for
Holy Week. Easter that year was on April 18th. Unamuno arrived in Alcalá the Sunday preceding.

In Alcalá, Unamuno read devotional books and the
Gospels, berated himself for the intellectualism of his
previous life, meditated on Christ and the Virgin Mary,
and poured out his feelings in the diary he had begun
to keep in a small, bound notebook. The tone of the
diary, up to a certain point, suggests that it is almost
the story of a converted intellectual—of a man who,
having once given up the language of the Church, its
practice and liturgy, in order to pursue his own secular
intellectual interests, at last returns to the faith, like a
Prodigal Son making his way back to his boyhood
home. The early entries in the diary show Unamuno

attempting to express in familiar, pious, and orthodox terms the significance of his wife's maternal exclamation.

But his effort to work out his salvation within the structure of the Roman Catholic Church in Spain did not succeed. On April 18th he found himself unable to perform his Easter obligation of making confession and receiving Communion. Lamenting his dryness of spirit, he returned to Salamanca, where he continued to pour his inner turmoil into his diary, struggling at great length with the questions of confession and Communion. His references to death (*muerte*) become so frequent that at last he comes to write the word simply as *M*.

The exact nature of Unamuno's religious position after the crisis has been a matter of great controversy. He has been called a thinker with a Protestant head and a Catholic heart; an atheist who dissimulated his disbelief with word-games and verbal tricks; a man who somehow got stuck halfway through a genuine process of conversion; a thinker flawed by a frivolous and unnecessary heterodoxy; Spain's greatest heretic and teacher of heresies; and a genuinely apostolical Christian of the twentieth century, perhaps its greatest. This list does not begin to exhaust the labels pinned on Unamuno—who was impatient of all labels in such matters.

Since questions about what someone *really* believed, apart from what he *said* he believed, are ultimately impossible to settle, I offer here only an interpretation of Unamuno's position which, first, takes seriously the genuineness of the 1897 crisis as it was recorded in his diaries, and, second, gives due consideration to the setting in which Unamuno tried to make himself be heard—Spain at the turn of the century, a country so divided that many of its intellectuals spoke quite seriously of "the two Spains": one liberal and forward-looking and secularist, the other conservative and traditional and clerical-minded.

Quite apart from the religious language in which he sought to express himself, Unamuno's agonized crisis brought him to the sharp recognition, already adumbrated in his dream of the death of a child, that to be authentically human means to live in the presence of death, to understand that mortality is the root of our condition—and to understand further that a great deal of human conduct can be understood as an evasion, a denial, a diversion whereby we seek not to accept the most fundamental reality of all, the fact that we will die.

Unamuno was not, of course, the first thinker in history to place an unflinching and steady meditation on the fact of mortality at the very center of his examination of man and society. Many of the writers of the Old Testament were there before him, as were Pascal and Tolstoy. Later, building on Tolstoy's *The Death of Ivan Ilytch*, Martin Heidegger, who seems not to have known Unamuno's work, argued that human-being was *Sein-zum-Tode*, being-towards-death, and that any self-understanding which is not grounded in this fundamental characteristic of *Dasein*, of that kind of existence which is human existence, is inauthentic—what Unamuno would have called "a vital lie." More recently, in a canon of works of increasing range and depth, climaxing in his posthumous masterpiece *The Denial of Death* (a book which unites psychoanalytic theory with Kierkegaardian ontology in a way that Unamuno would have approved wholeheartedly), the late Ernest Becker developed an understanding of the nature of human existence which dovetails completely with Unamuno's.

To state the points of congruence between these two thinkers, but using Becker's language and terminology, the predicament of all human beings can be stated as follows.

We human beings are born tiny in a world of people with larger bodies and sometimes ambiguous intents. We die without ever quite having gotten over the things that happened to us in early childhood. Between birth and death we live largely by words and symbols, the most urgent of which deal with the nasty little secret separating us from the rest of animal creation. We will die, *and we know it*. We are contingent creatures, and we have such an uncomfortable, intestinal knowledge of our contingency that we develop a panoply of cultural symbols, rituals, and institutions offering the illusion of perpetuity. Not daring to peer into the Abyss, we have invented culture, mechanisms of comfort and consolation which give meaning and significance to our existence.

This argument can be advanced into the territory of social history, via an exploration of what might be called the natural history of evil. To call the human lot secure is to falsify reality. Even apart from human-caused evil, creation is a "nightmare spectacular," the earth a blood-soaked arena where organisms gorge and feed on one another. Bosch and Goya are perhaps our truest painters. Ernest Becker believed that he detected "the rumble of panic underneath everything." Living beings are animated digestive tracts, equipped on one end with teeth capable of ripping up flesh, on the other with organs of excretion and stench.

For each of us, our own mortality is the greatest of personal evils, but culture provides us an apparent chance to mitigate contingency, to lose our sense of individual frailty and insignificance in larger affairs.

Since the culture to which we belong gives us meaning, we may be driven to absolutize it—to deny that it is as contingent as we are. Since our own cultural system gives us value and self-esteem, we conclude that other systems must be perverse and evil. Throughout history, humans have lashed out in all directions at other human beings who live by different mythologies of significance. Wars may seem to have their ultimate causes in politics or in economics, but only to those who are philosophically or psychologically myopic: politics and economics are part of a larger system of culture whose deepest roots lie in the denial of death.

This summary of Becker's *The Denial of Death* is also an almost perfect summary of Unamuno. He knew these things, albeit dimly, long before the 1897 crisis, and in the crisis itself they loomed with terrifying clarity in his consciousness. And he stated them magnificently in his last public act, on October 12th, 1936, when before an audience assembled for a solemn ceremony at the University of Salamanca he denounced General José Millán Astray—and by implication Generalísimo Franco and the Falange—for his necrophilous battle cry "*Viva la muerte!*"—"Long live death!—and for his odd desire to find psychological relief "in seeing mutilation around him."

But in his diary, on the heels of his spiritual crisis, Unamuno couched his meditation on death in traditional Christian theological terms of the resurrection of the flesh and the immortality of the soul. During the summer of 1897 he read devotional works, scholarly books (mostly by Protestants) on the history of Church doctrine, and the Bible, especially the Gospels

and the Acts of the Apostles. In October, with a letter
to Juan Arzadun, he began to attempt to communicate
directly to his friends, using strongly Biblical language, the content of his awakening. This period might
be called the iconographic stage of Unamuno's career:
he announces his intention to write a work called
Evangelical Meditations, composed of essays about New
Testament characters and incidents. In letters to various of his friends, he lists several such essays: "Jesus
and the Woman of Samaria," "The Evil of the Century," "The Social Kingdom of Jesus," "Nicodemus
the Pharisee," "The Prayer of Dimas," and "St. Paul
on the Areopagus." Of these, only "Nicodemus" was
published; it had been delivered at a meeting of the
Atheneum of Madrid in November of 1899.

Unamuno's friends, many of them atheists or ag-
nostics in religious matters, liberals and secularists in
political and economic matters, were not especially
sympathetic toward his apparent attempt to convert
them. He wrote Pedro Jiménez Ilundain in January
of 1898 about his crisis and his proposed *Evangelical
Meditations*, but Ilundain's reply in April was sharp.
Noting certain Protestant and heterodox elements in
Unamuno's letter, he pointed out that this "isn't something generally desired in Spain. *I fear greatly that
your words are being lost in the void*." Catholics would
not trust him, and non-Catholics would be indifferent
to what he said. Ilundain then questioned the use of
Biblical quotations and references to Jesus and other
Biblical figures as a suitable vehicle of communication.
He then suggested that Unamuno say what he had to
say in novels or essays—"not so obviously religious"—
and that in his criticism of tendencies in modern society
he not use as his "only base of argument the an-

nouncement that such things are condemned by Christ and his Gospel."

There is little doubt that Ilundain's warning that Unamuno's words were being "lost in the void" hit its mark. For eight months, Unamuno did not reply, and when he did, on December 23rd, 1898, it was to announce, first of all, that he was studying economics, and second, that he had begun a drama about "the struggle between the attraction of glory and the love of inner peace." The announcement of this drama marks the beginning of a new stage in Unamuno's attempt to communicate the sentiments that grew out of his personal crisis. The works on Biblical themes largely cease—with a few notable exceptions such as *The Christ of Velázquez* (1920)—and there begins an incredibly varied and prolific authorship: myriad occasional essays, book reviews, poems, novels, plays, prologues, public lectures, and a host of short stories. Again and again, Unamuno returned to religious questions in such works as *The Tragic Sense of Life* (1913) and *The Agony of Christianity* (1925, 1931), but he resorted to paradoxical, often ambiguous language designed to confound anyone who would catalogue him under some handy tag, such as "believer" or "nonbeliever." His writings, by his own account, were meant to raise questions, not to give answers; they were not "bread" but "yeast."

Throughout his long career after his crisis, Unamuno labored hard to avoid attracting an audience that was identified with any particular group. In *Tragic Sense of Life* he wrote:

> But the truth is that my work—my mission, I was about to say—is to shatter the faith of men, left, right, and center, their faith in affirmation, their faith in negation, their faith in abstention, and I do so from faith in faith itself. My

purpose is to war on all those who submit, whether to
Catholicism, or to rationalism, or to agnosticism. My aim
is to make all men live a life of restless longing.

In this position, Unamuno has at least two powerful
allies, one of them a profoundly Christian thinker who
has had an enormous influence on even secular philosophy in the twentieth century and the other a Lutheran theologian, martyred under Hitler, whose last
years had been spent in meditating over the peculiar
status of Christians living in a post-Christian age. Søren Kierkegaard was avidly read by Unamuno, and
the reason is obvious. In his intuition that true Christianity was almost impossible in "Christendom," in a
society where people become "Christians" in the same
way that they become citizens, merely by being born,
Kierkegaard resorted to what he called indirect communication, addressing his readers (what few there
were during his lifetime) by means of an elaborately
contrived system of fictitious authors representing
sometimes contradictory points of view. And the words
of the imprisoned Dietrich Bonhoeffer, written shortly
before his execution in 1945, serve to illumine Unamuno's decision to offer his fellow human beings yeast
instead of bread, even though bread is a much more
easily marketed commodity. Writes Bonhoeffer:

> Atonement and redemption, regeneration, the Holy Ghost,
> the love of our enemies, the cross and resurrection, life in
> Christ and Christian discipleship—all these things have
> become so problematic and so remote that we hardly dare
> to speak of them any more. In the traditional rite and
> ceremonies we are groping after something new and rev-
> olutionary without being able to understand it or utter it
> yet. That is our own fault. During these years the Church
> has fought for self-preservation as though it were an end
> in itself, and has thereby lost its chance to speak a word
> of reconciliation to mankind and to the world at large. So

Introduction

our traditional language must perforce remain powerless
and remain silent, and our Christianity today will be confined to praying for and doing right by our fellow men.

These words of Bonhoeffer—with which Unamuno
would probably have agreed from late in 1898 onward—make an admirable commentary on the materials contained in Unamuno's diary and in many of the
letters contained in this volume.

Unamuno's *Diario íntimo*, most of which was written
in the months immediately following his crisis, in five
bound notebooks, was circulated (except for the brief
and scanty entries from 1899 and 1902 contained in
the fifth notebook) to several of the author's closest
friends between 1898 and 1901, then hidden among
the papers in his study, forgotten by all save Don
Miguel himself. In 1927, during his exile, Unamuno
wrote Salomé, his eldest daughter, an anxious letter
about the possibility that she or his eldest son, Fernando, might have come across it in his absence. Its
existence was unknown to the growing band of Unamuno scholars until 1944, when Unamuno's letters to
his boyhood friend Juan Arzadun were published in
the Argentine review *Sur*, including the letter of October 30th, 1897, where he wrote, "Perhaps one day
I'll give you the notebooks in which for the past seven
months I've been writing everything that comes to
mind, everything that I feel and think and discover
inside myself." The first scholar to deal with Unamuno's religious crisis was Antonio Sánchez Barbudo,
in a rather unsympathetic series of articles published
in *Hispanic Review* and *La Revista Hispánica Moderna*
and later in his book *Estudios sobre Unamuno y Machado* (Madrid, 1960).

It was the Peruvian scholar and critic Armando Zubizarreta who, while working in the Unamuno Casa-Museo in Salamanca on his doctoral dissertation, a study of *How a Novel Is Made* (*Cómo se hace una novela*), discovered among Unamuno's papers the notebooks containing the *Diary*. It was not until 1966 that the *Diary* itself was published, but Zubizarreta published an account of its content and of the circumstances surrounding its writing in an article appearing in the *Mercurio Peruano* in April, 1957 and again in his critical study *Tras las huellas de Unamuno* (Madrid, 1960).

The *Diario íntimo* is by no means a polished piece of work. It was written *ad se ipsum*, even though he was willing for a time to share it with intimate friends, few of whom were sympathetic with the attempt to return to the faith of his childhood which is recorded in its pages. Even in the abridged version which is given in the present volume, few readers will fail to notice that it is obsessive, extremely repetitious, and often self-conscious in a rather theatrical way, nor that it lacks the literary merit that, even for relentless non-believers, distinguishes such other examples of confessional writing as St. Augustine's *Confessions* and Pascal's *Pensées*. But it is an important document for two reasons. First, it announces many of the themes that were to occupy Unamuno in later years, especially in *The Tragic Sense of Life* and *The Agony of Christianity*. Second, it provides a vivid picture of a sensitive and deeply intellectual man—deeply intellectual despite his negative words about "intellectualism"—who, in his inability to return to the neat simplicities of orthodox Christianity and in his recognition of the inadequacies of "modern and progressive" thought, may perhaps be the first post-modern man.

Introduction

Accompanying the *Diary* in this volume are some sixty-four letters, spanning the last forty-seven years of Unamuno's life, from 1890, when he was living on dreams and occasional tutoring jobs, seeking (for some time, in vain) a university teaching appointment and looking forward to marriage and fatherhood, until 1936, when he was secure in his international fame as Spain's most committed man of letters, but bereft of his wife and deep in despair over the tragic course of Spanish political history.

Unamuno was a prodigious letter-writer, although from 1910 onwards he complained that the press of his other duties forced him to neglect his correspondence—and he published in various Spanish and Latin American newspapers the kind of commentary on his readings and on the events of the day that a few years earlier would have gone into personal letters. He saved most of the letters he received, and many of those to whom he wrote saved his letters as well. His correspondents included close friends such as Juan Arzadun and Pedro Jiménez Ilundain, complete strangers, and such celebrated figures as Antonio Machado, Rubén Darío, José Ortega y Gasset, Jorge Luis Borges, and Giovanni Papini. By far the greater part of his correspondence (amounting to nearly forty thousand letters) remains unpublished, but those letters that have appeared in print (many of them in Latin America rather than in Spain, because of the Spanish political climate during the Franco years) are sufficient to fill a good-sized library shelf. Of necessity, therefore, the letters in this volume have been selected to represent the range of Unamuno's philosophical, religious, political, educational, and purely personal concerns. They reflect his early flirtation with socialism, his constant preoccupation with religion from the late 1890s onward, his sturdy political convictions, and his ever-shifting and ambivalent attitudes toward his native country, which he loved, often to his deep distress.

No one could ever accuse Unamuno of keeping his personal life and his public life in separate compartments. His public writings are filled with the intimate details of his life, sometimes directly, sometimes by allusion. And his private correspondence is seldom purely personal. Even with his close friends, the act of writing letters to them provided him with a pulpit from which to excoriate the Jesuits, lambaste devious politicians of every party and sect, lament the existence of stupid kings and moronic but powerful dictators, bemoan the mediocrity of public education, condemn German technocratic militarism and anti-Semitism, mock French literature for its triviality and Teutonic scholarship for its pedantry (although he held such German Protestant historians as Adolf von Harnack in high esteem), and point out the deficiencies of the separatist movements in Catalonia and the Basque provinces. He also used his personal correspondence as a sounding board for his work-in-progress, sometimes discussing books he planned but never wrote. (His biographer Emilio Salcedo lists over twenty such unwritten works, including a *Tristan and Isolde* and a book called *The Tragic Resentment of Life*, on which he was working during the last months of his life in 1936, when he was under house arrest in Salamanca at the order of Generalísimo Franco.)

Unamuno was a man of powerful, almost volcanic, energies; many of his letters show him in full eruption. He was also equipped with an indomitable ego and sometimes transgressed the boundaries of restrained behavior—in, for example, the two letters he wrote one day apart, in 1900, to the noted critic Leopoldo Alas ("Clarín"), where, at enormous length, he demanded to be noticed, even though at that stage in his career his accomplishments were slender. Not everything in Unamuno's letters is admirable, but much is. His critique of the illusions of progress was prescient, as was his distrust of Germany's intentions towards the rest of Europe. And he was capable of great tenderness, as in his letter to Matilde Brandau de Ross after the tragic death of her young husband Luis Ross, a Chilean for whom Unamuno felt the sort of affection that Socrates felt toward his youthful admirers.

The final letters in this volume are more personal and less political than the earlier ones, but the volcano was merely dormant, not extinct. In October of 1936, during a public ceremony in the Paraninfo or ceremonial hall of the University of Salamanca, Unamuno erupted in a fiery and deeply moving denunciation of the death-exalting and anti-intellectual tendencies of Franco's Falangist movement. He was not permitted to appear again in public, and when his voice was stilled for all time on the last day of 1936, the Falange buried him with its military rites, attempting most unjustly to claim him as its own. But the "last lecture" he delivered in October in the ceremonial hall to an audience that included Franco's wife was one of the most magnificent moments in his life. Thus we print here, as an epilogue to this volume, Luis Portillo's splendid account of the occasion.

There is, unfortunately, no biography of Unamuno in English that does justice to the complexity of the man. Until there is, it is hoped that the readers of this version of his *Diary* and this selection of his letters will find in these pages a fair picture of Don Miguel de Unamuno y Jugo, his life and times.

ALLEN LACY

Linwood, New Jersey
September, 1982

Chronology

Titles of works published in English are italicized.

1864	September 29; Miguel de Unamuno y Jugo born in Bilbao.
1874	Witnesses the Carlist siege of Bilbao.
1875-1880	Secondary education in his native city.
1880-1884	University of Madrid; doctorate in 1884.
1884-1891	Gives private lessons and does other teaching in Bilbao; writes articles for local newspapers; prepares for permanent teaching position.
1891	Marries Concepción Lizárraga; wins chair of Greek at the University of Salamanca, where he will live for the rest of his life except for the years of exile.
1895	The essays of *En torno al casticismo* (On Authentic Tradition) published separately; published as a book in 1902.
1897	Year of the religious crisis; starts writing the unpublished *Diario*; publishes first novel, *Paz en la guerra (Peace in War)*.
1898	Writes play *La esfinge* (The Sphinx).
1899	Publication of "Nicodemo el fariseo" (*Nicodemus the Pharisee*) and *De la ense-*

ñanza superior en España (On University Teaching in Spain); writes play, *La venda* (The Blindfold).

1900   Named rector of the university; publishes *Tres ensayos* (Three Essays).

1902   Publishes *En torno al casticismo* (On Authentic Tradition) in book form; the novel *Amor y pedagogía* (Love and Pedagogy); the travel sketches *Paisajes* (Landscapes).

1903   *De mi país* (From My Native Region).

1905   *La vida de Don Quijote y Sancho (The Life of Don Quixote and Sancho)*.

1907   *Poesías* (Poems).

1908   *Recuerdos de niñez y de mocedad* (Memories of Childhood and Youth).

1910   *Mi religión y otros ensayos breves (My Religion and Other Short Essays)*.

1911   *Por tierras de Portugal y de España* (Through Regions of Portugal and Spain), travel book; *Soliloquios y conversaciones* (Soliloquies and Conversations), essays; *Rosario de sonetos líricos* (Rosary of Lyrical Sonnets).

1912   *Contra esto y aquello* (Against This and That), essays; 1898 correspondence with Angel Ganivet published as *El porvenir de España* (The Future of Spain).

1913   Publication of Unamuno's central work *Del sentimiento trágico de la vida en los* hombres y en los pueblos *(On the Tragic Sense of Life in Men and Nations); El espejo de la muerte* (The Mirror of Death).

1914   Dismissed from rectorship; publication of the novel *Niebla (Mist)*.

1917   *Abel Sánchez*, novel.

1918   Publication of the long poem *El Cristo de Velázquez (The Christ of Velázquez); Tres novelas ejemplares y un prólogo (Three Exemplary Novels and a Prologue)*.

1922   *La tía Tula (Aunt Tula)*, novel; *Soledad* (Solitude) and *Raquel encadenada* (Rachel in Chains), both plays.

1922   *Andanzas y visiones españolas* (Spanish Travels and Vistas).

1923   *Rimas de dentro* (Rhymes from Within), poetry.

1924   21 February: Unamuno leaves Salamanca for exile in Fuerteventura, one of the Canary Islands, where he arrives 10 March. Escapes from the island and arrives in Paris 28 July. Publication of *Teresa*, poetry.

1925   Middle of August: Unamuno moves to Hendaye where he spends the remainder of his exile. Publication of *De Fuerteventura a París* (From Fuerteventura to Paris), sonnets of exile. *L'Agonie du christianisme (The Agony of Christianity)* published in the French translation of Jean

Cassou; in 1931 it is published in Spanish as *La agonía del cristianismo*.

1926   *Sombras de sueño* (Dream Shadows), *El Otro (The Other)*, both plays.

1927   Publication in Buenos Aires of *Cómo se hace una novela (How a Novel Is Made)*, which appeared in 1926 in Cassou's French translation as *Comment on fait un roman*.

1928   *Romancero del destierro* (Ballads of Exile).

1929   *El hermano Juan o el mundo es teatro* (Brother John or The World Is a Stage), a play.

1930   9 February: Unamuno crosses the border back to Spain. Publication of *Dos artículos y dos discursos* (Two Articles and Two Speeches).

1931   14 April: Spain is declared a Republic; Unamuno reappointed rector of the University of Salamanca.

1933   Publication of *San Manuel Bueno, mártir y tres historias más* (*St. Manuel Bueno, Martyr, and Three More Stories*); 14 July: death of his oldest daughter Salomé.

1934   May 15: Unamuno's wife dies; 30 September: Unamuno is retired as a professor and named lifetime rector of the university.

1936   Receives honorary doctorate from Oxford in late February. The Civil War

I
The Diary

Notebook 1

+

HOLD ALL worldly wisdom and all human self-satisfaction in less esteem.

The mystery of freedom is the very mystery of reflective consciousness and of reason. Man is nature's consciousness, and his true freedom consists in his aspiration towards grace. That man is free who is able to receive divine grace and be saved by it.

One must seek for the truth of things, not their reason, and truth is sought in humility.

Leopardi, Amiel, *Obermann*—

With my reason I was seeking a rational God, who kept disappearing, being purely an idea, and who turned into the Nothingness-God which pantheism leads to and into the pure phenomenism which is the root of my intuition of the void. I did not feel the living God who dwells within us and reveals himself to us through acts of love, not through the vain conceits of pride. But then He called out to my heart and put me in the fear of death.

Know thyself.

"But if they should hear about themselves from you, they cannot say, 'The Lord lies!' What else is it for them to hear from you about themselves except to know themselves?"

St. Augustine, Confessions, X, 3.

I had taken note of that proposition of Spinoza which says that the free man thinks about everything but death, since his life is a meditation on life itself, not on death.

And I did not understand that to become a free man in spirit and in truth it was necessary to become a slave and, once having become a slave, to await from the Lord the freedom which permits us to live in meditation on Life itself, on Christ Jesus.

He who wants everything to happen that does happen brings it about that everything happens as he wishes. Human omnipotence, by means of resignation. But I did not understand that such resignation is reached only through grace, through faith and love.

For a long time in my study two drawings, one a portrait of Spencer and the other my own drawing of Homer, beneath which I had copied out those verses from the *Odyssey* that read "the gods weave and accomplish the destruction of men in order that their posterity may have something to sing." And that is the quintessence of the vain spirit of paganism, of the sterile aestheticism which kills all spiritual substance and all beauty.

I have often written about the difference between reason and truth, without understanding that difference very well. In this world, amid the disputes to which God delivered us we may manage by reason to prove that we are right—but truth is wisdom and peace.

*4**

Just as God made procreation and nutrition matters of delight, so that we gladly do what we might not do out of mere duty, so He added the delight of vainglory in works of art and science so that we might carry them out. But just as that carnal delight, that concupiscence, causes many to die, so is this spiritual delight also a cause of death when it feeds on spiritual pride. Happy are those who raise children with their gaze fixed on the service and glory of God; happy are those who spread their thoughts abroad for the glory of the Lord and the good of their neighbor!

Through humility one reaches the wisdom of the simple, which is to know how to live in peace with oneself and with the world, to live in the peace of the Lord, trusting in truth, not reason.

I enter on faith with the pride of my past years of sleep, so that everything turns to arranging my own vainglory, making God serve me rather than me Him. I was thinking about famous converts and about the vanities of a showy Catholicism. I ask God to strip me of myself.

I would not like to make truth into reason, to turn ineffable truth into reason subject to the figures of logic. I would ask, not argue, that your name be hallowed, Lord, not with vain words but with acts, and with words that be also acts, words of love.

I have never been able to be a sectarian. I have always battled against every kind of dogmatism, allegedly for the sake of liberty. But really it was from pride, in order not to have to get in line, recognize a superior, or discipline myself. Now I want to listen to life and death in the army of the humble, joining my prayers to theirs in the holy freedom of the obedient.

I have tempted the Lord, asking of Him something prodigious, an open miracle, with my eyes closed to the living miracle of the universe and to the miracle of the change in me.

The comedy of life. A stubborn tendency to sink into sleep and to play a role without seeing reality. And there comes a point when one plays the comedy all alone, plays the comedian for oneself alone, wanting to keep up a pretense before Thee, who reads our hearts. Not even to ourselves are we sincere and simple! That's how blind we are, and hidden from our own eyes.

To know ourselves in the Lord is the beginning of salvation.

I must be careful not to fall into the comedy of religious conversion and not to let my tears be theatrical ones. No one, Lord, can deceive You.

"Often, out of very contempt of glory a man derives an emptier glory. No longer, therefore, does he glory in contempt of vainglory: he does not despise it, inasmuch as he glories over it."

St. Augustine, *Confessions*, X, 63.

Socialism and Communism. The holy communism of Communion, of all taking part in the same God: Communion in spirit.

What makes a community of a people but its religion? What unites them *beneath* history, in the dark course of their humble daily labors? Self-interest only appears to be the link that ties them together; it is religion that produces communal spirit. Religion creates a nation and is the spiritual fatherland.

Childhood. I've often thought that God does not destroy us because of the just men of Sodom.

"Suffer little children to come unto me." "Whosoever shall not receive the kingdom of God as a little child shall in no wise enter therein."

From D. J. J.

I don't want to be anything nor have anyone remember me. Work? What for? I immure myself here among a few old men, and—on with life? My aspirations are already satisfied. A nihilist.

At the beginning I asked only for peace and serenity, thinking only of myself. But one day, at Alcalá, opening *The Imitation of Christ*, I read: "I have no words to speak but only this: I have sinned, Lord, I have sinned. Have mercy on me and forgive me." And I realized immediately that I should have asked forgiveness, not peace. Forgiveness and nothing else! Until then it had not occurred to me clearly that I had sinned much against the Lord.

When I prayed, my heart recognized the God my reason denied.

If I come to believe, what better proof of the truth of faith? It will be a miracle, a true miracle, a testimonial to the truth of faith.

Diary

The tears I wept when the crisis broke upon me were the tears of anguish, not those of repentance. The latter cleanse, the former irritate and excite.

———

How often I have written about living in eternity and not in time, about living amid what is permanent rather than in passing events—but with no true feeling!

———

Tonight, musing here on the balcony in the calm of Alcalá, feeling myself drying up and thinking about death, I had this idea: I have no soul, no spiritual substance; I have only states of consciousness which will vanish along with the body which sustains them. I have lost my soul, or rather I have a soul which has died from sin. It is a carnal soul, not a spiritual one.

Return to me my soul, O Lord.

———

One act, only one act of fervent charity, of warm affection, of true love, and I am saved. But what will bring me to this one act when my spirit contains only concepts? I cannot weep.

Acts, acts, acts!

———

"The true dates in the life of a man are the days and hours when he acquired a new view of God. Perhaps for all men, but surely at least for all reflective and virtuous men, all of life is a continuously growing sense of God. It may occur that in any given year—this year—we know no more theology than the year before, but we have indubitably acquired new knowledge of God. Time itself unfolds the mystery of His perfections: the workings of grace make us know Him even better."

Fr. Faber, *The Precious Blood*, I.

———

And Faber continues: "Ancient truths are strengthened, obscure truths are clarified, and other new truths appear on the horizon of our intelligence. But a new concept of God is like a new birth."

———

What greater miracle than that there should have been millions of men over long generations who have believed in things incomprehensible, in mysteries repugnant to human reason? It is a miracle, a miracle of collective humility. Why do so many men believe? Why is reason not stronger?

The truth of faith is proved by its existence, and by its existence alone.

———

In conversations it often happens that a point is reached which people call philosophy: the shortness of life, the vanity of all things. And then someone almost always says, "Better not think about it or life will be impossible."

Nevertheless, it is better to think about it, for only then is it possible to live our lives awake and not in the dream of life.

———

In us lives the memory of the people we have loved who have died. But when we die, will that memory die? We will die, and the memory of us will remain on this earth. But what is that memory? When those who piously preserve memory of us themselves die, our memory will die on the earth.

I leave behind a name: is it any more than a name? What more can I be than the fictitious characters I have created in my imagination? What more is Cervantes today, on this earth, than Don Quixote?

———

I desire consolation in life and the power to think serenely on death. Give me faith, my God, for if I manage to have faith in another life, then the afterlife exists.

Death is a mystery? But then birth is too. How can men come from men?

To know how to weep: what great wisdom! The wisdom of simplicity, of substance, and of life.

Gratias agimus tibi, propter magnam gloriam tuam. We give Thee thanks for Thy great glory, thanks for being allowed to see it. Have we really understood these words the faithful sing? To give God thanks, as for a beneficence He has granted us, for the gift of His glory; not for his bounty and goodness towards us, not for having snatched us out of nothingness into being, not for having made us His children, but thanks for His glory, for that glory which was all of life before the creation of the world.

In the midst of this drought, this inability to break out weeping and find some relief, why do I feel this tendency to pray, even though it be coldly and mechanically? Why this seeking out the temple, this soft inclination towards the things which gave me a spiritual life as a child?

Since death is the natural end of life, the natural way of life is a passage towards death, and its natural light the light at the end. Life can be understood only in the light of death. To prepare oneself to die is to live naturally.

Simplicity, simplicity! Give me, Lord, simplicity, that I not play out the comedy of conversion, not play it as a spectacle, but do it for myself alone.

Philosophers appear in a series. One disappears as another appears to destroy what his predecessor built up. [. . .]

The Church is a permanent unfolding. All her saints and all her doctors live in her, and each new member is added to those who came before. And to her thinkers and poets and saints is joined the multitude which prays and loves in silence. The high speculative contemplation which love wrings from those of her sons who glorify the faith rises up from the common prayer of the humble. Beneath the fiery words of each of her doctors breathe the tears of the humble, the abnegations of the simple, the feelings of the people. In religion, science and poetry and action are unified.

The life of the Church is a fact, a great and astonishing fact. It traverses the ages in defiance of mere discursive reason. The Absurd lives on and, what's more, gives life to the existence of the humble.

To live, to truly live, to live spontaneously, without ulterior motives, to live in order to die so as to go on living: that is what is gained with the holy simplicity God grants those who humble themselves.

I went as far as intellectual atheism, to the point of imagining a world without God, but now I see that I always kept a hidden faith in the Virgin Mary. In moments of affliction I would find myself mechanically exclaiming, "Mother of Mercy, help me!" I even sketched out a little poem about a prodigal son who abandons his maternal religion. As he takes his leave of his spiritual home, the Virgin accompanies him to the threshold where she says a sad farewell and gives him counsel for his journey. From time to time the prodigal son turns around, and there, still standing at the beginning of the long and dusty road which leads to the horizon before him, he sees the Virgin, standing in the doorway, watching her son go away. And when he finally returns in weary disarray, he finds her still waiting for him at the threshold of the ancient house; she opens her arms to him and leads him to the Father.

Of all mysteries, Mary is the sweetest. Woman is the basis of tradition in all societies. She is calm in the midst of turmoil, repose in struggle. The Virgin is simplicity, the mother of tenderness.

The Man-God was born of woman, out of the calm part of humanity, out of its simplicity.

One hears blasphemies against God and Christ, mixed with obscene expressions, but one hears no blasphemies against the Virgin. Christ said that sins against Him would be forgiven but not sins against the Holy Spirit, and one of the greatest sins against the Holy Spirit is to insult His Wife and blaspheme against her.

"Amends can be made for all of life's actions, except for the last one (death), which no process, not even a supernatural one, can undo. That last act determines all the rest and gives them their definitive meaning."

Fr. Faber

I can already think calmly of death. Thank you, Lord.

Sedes sapientiae. Mark well, *sapientiae*, not *scientiae*: throne of wisdom. Mary, the mystery of humility and love, is the throne of all wisdom. Empires, theories, doctrines, glories, entire worlds all pass away while, in eternal calm, eternal Virginity and eternal Maternity, the mystery of purity and the mystery of fertility, remain.

Sedes sapientiae; ora pro nobis.

12*

Notebook 1
[. . .]

Only one man, as far as the Gospels are concerned, was clearly saved. Only one man is canonized in the Gospels. To only one man does Jesus say: *mecum eris in paradiso*. And this man was a thief, a sinner of whom we know only that he was a thief. He had a bad life and a saint's death, even as Judas led the life of an apostle and died in despair. It would be well to meditate a great deal on the contrast between the life of Judas and that of Dimas.

Why was the thief saved? "Dost not thou fear God, seeing thou art in the same condemnation?" "And we indeed justly; for we receive the due reward of our deeds: but this man hath done nothing amiss." [Luke 23:40-41] He humbly recognizes his sin and the innocence of Jesus, and he believes he himself deserves the punishment he suffers. And then he turns to the Lord and says, "Lord, remember me when thou comest into thy kingdom." Herein lies his act of faith.

———

Holy Wednesday

A deathly calm, an enormous aridity. I see my case only intellectually. All of my feeling has dried up. I think about surrendering myself to the Lord, I mean to do so, but is it not wrong of me not to stir myself up into feeling something?

———

Maundy Thursday

Learn to live in God and you will not fear death, for God is immortal.

———

For years now what has most of my talk added up to? No more than gossip. I have spent my days judging others and accusing almost everyone else of foolishness. I was at the center of my universe—and thus, my fear

*13**

of death. I came to believe that the world would come to an end at my death.

Often I have observed that the sad thing about all worldly conversations is that they are not dialogues at all but intermingled monologues. Those who talk remain strangers to one another, each one following his own line of thought. No one listens with benevolent attention. Each one is impatient to speak his piece, which always seems more important than anyone else's. Almost never is there any mingling of feelings, any unity of intent, any communion of spirit, in what is said. The frequency of interruption in any worldly conversation is worth noting as a symptom of a very painful disease.

It would not be thus if one conversed in God, simply and humbly, making conversation an act of love toward one's neighbor, and trying not to talk of oneself nor set oneself up as the center of the universe.

That holy mingling of feelings of which I have sometimes dreamed is to be achieved only in God.

Never argue. Christ did not argue. He preached and avoided all argument. No use refuting others' opinions, for such refutation merely indicates a desire to appear stronger than your neighbor and to dominate him. Set forth your opinion with sincerity and simplicity, and allow the truth to work in its own way on your brother's mind. Let the truth win him over instead of besting him yourself. The truth you proffer is not yours; it is above you and sufficient unto itself.

The Social Question.

The worst evil of poverty is that it dissipates energy, stupefying the spirit and preventing it from looking after its own salvation and the glory of God. Care for the morrow prevents taking thought for eternity. Rare today are the poor who live like lilies of the field or the birds of the air, without worrying about what they will eat and drink and letting each day bring its daily care. At the same time, poverty, or rather, wretched misery, incites discontent and rancor and leads to theft and perjury, as it says in Ecclesiasticus.

For all these reasons, the poor in spirit are called blessed, even if they are rich in fortune. Economic well-being can be a blessing insofar as it frees man from the concern for our daily bread and allows him to turn to himself and think of his eternal salvation and that of his fellow human beings. A person with enough to provide for his material life can more freely look to his spiritual life. Happy are those who have wealth as if they didn't.

But wealth, which should be a blessing, often becomes a curse; that which should set us free of the world often makes us even more its prisoner.

Poverty, when it means having only the necessities, is a blessing, even a fortune in itself. Actual poverty is a disaster, but then wealth can also be disastrous.

As it is with individuals, so with nations. Progress and culture and a wealth of material means are the same for a nation as for an individual. The result should be to free them to dedicate their energies to the glory of God. But wealth can be used as badly as Adam used his freedom.

Progress, a godly gift, works to the perdition of many nations which do not use it for their salvation, even when their souls are freed from natural animality. And thus civilizations and nations fall into decadence.

Culture is a gift of God when it is used for His greater glory.

Justice elevates people. It is sin that makes nations wretched.

There is no other philosophy of history.

———————

"What is truth?" Pilate asked Jesus, and without waiting for a reply he went forth to speak to the Jews and tell them he found Christ without fault. What is truth? That is the question put by all those who see what is just and right but do not have the strength to accomplish it. This is the question implicit in every form of rationalism, which seeks truth in reason rather than in faith. "Blessed is he whom truth herself teacheth, not by figures and voices that pass, but as it is." (*Imitation of Christ*, I, III, 1.)

Thy Kingdom come: the Kingdom of Truth, not of reason.

———————

My rebellion against faith began with Hell. The first point of faith I rejected was the belief in Hell, as being an immoral absurdity.

I have always been terrified by the thought of annihilation, nullification, the nothingness beyond the tomb. Why a further Hell, I asked myself. The thought tormented me. But then I said to myself: in Hell, one suffers—but one lives. The point is to live, to be, even if in suffering.

The terror of nothingness is a pagan terror. Give me, my God, faith in Hell. If I can believe in it, it exists.

Immense mystery of Hell! Eternal suffering! But it is a suffering which, outside the sufferer, is not positive, a suffering which glorifies God. A terrible mystery, and perhaps the touchstone of true faith.

We ought to believe in Hell. This is the whole point. Does it exist? We ought to believe in it, and when we believe in it it will exist. And if by believing in it it exists, then it must exist.

The impenetrable darkness beyond the tomb for our natural light, for our reason, ought to be a supernatural light, the light of our life.

A life which is pure darkness and continuous death and dissolution forever and forever and forever, centuries upon centuries and centuries.

Each one of us is the confluence of an eternity and an immensity. Everything is linked together, and everything works on everything else by direct or indirect action: primary, secondary, tertiary—milliary. The movement of the farthest star is part of the action of our earth. We are products of the workings of all the concomitants of our acts and of all the antecedents of these concomitants and the concomitants of these antecedents. Each and every phenomenon is the result of the entire life of the universe, an effect of the single Cause.

In the same manner every act of ours affects and works upon others and these others on others still, thus extending toward the immensity of everlastingness. The fall of a single pebble would be enough to topple an immense planetary system in unstable equilibrium—and even if it does not topple it or have any visible effect, must it not modify the whole of it?

Should we really be surprised by the idea of the infinite effect of our guilt, of the infinitude of our sin?

An ocean of bitterness surrounds all humanity, and each new sin embitters that ocean all the more, and that greater bitterness extends to all men. Does it seem that the additional bitterness of one more sin in such an immense sea is infinitely small? That one drop more will not make the ocean overflow? But it might serve

17

to doom a soul already on the edge of the abyss, one for whom even a tiny droplet would be sufficient to work his doom.

The tremendous mystery of free will! Free will is not a matter of reason but of truth. To attempt to rationalize it is to destroy it. How can the idea of an intention *created* by our will have occurred to any human mind? The truth is that we are of God, made in His likeness, and our free will is a likeness of His creative power. The course of phenomena, exterior as well as interior, material as well as psychic, is determined; every event in the exterior world and every state of consciousness follow by law on those which precede and accompany them. But underneath there is free will, which makes us feel a sense of responsibility and which raises us above time. By free will we live in eternity. Virtue creates acts by its motives. It is a tremendous mystery, which like the mystery of Hell ought to immerse us in God, sanctifying the holy name of our Father which is in Heaven. Thus we can ask for the coming of His kingdom, the kingdom of grace; our free will immersed in grace, we will want what God wants. Then we can say: thy will be done on earth as it is in heaven, in the realm of the ideal and in our souls just as in the realm of reality and our bodies.

Human reason, left to itself, leads to nihilism. Any acceptance of anything substantial and transcendent is a matter of imagination or of imitation faith. The Idea, the Absolute, the Will, the Unknowable—what is any of these but an idea of our own, a phenomenon of our mind? And our mind—what is it but a phenomenon, an appearance? As far as reason is concerned there is no other reality but appearance. But reason cries out in mental necessity for something solid and permanent, some subject uniting the appearances, because it does not merely know itself: it also feels itself and knows that it is.

And it arrives at that desolating
Infinite vanity of all that is
at the vanity of vanities and all is vanity, the last point that human wisdom can reach.

And left to itself in this desolation, it finds itself terrified to face the nothingness it has created and in which it sees itself submerged. It is seized by vertigo, the terrible dizziness of trying to conceive of itself as not being, of having a state of consciousness in which there is no state of consciousness. Nothingness is inconceivable.

And from there to God, whose glory issues from the desolation of nothingness. A new, sublime creation! It is the creation of faith, because where reason combines and analyzes, faith creates.

———

Through faith we receive the substance of truth; through reason, its form.

———

Ecclesiastes is the highest point reason can reach. It is, accordingly, one of the best preparations for receiving faith.

———

What a great deal of activity there is in the world which is really nothing but laziness! How much work which is simply idleness! We fall into a slumber at certain activities, into the heat of certain studies, and we don't wish to awake from our dream into reality. Much damage is done by letting onself be wrapped up in a consuming passion, however elevated it may appear.

Some people who are dedicated to scientific investigation despise people who spend much of their day playing dominoes, never seeing that in their own activities they are moved by a spirit in no wise different.

In the eyes of the world, many great saints appear only to be idlers. And prayer is called idling.

Men of the world busy themselves at their vain work so as to avoid the godly whisper, which is to be heard only by a soul in repose, in quiet, in silence.

The more one flees from death, the closer it gets. Days of all-absorbing occupation pass by in the same way as days of quiet contemplation.

Stupefy yourself with work: here you have the world's ultimate maxim. "Wherefore I perceive that there is nothing better, than that a man should rejoice in his own works; for that is his portion: for who shall bring him to see what shall be after him?" (Ecclesiastes 3:22) This is the wisdom of one who says that the death of donkeys and of men is one and the same, and that the condition of both is equal; that men die like donkeys; that men have nothing that donkeys don't have; that everyone is a victim of vanity; that everything ends up in the same place, since everything is made of earth, to which it returns; and that—who knows if the spirits of the sons of Adam ascend and those of donkeys descend? Given such wisdom, there is nothing left for a man but to rejoice in work—and stun his free will. But if a man abandons himself to grace and his heart rejoices in the Lord, he reaches another kind of wisdom, the wisdom of faith, which raises him above the donkeys.

Laboriousness! But how much labor is only that of the donkey on a treadmill.

One must look carefully at the so-called "religion of work," a religion with which I have for so long tried to stun myself.

Work! For what? Work in order to work some more? Production for the sake of consumption and consumption for the sake of production, in the vicious circle of a donkey? Here we have the essence of the social question. If the human race is no more than an endless series of men without a permanent common substance, if there is no communion between the living and the dead, and if the dead live only in the memory of the living, then what is the point of progress?

The thirst for infinity is a tremendous mystery, man's aspiration towards God. All progress starts from the promise *ye shall be as gods*, *knowing good and evil*, and out of this progress, originating in the guilt that condemned man to work, God provides the elements for our salvation. *O felix culpa!*

But now that I am back in the Christian community, I find myself with a faith which consists in wanting to believe, rather than in believing, and with it all of the ancient doctrine has come back in a solid block, without details or dogmas. Without thinking about any particular beliefs, I find myself with an unconscious faith. What's more, whenever I have considered some special teaching, I have rebelled and seen it as I saw it during my long sleep. But now, out of this dark nebula, out of this compact faith without lines or letters, the harmonious fabric of the divine doctrine begins to emerge and I am starting to see its line and form. It is as if, as I come closer and closer, its lineaments begin to appear. Little by little the dream is rent apart and I can see the reality.

How frequent it is to see a man spending his life fleeing from himself—so frequent that one wonders that it is seldom thought about. But where can a man go that he will not find himself? He runs and runs, in desperate flight, trying to lose his sense of self. He flings himself into the world and into a deceptive dream in order to free himself from himself; unconsciously, he dreams his life. How many suicides are trying to free themselves of self, rather than of the difficulties of their lives! The suicide wants to get rid of himself, not of his life. He wants to be rid of his soul and his consciousness, not of the wretched death's body from which the Apostle asked to be freed. And there are many moral suicides, who strive to drown their souls in tumult and dissipation, like those unfortunates who drink to dull their awareness or stun it.

Unhappy souls who live in flight from themselves! Where will they find rest?

Seek yourself in the Lord. There you will find true peace and be able to look face to face at yourself. Embrace yourself in holy charity and you will feel the permanent substance of your soul, summoned by Christ to eternal life. To love oneself is much more difficult than is generally believed, and it is the beginning of true charity. How few know how to love themselves in Christ! To become substantial and to unite oneself with the Lord is a mighty task, as is the task of living with oneself, in a close embrace with one's wretchedness, truly knowing and loving oneself. Ordinarily we think of ourselves as we think of a stranger. And there are times when we see ourselves outside ourselves, aliens to ourselves, a saddening vision because we see ourselves, in all our vanity, as passing shadows. I can remember once staring at myself in the mirror until I became two different people and my own image became that of a stranger. While standing there I spoke my own name in a low voice and heard it as the voice of someone else calling out to me. I was overcome, as if feeling myself at the abyss of nothingness, a vain, passing shadow. What sorrow I felt! One is submerged in fathomless depths which cut short the breath; everything vanishes, and one faces nothingness and the void, eternal death.

"Let not the waterflood overflow me, neither let the deep swallow me up, and let not the pit shut her mouth upon me.

"Hear me, O Lord; for thy lovingkindness is good: turn unto me according to the multitude of thy tender mercies." (Psalm 69:15-16)

Know thyself! This phrase is often repeated and taken to be a principle of philosophy by the worldly wise. But the phrase is taken to mean observation of oneself as if one were a stranger, a mere example of humanity, a scientific or psychological object. These people reduce "know thyself" to a cold formula for purely intellectual knowledge, to an anatomical science and nothing more; their "self-knowledge" does not embrace knowing oneself as a concrete and living individual, as an individual and concrete "I," a vessel of miseries and sins, of pettiness—and greatness.

Some people fall into a sterile and noxious psychologism, prying into themselves and using themselves like laboratory animals for pointless experiments. What would one say of a surgeon who mangled his arm by way of experiment, or a doctor who gave himself tuberculosis so as to study the disease in himself? But many people behave this way as regards their souls.

An immense sorrow runs through the world of the literati, drowning their souls: the sorrow of the vanity of vanities and all is vanity. The drunken spree of progress occasionally gives way to clarity of vision, and the spirits of men sense the abyss at their feet. Then, over the waters of the flood, the Ark which was thought to have been lost and sunk is seen floating, and the drowning strive to cling to it.

"And he said unto them, Go ye unto all the world, and preach the gospel to every creature."

Mark 16:15

"He answered them, I have told you already, and ye did not hear; wherefore would ye hear it again? will ye also be his disciples?"

John 9:27

[Easter Sunday]

Last night, Holy Saturday, at evening prayers an inner struggle. Later I could not sleep a wink. An enormous aridity. Today is the Sunday of the Resurrection, and I have not yet been resurrected to the communion of the faithful.

"Let your women keep silence in the churches: for it is not permitted unto them to speak; but they are commanded to be under obedience, as also saith the law."

I Cor. 14:34

The conservation of faith is perhaps due to women, for they maintain the tradition of piety with their silence.

Mankind's ascent to God is symbolized by Mary's ascent to God aided by His grace; Christ is God's descent to mankind, to Mary.

The *Magnificat* is the song of humanity, just as the *Pater Noster* is its prayer.

It was to a woman, to Magdalen, a reborn sinner, the first human being so favored, that the crucified Christ appeared, calling her by name, Mary. Women who had come from Galilee to serve him followed Him to Calvary, while the men, his disciples, fled. His resurrection was announced to His apostles by the holy women. "And their words seemed to them as idle tales, and they believed them not." (Luke 24:11)

Christ has been resurrected in me, to give me faith in His resurrection, the beginning of His doctrine of salvation. "Blessed are they that have not seen, and yet have believed." [John 20:29.] A year ago I would have said that it would be as miraculous for me to believe again in the Man-God as in His having been raised from the dead. Give me, Lord, absolute faith and it will be the proof of its own truth.

No divine text, no Holy Writ, no tables of the Law have descended from Heaven bearing obvious signs. The Gospel is essentially an oral tradition, an oral tradition inserted in a human way in a text whose original codices are a matter of dispute. The Word was made flesh among men, not the Law, not Scripture.

All Christian life through the generations is based on divine revelation, an oral revelation set down in writing in a human manner in Scripture, in tradition and not in material permanence. The spirit gives life, the letter kills.

The Church is the body in which tradition lives, in which the Word is made flesh. Where do the Protestants get their Scriptures?

Protestantism wavers between slavish literalism and rationalism, which makes the life of faith evaporate. If the Catholic Church were to disappear, the Protestant confessions would vanish, but not vice versa.

Protestantism will have to run full cycle, lose itself

in the rationalism which kills all spiritual life, in order again to fall back into the faith from which it came.

Freedom, freedom! When has any Protestant attained the freedom of the Catholic mystics? They fall either into the slavery of the letter or into the nihilism of reason.

They have wanted to subject faith to progress. But faith lives quietly and enduringly under progress and within it, as truth lives within reason.

The Superman, *Uebermensch*. He is the Christian. "Be ye therefore perfect, even as your Father which is in heaven is perfect." The poor inventor of this business about a Superman has become an idiot, a new Nebuchadnezzar. Naturalism leads to deification, to Nietzsche's *Uebermensch*, to Max Stirner's *Der Einzige*, and it all ends in nihilism. I-ism and nihilism are concepts which finally become identical with one another.

Nevertheless, there is a natural aspiration in anarchism, an urge for freedom from external law, from the letter that kills, a longing to live in accord with the spirit and with justice.

Our Father.

Father! This is Christ's revelation, for in all the old Law God did not appear as a father, The most characteristic thing about Christianity is its teaching of the fatherhood of God, making men the children of the Creator, not creatures merely, but children.

Father! Our children seek our protection. The child gives his father a smiling look and asks of him no definite favor, no action which will enrich his life, but only a caress. "Papa!" my son calls out to me, and if I answer him by saying "What?" he is sorry, for he wants me to answer by saying "Yes, my love?" And he snuggles up to me, hugs against me, and stays there, enjoying himself in feeling my favor and my touch, in having me next to him, looking into my eyes from time to time to see if I return his glance with affection. Thus with our Heavenly Father we do not ask of Him the favors of material progress, nor riches, nor health, nor pleasures, nor honors, only His nearness and His warmth, only that He watch over us spiritually, that we feel ourselves under His holy providence.

The majestic mystery of love! It is love's existence that proves the existence of God. Love! It is not a bond of mutual benefit or interest, but the pure delight in feeling ourselves joined, of feeling ourselves brothers, of feeling ourselves alongside one another.

Our Father which art in heaven. In heaven, above us all, in the common sky above us which is common to us all, one Father for all, a common Father.

Hail Mary, full of grace.

All the grace which God was to shower on men he concentrated on Mary, the symbol of sanctified humanity. Mary is the depository of grace. . . . The grace which God has granted generations of humans over the centuries was deposited in Mary, who received it in all humility: "Behold the handmaiden of the Lord; be it unto me according to thy word." Her words express the most sublime obedience, which is the root of all freedom. As Christians, we conquer our own freedom by means of this obedience. "Behold the servant of the Lord; be it unto me according to thy word." Thus each one of us individually translates "Thy will be done" which we intone together to the Lord.

"Not unto us, O Lord, not unto us, but unto thy name give glory."

Psalm 115:1

"Give to God what is his and ascribe to thyself what is thine: give God thanks for his grace and to thyself guilt and pain known to be due to thee for thy guilt."

Imitation of Christ, II, X, 11

We must lose ourselves in the nothingness which terrifies us in order to achieve eternal life and to become all. Only by making ourselves nothing can we become everything. Only by recognizing the nothingness of our reason can we reach by faith that all and everything which is truth.

In the most vigorous flight of rationalistic human philosophy, the idealism of Hegel, the point of departure is the formula that pure Being is identical to pure Nothingness: rationalist nihilism.

Easter Monday

To rationalize faith. I wanted to become its master and not its slave—and thus I fell into slavery instead of gaining freedom in Christ.

Mary is like the node of Christian life. The prayers of the faithful are concentrated in her to reach the Lord, and His grace is deposited in her to pour on mankind. She and her virtue are like a powerful spiritual lens through which mankind and God are brought into a focussed relationship.

A constant tension drives me to spiritual rumination, to a life in which I delve like a mole into my soul. In the course of a purely contemplative life I might have perhaps been carried away by excesses. I will have to cultivate the active life of a writer, making my pen into a weapon of combat for Christ.

There was a time when I dreamed of entering the cloister, but God has taken me along a different way. God be praised! Thy will be done.

Christ suffered and paid for future sins. Sin has a retroactive action, inasmuch as it is committed in eternity. Temporal passion and eternal passion. Where are those sorrows given substance? The Eucharist.

Fifth festive mystery: the child lost and then found in the temple.

Mary found her lost son in the temple, sitting in the midst of the doctors, giving them instruction. Christ is to be found in the temple and not in vain disputations, if to our misfortune we have lost him. And we have to seek him as a simple and humble child.

I have a letter from Leopoldo in which he tells me all that has been let loose against me. They are attributing my rebirth to my desire for a professorial chair in Madrid, to my seeking notoriety and wanting always to be in a position of authority, to my wanting a greater public, and to my failures.

Erquiza died suddenly; how did he die?

The saddest thing is that Navarro and Torres lament the step I have taken, attributing it to an excess of feelings. Is such a thing possible—an excess of feelings? When the dangerous excess lies in an excess of reason?

Thank God I don't hear everything people may be saying about me. And in addition to the insults of some there is the joy of others, especially those who truly love me.

Now more than ever I must avoid playing out a role.

I am told that Maundy Thursday was the day in which they most spoke ill of me, at the table where I used to engage in outrageous talk. In the meantime I was tranquil in Alcalá, knowing nothing of this. What is the difference between the insults we hear and those which do not reach our ears? Why must we be upset and sad about disparaging remarks we have not ourselves heard? The sad thing is that they are giving vent to their evil passions.

I am withered as in a drought. I am unable even to summon up the great fear of death which recently wrenched me, nor the tears I wept when D.J.J. spoke to me in the choir-loft and said, "Perhaps this is the way." Nor can I relive the struggle through the night of Holy Saturday, nor the grief in the railroad coach on the way back from Chamartín. These visitations do not come upon me when I seek them, but only when You choose to test me.

I write these very words with a calm I'd rather not possess.

But simplicity and purity—the two wings with which we lift ourselves—must prevail. No theatrics, no illusions, no self-chastisement to work myself into deceitful states of auto-suggestion. Better to abandon self altogether.

We ask for signs, ignoring the fact that the most evident sign is that we ask for them.

In the first pangs of my rebirth, the Lord willed that I manifest the beginnings of the process to others and that the news should spread among those who know me. Thus was I bound to my duty. And now the enemy wishes me to leave off, to consider it all a temporary departure from my senses, to endure their explanations, leaving me with no benefit of the doubt. Vainglory puts on the cloak of humility. They were probably right then to say that all I seek is notoriety and that to speak of my spiritual crisis is vanity.

In this state of calm I am not calm. In this calm I seek inner agitation, though I wish for it calmly. And that is the greatest proof of God's goodness.

Notebook 2

✝

I MUST LIVE in the world—but may I not find ascetic perfection in it? By intention and by desire, yes.

The life of the Stylites was a matter of perpetual warning and example. The monk's virginity shows the worldly man the virginity in desire. Virginity is the specifically Christian virtue (Harnack, II, p. 10). Women must be had as if not had, and the same with riches.

The exercise of the virtues of chastity and of poverty among monks, among the select, continues to show Christianity how to appreciate and practice these virtues in spirit—and not in accord with the letter. Yet, if no one lived in accord with the letter of virtue, thus conserving its spirit, the spirit would at last be lost.

Christ told us to imitate Him. But who would dare believe himself a Christ, God of God and light of light?

Race horses seem solely fit for racing, but fine cross-breeding among them produces excellent hunters and conserves the purity of the race. Spiritual men conserve the purity of Christianity by their spiritual cross-breeding. Monasticism prevented Christianity from falling into the heathenish superstition of the third and fourth centuries (Harnack, II, p. 9).

When we consider that there are men who live chastely in accord with both the letter and the spirit, we who are not bound to the letter should mourn if we are not able to keep at least to the spirit.

_____

*32**

On Death.

The sorrow of waking at night to find my hand asleep. I hasten to move it, to touch it, wondering if it has gone dead and cold on me, and if death comes this way.

Terror of the night when I get up with palpitations.

A long-time madness of mine: immortality by force of intensity. Some people live more than others in a given period of time. One man will live more in four years than another in twenty, live a more varied life. Thus it would be possible to live an eternity of intensity in a limited time, for all extension is infinite insofar as it contains infinite parts. Yes, but following that metaphor, it is infinite in nothings, in infinite zeroes. The vanity of vanities. Eternal life lies not in change and variety but in the constancy of faith and grace.

And what of waking in the night and asking myself if I am alive? Am I already dead? Will my existence from now on consist in remaining as I am now, here, like this, all alone with myself and my thoughts, forever and ever and ever? Why any further Hell? Take a man at any moment of his life, even when he thinks he is the happiest, and make him believe that that moment will lengthen into eternity and everlastingness—and as soon as he stops to think about it he will see it as Hell.

It would at times be a great consolation to detain some passing moment in the flux of time and give it substance, but if this consolation were prolonged forever it would become our worst torment.

Speaking of the last stage, the moment of death, Maestro Granada says, "To go back is impossible, to go forward is intolerable, and to remain as one is is not granted. What is to be done, then?"

Diary

The terrible mystery of time! When shall we ever be free of time, of irreversible and irreparable time?

If we suddenly found ourselves going blind even while enjoying sound health, objects becoming blurred, darkness advancing upon us, would not terror seize us? And what relation is there between going blind and dying? The mind which conceives of its own disappearance will go on disappearing, conceiving of it ever more obscurely, and then, ever more terrified by the gradual dulling of all perception—a certain sign of the end. We shall resist like a person trying to open his eyes when he has been overtaken by sleep. Anyone who has experienced the struggle against sleep has already had a glimpse of the struggle against death. To want to speak and not be able; to want to get up and find one's legs not obeying; to want the strength to put down evil and find a total lack of strength.

A dying man, wasting away, speechless, unable to move his limbs, his breathing the only sign that he's alive: who knows what great battles wage within or how he suffers without being able to express it? He may not have the strength to express his ideas and feelings, but they are all that is left in his worn-out body. Surely these feelings fill him entirely, just as the stars fill the sky when the sun goes down. Those who look on do not know what is taking place in this last stage of life. Since this event is unique and since no one has ever returned to tell of it, we know nothing. It is the one stage of life we have no experience of: one dies only the once. Is it not perhaps worth living to experience this one act? To live in order to die?

We shouldn't think of it, we are told, for if we give ourselves over to fretting over death, life will become impossible. But one must think of it. The beginning of any remedy is to know the disease, and since death is humanity's malady, to know it is to begin to remedy it. On the day when that idea of death, which today paralyzes my efforts and sinks me deep in sorrow and powerlessness, comes to spur me onward to work for the eternity of my soul rather than trying to immortalize my name among mortals, on that day shall I be cured.

In the dream of the world everything is a vanity fair of mutual praise, of giving glory in order to get glory, declaring that this man or that is "immortal."

Of learning of the change in me, some people have told me: this will pass; it's only the the effect of mental fatigue, of too much work. I even came to think that myself.

Thus Festus spoke to St. Paul: "Paul, thou art beside thyself; much learning doth make thee mad." But he said, "I am not mad, most noble Festus, but speak forth the words of truth and soberness" (Acts 26:24-25).

And if he had been mad, it would have been with the holy madness of Christ! Would that I suffered such madness!

On Death.

If the end of the world were announced to take place on a definite day, any time between now and fifty years from now, into what a state people's feelings would fall! But for each one of us death is the end of the world: the sun will go out, all sounds die away, all things dissolve into nothingness.

Quasimodo Sunday, 25 April.

A conventual Mass at the parish church, a sermon by the priest about the fact that many believe that going to church is doing God a favor, when it is we who need God, not He us.

How is it that I imagine myself to be a great personage, one destined to create a sensation in the Church, my conversion providing a model for others? How many ways pride has of surviving!

I suffer from abulia. Without some outside stimulation I cannot resolve to work, and my only recourse is to try to seek such stimulation. Once the mad thought occurred to me to wish for a serious illness or an accident, which by putting me near death would move me to seek Confession and break this state of mind.

Hell.

That horror of nothingness—is it not perhaps a warning? Would not an eternity of solitude, alone with one's own nothingness, be worse than nothingness itself? Because you have thought only of yourself, have sought only yourself, and thought yourself the center of the universe, you would be with yourself and only with yourself for all eternity, trapped in your interior world, with everything outside yourself scrubbed from your senses. Thus you would soon plumb your own nothingness and have it for company eternally.

Intellectualism is a terrible disease, and all the more terrible when one lives in it in unknowing tranquillity. It is as terrible as madness or idiocy. It is said that neither madmen nor idiots suffer. Because they do not know of their illness, they are even able to live contentedly. My little Raimundín does nothing but laugh.

Received Denifle's book today, and was soon taking bibliographical notes. Books for books' sake! This damned curiosity. This dryness is incurable. Curiosity triumphs over everything: I only think about mysticism as a new area of curiosities.

[. . .] I though I had encountered a book of erudition and I find myself with a devotional book. What good will it be for me to know how to define pity or sorrow without feeling it?

I have been flattered to be called a mystic, believing that a mystic is of a more powerful spiritual rank than the philosopher, just as the philosopher is higher than the scientist. But the necessary thing is to be good.

How much danger there is in this neo-mysticism, this false mysticism of the proud, the sensual, and the drunken. The thing is, to be good.

The most insignificant event, a phrase, an innocent word overheard, something my son says—everything strikes me as a warning and a symbol, something with a hidden meaning, and I relate everything to my state of mind. If I go on this way I am bound to fall into superstition. The church bells never toll but I think they are summoning me. I am convinced that every cleric I see is on his way to question me and ask what is wrong.

I feel a great desire to announce my state of mind to everyone, a great facility for confessing to anyone at all—and an enormous dry indifference at the thought of confessing as the Church directs.

I suffer from a great debility of the will and am unable to decide anything. For days I have meant to visit the parish priest, but every day I put it off, hoping to run into him by chance on the street and make an appointment. I even dream that he will come to see me at my house, since I know he saw me at Mass. What sim-

Diary

plemindedness! I cannot make up my mind. I have no will—but will without grace is nothing.

"I am nothing, nothing, nothing," I thought as I came out of Mass today. And when I got home I happened to read Chapter III of Book II of the *Imitation* and its grand prayer imploring the grace of devotion. "Behold, Lord, that I am nothing, that I have nothing, and that, of myself, I am worth nothing. You only are good, righteous, and holy. You put all things in order. You give all things, and You fill all things with your goodness, leaving only the wretched sinner barren and devoid of heavenly comfort." [. . .]

———————

Death.

"The fear of death is the beginning of wisdom" (Sirach 1:16). The beginning of wisdom is the fear of God. The fear of death is the fear of God or its beginning.

"Think about your final moment and you will not sin" (Sirach 7:40).

"If an herb were known whose effects were to drive off old age and sickness so long as it was kept nearby, it would fetch a high price. Death is such an herb. Whoever keeps it constantly in mind will never grow old through sin" (Denifle, *Das geistliche Leben*, p. 32).

There comes a moment in which, although the imagination is not constantly dwelling on the image of death and the mind is not occupied in thinking about it, the recollection of death has nevertheless become the substance of our being, something ever present with us, which unconsciously animates all our psychic processes. We can then say that we have a full and true consciousness of life, since life is an ongoing process of dying.

*38**

What is all your past? Where but in your memory? And if your memory vanishes, then where is it?

Can one speak of the memory of death? Remembering death, we recall it.

We live dying; each moment we die and are reborn. The fugitive present flows between the death of the past and the birth of the future: and this birth is, like our own, at the risk of death.

———

If you want always to be master of yourself, stay always in God's presence. Don't do like children who close their eyes so that no one will see them. Adam hid after his sin of disobedience.

———

Whenever it occurs to you to doubt the truths of faith and you ask yourself "What is truth?" remember that these are Pilate's words when he handed over the Christ.

———

Wednesday, 28 April.

Read the ninth chapter of the Gospel of St. John.

I am a blind man in whom the works of God must be made manifest.

Anoint my eyes with clay, Lord, and lead me to wash in the pool of Siloam, in the confessional, so that I may return with sight restored. Give me strength, for I have no will.

And later I will say, to your glory: yes, I am he who sat and begged for human glory. Jesus took clay and annointed my eyes and said to go to the pool of Siloam, and I went, and once I had washed, I saw.

The Lord has made clay out of the dust to which I reduced everything by means of analysis in my passage across the desert of intellectualism, and He has placed it upon my eyes, so that I might desire to see, and then go and wash and see.

In myself I am nothing, truly nothing. Whatever of
being is in me is divine; whatever I have of being is
of God. And if I am abandoned by God I will feel my
own nothingness, and this eternal vision of my nothingness would be eternal torment, eternal death.

One should attempt from time to time to conceive
of oneself as non-existent, feel oneself not being. Out
of such horror comes the fear of God—and hope.

Integralists, Carlists, Mestizos, Neos, and Other Partisans—

God handed the world over to the disputes of men.

What a lack of charity! How much spiritual damage
is done by this wrangling! It would all be different if
we looked to the reform of the inner man, to our own
renewal in Christ. If instead of wasting our energies
in thinking how best to deal with others and what
others are like and how they think and how we are to
relate to society, we were to scrutinize ourselves and
tirelessly cultivate ourselves, then just and charitable
relations might spontaneously well up among us all.
[. . .]

All those people who engage in disputes in the street,
in the newspapers, and in the societies they belong to,
come together in their common hour of prayer and
worship. Let them pray more, argue less. The longer
they come together and the less they dispute with one
another, the better they will agree.

[. . .] We should practice spiritual obedience, spiritual poverty, spiritual chastity, and develop thereby
true Catholic unity, which ought to be the communion
of the faithful.

It is a matter of using our knees more than our
elbows.

Thursday, 29 April.

Chapter 10 of the Gospel of St. John.

By not confessing and communing with the faithful, I enter the Church of God like a thief: not by the door.

What does it mean to live outwardly like the people, attending to their sacrifices and prayers, but meanwhile setting up internally a kingdom apart—and not entering through the door?

Give me, Lord, strength so that I may wash at the pool of Siloam, the pool of your messenger.

Why should I kill my soul and drown its aspirations so as to seem logical and consistent to others?

It is a terrible thing to be a slave to what others think of us. The slavery of vainglory is a terrible one.

A change, the others will say. No, a progress.

It's not for them but for myself that I must answer. Freedom, freedom, freedom.

God has called me, I must hear him. If the others don't understand that call, must I live as their slave?

One must live one's own reality, not the appearance of oneself that others create: live in our own spirit and not in an alien concept.

John 11:4 (Friday, 30 April).

Here is a ray of hope, of true hope.

It is not for death but for the glorification of the Son of God.

This eleventh chapter must be re-read many times.

Not the Sadducees but the Pharisees persecuted Jesus the most. It was against them that he directed most of his invective, and it was the Pharisees who believed in the resurrection of the flesh. They were the idealists of that time.

Idealism debilitates, and it is more prideful than positivism.

One must be on strict guard against sentimentalism, which passes itself off as rational faith.

––––––––––

The worst of it is not having to break with my former self. My worst fear is that I will carry the spirit of my old life into the new, that I will be Catholic as I was an Anarchist, and for the same reasons: that I will turn Catholic thinking of myself and of making a name for myself in the Church. The theatrics of conversion prevents true conversion. A terrible thing.

Simplicity, my Jesus, give me simplicity!

––––––––––

Last night, at Pepe's house, I read part of the life of Father Faber. What a soul! And what a conversion! Out of pure religion he came to Catholicism.

Before he converted he said, "A year from now either I will be a Catholic or I will be a madman." Can't I say the same thing?

––––––––––

If I were suddenly certain that I wasn't going to live more than two days, I would surely go to Confession? Why don't I do so now?

––––––––––

A terrible habit: I read books of devotion and cull only quotable matter, striving to pile up bibliographical erudition on the subject to satisfy my curiosity. I must rid myself of this atrocious bibliomania, this stubble of moral intellectualism. Is not the beginning of perdition to regard mysticism and asceticism as a branch of literature?

Notebook 2

Literatism and aestheticism are the poisonous flowers of the pagan spirit.

I've long kept the image of Homer in my study with
his exquisitely venomous verse, his blasphemy, to the
effect that the gods weave men's destruction so that
future generations may have a theme to sing! The
gods, yes; that is, demons, but not God. Demons weave
and carry out the destruction of men so that future
generations may sing the feats of the damned. How
many doomed heroes are turned into legendary heroes
by the requirements of poetry!

Art for art's sake! That's like saying life for life's
sake. No, life for death's sake, life for the sake of eternal
life, and art for the sake of eternal life, for religion.

Time.

What's past is past! What's done is done! Terrible
phrases!

What's past is past, yes, for those who live in fugitive
time, for those whose life's course is like that of a
moving body along a trajectory, like the earth through
its orbit. [. . .]

Life should be lived recovering the past, following
and keeping to time's series, receiving the present from
the treasure of the past, in true progression and not
mere progress.

And how? By storing up merit for eternity, knowing
that today we are better than we were yesterday, radically better, that today we are *more* than yesterday—
more truly *beings*, more divine.

To do good is not the same thing as to be good. It
is not enough to do good, one must be good. It is not
enough to do more good works today than yesterday;
it is necessary to be better today than yesterday. In
fact, what kind of good works are those that have not

made you better as you have gone on accumulating them and piling them up? Good works which don't make you a better person as you treasure them up for yourself are vain, merely apparent, the good works of vanity.

An infamous proverb says, "A miracle is a miracle, even if the Devil did it." Worldly ethics is concerned only with the deed, not the agent: the point is to remove the harm in any act. It matters little if men live with feelings of hatred, so long as social progress keeps them from actively harming each other. It doesn't matter that men become better, for what's important is that they cannot damage one another. But it's more important to be good, even if occasional wrong is done, than to be bad and do the seeming good.

It may be that for a certain type of man committing a crime will free him from the poison of his obsession, and perhaps a vengeful man avenged will return to himself, truly repentant and purified of his vengefulness. If such be the case, better thus, than to live consumed by his rancor.

———————

Slavery.

With our conduct—our acts, deeds, and words—we weave a poor imitation of ourselves, which ends by enslaving us. Instead of being judges before God of our acts and words, instead of judging them in the tribunal of our conscience, where our Lord has his special abode, we pay attention only to the impression our acts and words make on our neighbors. We are swayed by the praise and applause of others and cling to the deeds and words of which they approve, meanwhile abandoning those that they judge to be products of a weak spirit or a small wit. [. . .]

And thus we find ourselves with an I which the

world has made for us or which we have fashioned in our slavishness to the world, and we put every effort into keeping up the role we have been assigned in this wretched drama, playing it in whatever way will win us the most applause. And when we seemingly scorn the applause and play our role only for our own satisfaction, it's even worse, for the fact then is that we have completely identified with our role. Playing it to ourselves as the audience is masturbatory pride.

It's a terrible thing to live as a slave to the I which the world has given us, to be faithful to the role assigned, responding only to the demands of the theater without ever glancing at the huge splendor of the heavens outside the theater, without ever seeing the terrible reality of death. The poor actor may be feeling sharp pain, but he can neither complain nor cry out, for then the public would hiss him. He would be a sincere man, but not a good actor. People who say that the world is a comedy do not carefully consider the horror of what they are saying.

Perhaps the poor comedian remembers that the comedy will come to an end and that he will find no way out of his troubles. If he begins to cry, and if tears are not part of his role, the public will say that the poor man has gone mad.

Freedom, Lord, freedom! Let me live in Thee, not in the minds of those whose skulls will be reduced to dust.

The I which the world has given me will perish along with the minds in which it lives, and scarcely more than my name will remain. Living with that I, can I fail to tremble before nothingness? But my own I, the one plucked from nothingness by Thee, will live in Thee.

John 14:12. If He brought Lazarus back from the dead, why would He not bring back from the dead whoever believes in Him?

Every day I make new discoveries in the old faith. It is as if the light of dawn were spreading and illuminating the dark landscape, so that what had been a formless mass began to take on outline and shape and figure and life. When will the Sun itself appear?

"But the Comforter, which is the Holy Ghost, whom the Father will send in my name, he shall teach you all things, and bring all things to your remembrance, whatsoever I have said unto you" (John 14:26). One must read and read again this fourteenth chapter of St. John.

Attending first of all to one's own personal salvation, to one's personal destiny beyond the grave, is said to demonstrate the most refined egotism, and egotism is also the name given to whatever it is that drives someone to a Trappist monastery. Blessed egotism, which produces works of charity!

It is considered noble, elevated, and great not to think of oneself nor of one's eternal salvation, but to work for Mankind. But what is this Mankind—a mass of human beings whom death will annihilate, reduce to nothingness along with all of their descendants? Is it nobler to work for the temporary and passing well-being of human beings who must suffer annihilation or to awaken in them a sense of the Beyond? Humanity! If humanity is a series of generations of men who must perish, if there is nothing permanent in it, if there is no communion of the living with the dead, then humanitarian altruism is a pathetic thing indeed!

Is there any greater charity than to bring men back to themselves?

Altruism, altruism! The altruism that makes sense is Schopenhauer's—to preach cosmic or collective suicide.

But if each of us were to think seriously about his salvation, what a flood of charity would there be on this earth!

To save everyone else by saving yourself is the same thing as to save yourself by saving everyone else.

It's a sad notion: each person sacrificing himself to humanity, one and all. We, the sacrificed, are made into an abstraction. What then is this so-called Humanity? This is really pure idolatry, and of the worst kind.

No, the Humanity to which we *should* sacrifice ourselves is Christ, old Adam's recapitulation (according to the formula of a saintly Father), who sacrificed Himself for all, for each of us. We Christians are mystic members of Him, who is a reality outside ourselves. [. . .]

Altruism, generosity, abnegation! These vain words separate men from their own salvation.

There's no sense in beating around the bush. If we believe that we and everyone else return to nothingness, then battling for the redemption of others is a sad task, a work of death. Make others happier, until their increased happiness becomes—in the face of annihilation—*unhappiness*! Nothing could be clearer: if mankind progresses in culture, in the ease of life, if men give themselves over more freely to the fascinations of art and science, then culture becomes more elevated and consciousness becomes clearer and more sensitive. And if the perception of nothingness becomes clearer and more sensitive, then men become ever more unhappy. The more sweet and pleasing and enchanting life becomes, the more horrible the idea of losing it. Thus do cultures ripen and rot and decay. Every day the vanity of vanities becomes more evident.

But out of the depths of sorrow, misery, and misfortune a godly hope in eternal life springs up, a hope which sweetens and sanctifies the sorrow, while from the very bosom of a life of ease and gratification there flows the despair of sinking into nothingness. Though it seems a paradox, there's such a thing as the unhappiness of happiness. Those who live in well-being and pleasure taste the bitter fruit of spleen, boredom, and despair.

Man's end in life is not to be cultured or refined, an exquisite aesthete, but to make himself truly happy. And if worldly happiness leads to despair, worldly happiness is not true happiness.

The whole point: whether or not there is a life beyond the grave. If there is no such life, or if we come to believe that there is none, then civilization and progress will only serve to make man more sensitive to that idea and turn his happiness into unhappiness, turn the increased ease of his life into the source of his woes.

Few periods in history are more instructive than the period of Latin decadence, at the time Christianity arrived in Rome. The unhappiness of happiness ruled. Suicide was common. Stoicism turned men's souls to stone, and Epicureanism liquified them.

Not to think about death: impossible! The more one enjoys life, the more one thinks about death. Happy is he who thinks about it from the depth of sorrow.

The attempt is made to flee from the thought of death and the shadow of eternity by plunging into the study of science, the cultivation of art, or the pursuit of public life. These are all means of self-deception, of

playing deaf. The cultivation of science leads to intellectualism, to a sad dryness of the spirit. The cultivation of art leads to aestheticism, literatism, and other
terrible sicknesses. The ultimate course of these sicknesses is horrendous, as one falls into what is called
the mysticism of sensuality.

And philosophy? There's nothing more horrible than
to study our origin, essence, goal, and destiny as a
mere curiosity to satisfy the mind.

One must live with one's whole soul, and to live
with all one's soul is to live with the faith that comes
from knowledge, the hope which arises from feeling,
and the charity which springs up from love.

I've long been concerned with the redemption of the
poor, the worker, the wretched—though I've always
believed that the rich were also wretched. But as I've
come to my senses and begun to think about my own
eternal salvation, I've come to understand that working
to make people happy, while not thinking about their
eternal salvation, was to work to make them unhappy.
More than once I've stated that the rich man needs to
be saved from his riches just as much as the poor man
needs to be saved from his poverty. Today I better
understand this truth. We all need to be redeemed
from the source of our sin.

The usual convenient slogan is charity in the rich
and resignation in the poor. It should be charity and
resignation—or better, abnegation—in both the rich
and the poor. What a need for the poor man to feel
charitable toward the rich, and for the rich man to
resign himself to the poor! The rich man who is resigned to his wealth in effect renounces it, and the poor
man who feels charitable toward the rich man elevates
himself above his poverty and makes an advantage of
it.

Diary

[. . .] "God wills," said Fénelon to someone, "that you be wise, not on the basis of much reflection, but, on the contrary, by obliterating all the uneasy reflections based on your false wisdom. When you no longer act from natural vivacity, then you will be wise without your wisdom. The movements of grace are simple and ingenuous. Impetuous natures think much and speak much. Grace discourses and reasons very little, for it is sensitive, peaceful, and drawn in on itself."

Silence, silence, to hear the Lord!

I am astounded that there can be people who are not overcome by the idea of annihilation, or who coldly accept the thought and go on living, or who live without thinking that they must die. Are they made of some different material than I? Was I myself of different material for years? But no, because even if it's true that only now have I returned, after some years, to the *emotion* of death, the *idea* of death has always been with me.

I am going to live a life of internal sorrow. The thought torments me that my presently renewed faith is only nature's illusory lure to let me go on living. The idea has occurred to me that I should believe so that I can live peacefully in hope, whatever the reality later turns out to be—even if I must eventually sink into nothingness. At other times the Satanic notion has struck me that if I follow this course I will end up wanting to lose myself in God, annihilating myself pantheistically—and that it is God who is taking me in that direction. Belief in a providence permeates all these ideas, whether it is that I am being lured on to go on living without despair, or that I am being led to accept what I fear. But if there is a providence, why

not life eternal? "Truth was not made for the consolation of men." How I shall have to purge myself of
that blasphemy I've repeated so often. I will possess
the truth—and it will not console me.

All insufferable. I ask for a sign, just one evident
sign, and yet I see in advance that if I were to receive
one I would be bound to analyze it, to assay it. And
yet, to ask for a sign, is that not already a sign of the
very thing one asks for?

Impossible to go on living this way, I tell myself.
But this is precisely the way I must live, battling with
these temptations, getting used to death.

Who if not God himself has moved me to seek Him?
I have long mocked doubt. Today I live in doubt.

Logic, logic! Logic makes us derive conclusions from
established principles, from data, from premises, but
it does not give us new premises or new first principles.
To ask for logic is to ask that we not go beyond the
principles furnished by reason. And why should I live
a slave to these?

No, I do not want to be logical, because other principles have opened themselves to me, and not by means
of logic.

In the name of logic a nation of deaf men would
condemn the only person among them who could hear,
and he would have no means of explaining himself.

Why should I be logical with my antecedents? Why
not be logical with my heart? Are my antecedents
worth more than my heart?

Logic is generally another form of slavery to the
world, that slavery in the form of an ideal.

It is not a question of logic, but of first principles.
And first principles do not come from logic. Logic
does not give us the intuitions upon which it operates.

Diary

The only role for logic in the case of a man blind from birth who gains his sight is to establish a concordance of his new impressions with the system of the old ones, rectifying their interpretations. Such is the role of logic in faith.

And here is how I, who fled all intellectualism, will again fall prey to it. I killed my faith by trying to rationalize it. It is only right that now I should vivify my rational acquisitions with faith and give my time to this task.

All of which is enough to drive me mad.

Notebook 3

CATHOLIC RATIONALISM.

As regards those "doubtful disputations" and the giving and taking away of patents of Catholicism and the judging of one's peers and deciding what they should do or believe, see Romans 14.

———

Those souls are fortunate whose days are all alike! For them, one day is the same as another, and a month is like any one of the days, and a year like any of the months. They have conquered time, living above it, not subject to it. They only see the differences between dawn, morning, noontide, afternoon, and dusk; they note only the differences between spring, summer, autumn, and winter. They go to bed in peace to await the new day, and when it comes they rise happy to live it. They live the same day over and over again. They rarely form any *idea* of their Lord, for they do not think of Him but live Him. They live God, which is more than thinking, sensing, or loving Him. Their prayers are not something separate and apart from their other acts, nor do they need to draw apart to say them, for their whole life is a prayer. They pray by living. And at last they die, in the same way the light of day dies away at nightfall and goes to shine elsewhere.

Holy simplicity! Once lost, it is not recovered.

———

[10 May]
Yesterday, Sunday, at Canillas. What peace there! If

one could live and die like they do. We went to the burial at Calzada of a poor fellow who had died of paralysis. I kept thinking about spiritual paralysis. They told me that he died saying, "What a sweet dream!" He seemed asleep there, at the door of the church.

Later the fields were blessed. The young girls brought all their presents in a procession, shawls, kerchiefs, all strung up on a pole.

———————

Pompeyo Gener sent his book, *Amigos y maestros*, a study of various writers. It concludes with the "philosophers of the ascendant life," who celebrate the struggle for life: Darwin, Spencer, Taine, Renan. He pronounces against all neo-mysticism, decadence, and so on. Well done. But the point is that all those things are in the same camp as the most "sane" positivism: it's all a matter of objectifying oneself and then sitting back to think about humanity.

One must come back to oneself and pose the real problem: what will become of me? Do I return to nothingness at my death? Anything else amounts to sacrificing one's soul to a name, to sacrificing our reality to our appearance.

———————

We are distracted from thinking about death, and the final awakening, by youth, nature, spring, health, the sun, all of which intoxicate us with life.

How many dying people must ask: just four more days, Lord! A week, just a little more time, please, this is all so unexpected! Terrible it is that death arrives unexpectedly.

Life! Everything is a hymn to life, an exaltation of life. Sheer intoxication. This damned literature produces the fatal illusion that life never ends, that it goes on after our own death.

No: once you are dead, nothing of all this around here lives on for you.

———————

Death.

If the occasion comes up for you to look at a cadaver, ask yourself, what have we here but someone asleep? What kind of sleep is this? But if you jab or wound a sleeping man he wakes up, moves excitedly, and cries out. A dead man's insides may be opened, his flesh cut, and his viscera exposed, but he does not move.

———————

Death.

Nothing is destroyed, everything is transformed: so they say by way of consolation. Matter is in perpetual change. And in the same way, they add, the spirit's matter is not lost. Our ideas are not lost either, but keep bearing fruit. We leave behind us the effects of our work. Everything we do remains in one form or another. We all contribute to progress.

A sad consolation! And my I, my own consciousness, what becomes of it? What becomes of me—never mind my matter. If I disappear forever, if my personal consciousness goes, then the world goes with it as far as I am concerned. If my I is no more than a passing phenomenon, the world in which I live is a passing phenomenon.

It seems impossible that there should be people who live calmly with the belief that their personal consciousness returns to nothingness.

But after all, this constant preoccupation of mine with my own finality and destiny is not exactly pure. Perhaps it's an acute form of egotism. Instead of trying to find myself in God, I try to find God in myself.

I have a premonition that I will never again know joy. Sadness will be my lot while I live.

Diary

I have lived dreaming of leaving a name in the world, and I will live now obsessed with saving my soul.

In this unbearable situation I am now haunted by the idea of suicide. Just a few moments ago I thought of injecting myself with a strong dose of morphine to go to sleep forever. And I saw myself, once the injection were made, terrified in the face of death, announcing what I had done so that help would come, or, in despair, starting to run, breaking into a sweat, and by violent motion trying to overcome the sleep and the morphine.

And if God has created us, why should we give thanks if we are to return to the nothingness from which He brought us?

And why should we praise His works? What for? Can our praise add one whit to His glory or greatness?

It is a duty? What is this business about duty?

The serene contemplation of the world, the long vision of history, working for progress, respect for others—it is all vanity if we are altogether finished at death.

It's impossible to live like this. Precautions are no use, nor philosophical convictions, nor the deceptions and frauds of the heart, nor sentimentalism. What's needed is faith, robust faith, immoveable faith. And this faith can only be taken from the people. It must be their faith, the faith of others, the faith of the simple.

I can find no support in myself. It's useless to deceive myself or to insist on living on illusions and feeding on them. I need realities.

What does all this mean? Is it not already a sign?

I lived in a trance, without thinking such thoughts as these, lost in my projects and my studies, trusting in reason—the way others live. I lived happily, not thinking about death except in the way that one thinks about a scientific proposition. The thought left me as lukewarm as the thought that one day the sun will be extinguished. I have lived like most of my friends live, letting myself live and dreaming of leaving something behind, adding my little share to the work of progress. I have lived discussing philosophy, arts, and letters— as if these all were eternal. I have lived like those do who are called healthy-minded, balanced, and normal, considering death to be a law of nature and a necessary condition of life. And now I can't go on living like that. I look back on those spirited years, those years of energetic struggle, of projects and joy, as years of spiritual death and sleep. I cannot but view them with a certain sadness. I thought I had lived happily, and now I see myself wrenched from that happiness. But I cannot repent of those years. I sigh for the fleshpots of Egypt.

But there is now another reality. I will not return to that life. I will not be "cured," as my friends put it. I will no longer be able to live as I have lived. Who tore me out of that sleep? What happened?

The crisis incubated slowly, and I didn't understand it until it was on me. I find myself in another country, with other horizons, with another life. The perspective seems to have changed completely. And just as in those years I considered the judgment of the believer to be something strange but worth knowing about and studying, as something that might correct the means of my own judgment, now I find that everything I acquired in those years strikes me as somewhat strange, a structure outside myself, something that has not taken on flesh in my spirit.

How right was Martínez Ruiz to write that I did not know where I was going! How right Navarro

Ledesma to present me as the first victim of intellectualism! And it was against these two, who saw me
so clearly, that I inwardly rebelled.

I took up the study of religion as a curiosity, as a
phenomenon that was fodder for my curiosity. I outlined a philosophy of religion and became absorbed in
Harnack's *History of Dogma*. And today my former
theories strike me as mere curiosities.

Death.

There are people who are in horror of the grave,
and when they see an open pit in a cemetery they think:
I'll be in there, in the dark, with no air, unable to
move, eaten by worms, exposed to the frosts of winter,
soaked with wet, my body rotting away. It doesn't
occur to them that they will not see the darkness, nor
hear the silence, nor note the lack of air, nor feel the
cold or anything at all. Nor will they be there in the
grave. Contrary to what they think, they won't "be"
anywhere at all. Their imagination tortures them with
an absurdity—the invention of a live consciousness for
a dead body.

It tortures the imagination much more to try to
imagine yourself as not existing. Try thinking that you
do not exist and you will feel the horror of spiritual
burial: that terrible state of consciousness in which we
imagine there is no state of consciousness. The thought
that we will not think brings on a dizziness which
reason cannot cure.

[. . .]

One must die in Adam in order to come to life in
the Christ sleeping in Jesus.

"For if the dead rise not, then is not Christ raised.
And if Christ be not raised, your faith is vain; ye are

yet in your sins. Then they also which are fallen asleep in Christ are perished. If in this life only we have hope in Christ, we are of all men most miserable."

(I Cor. 15:16-19)

If there is no other life, the Christian faith is vain and vain its work. There is no reason for it to bear fruit and spread. If there is no other life and the Christian spirit serves only for this life, we Christians are the most miserable of men. No, it is not possible: even if man were by nature and essence mortal, so many longings and strivings would already have created another life for him. Whence comes this encompassing obsession with another life, with the Beyond? Are we no more than a transitory phenomenon in this world? Why shouldn't the world be no more than a transitory phenomenon in us?

———————

Must wise men be more right than saints? Must the reason of Spinoza or Spencer be a better voice for truth than the heart of St. Francis of Assisi or some other saint?

I once wrote that if faith is observed in good people, it isn't that they are good because they believe but that they believe because they are good; that their goodness does not come from their faith in glory, but that their goodness creates the glory for them. Goodness: is it not a criterion of truth?

No need to discuss whether the Christian faith produced the miracles of saintliness and charity. These qualities, wherever they came from, gave birth to hope, and hope gave birth to faith. It's all the same thing.

———————

Many say they wish to believe, that they would really like to believe. And some add: if I could believe and did believe I would lead a more sober and penitent life, imitating the life of a saint. So? You want to believe? Then just imitate the life of a saint and you will end by believing. Act as if you did believe and you will come to believe. You say that you cannot act thus because you don't believe? Then the truth is that you don't really want to believe, even though you think you do. Your desire for faith is an illusion.

The surest way to arrive at belief in the Credo is perhaps to say it every day with the greatest fervor possible.

You say that would be auto-suggestion? But what is that? Does it mean that I am both the suggester and the suggested, the influencer and the influenced? Can the one influenced be the one who influences? Whence has the influence, the suggestion, come to me?

———————

From the prologue to Arzadun's work.

Childhood! The remembrance, more or less clear, of our childhood is the balsam which prevents the mummification of our spirit. In times of aridity and abandonment, when the terrifying vanity of vanities sounds and resounds in our ears, when the soul is exhausted by its wanderings in the desert and finally arrives at the terrible mystery of time to behold the bottomless abyss of nothingness, then the sweet echoes of distant childhood are heard in the silence, like the murmur of fresh and living water that had gone on flowing beneath the hot dry sands. And then, when the throat is parched and the innermost spirit is torn apart, when the soul thirsts in its agony, you scrape your hands in clawing the earth as you fall to your knees to drink deeply to restore your life from this flowing underground spring which has kept its freshness and purity.

———————

But what is all this about wanting everything to work out between God and me? And waiting for signs or for him to complete His work? What does my incapacity to hand myself over to any man whatsoever mean? I constantly talk of humility—and then I will not humble myself before another man and I spurn all intermediaries. When Jesus comes in all His glory to judge us it will be too late to believe: it is necessary to believe in Him as a man. Many believe in the divinity of Christ but not in His humanity; these people do not believe in the God-Man. Many believe in an ideal Christ who floats in a certain mystical vagueness and who is forged in the regions of pure thought, without believing in the human Christ who appears to us in His Church, clothed in all that is human in the ritual, the liturgy, and the priesthood. The Eucharist is the form of this Christ made human. It is a great scandal to the idealists, a great contradiction to the proud— and the touchstone of humility.

Now I'm trying auto-suggestion on myself. It seems incredible that I should write these things and then rebel against them. Am I not sincere when I write them? Or am I not sincere when I rebel against them? Or is it that in me there are two I's, one who writes these lines and another who rejects them as delirium? Is this the struggle St. Paul spoke of when he cried out, "O wretched man that I am!"? Or does God move my hand so that what I write is not mine but the work of a spirit dwelling in me? In any case, it's something to think about deeply. The fact is that I am preaching to myself, converting myself, and that on one day I write things which seem the next day to have been written by someone else, not by me. How slow and tedious it is to shed one's old self!

And I see that the sleeping man lingers on in me,

and that I keep with me everything that I treasured up in those years of human science. I don't think these things contradict what is new. It's as if I received the new faith on top of the old convictions, in order to crown them and give them life. My idealism, my socialism, my anarchism, my theoretical phenomenalism, all seem transfigured in a new light. But does the most terrible of tests await me? Could it be that after combining my rational convictions with a supernatural faith, this faith will kill these convictions, and that I still face the hardest trial, that of getting rid of them? Must I, in the end, sacrifice my reason? That would be horrible. But Thy will be done, O Lord, and not my own. If reason endangers me, take away my reason; give me peace and salvation, even if in these things must lie imbecility.

Meanwhile I resist submission to any man, obstinately not believing in the humanity of Christ. I cannot see beyond all the defects and ignorance of His ministers. I am more and more resistant to the idea that the confessor is Christ, and I feel myself pushed more and more towards Him. I would have the priests come to me, rather than my going to them. And I waste my time wondering about which of them to confide in— as if they were not all the same, all of them merely representatives, mere figures. If I knew a saint I would place myself in his hands. But how will I know a saint if I see one?

It is strange to feel myself attracted by everything I have most scorned, even while I still see all the weaknesses I saw in it before. Everything that can be said against auricular confession by those who are most opposed to it and most deeply repelled by it, I have already said myself and still repeat, but I still feel myself drawn to the confessional. It strikes me that the more superstitious I find it, the more it attracts me. Yes, because the more superstitious and vulgar and fetishistic, the more humiliation to be found in submission to it, the greater is the humility in accepting it. Will I then fall into superstition?

Superstition! What is superstition! Superstitious Pilate asked Jesus: What is truth? And then without waiting for an answer he went to wash his hands. We children of truth ought to ask the Devil: What is truth? And without waiting for an answer go to wash ourselves in penitence at his tribunal. Without waiting for an answer, so as to remain in terrible doubt! All of this is intolerable.

How my state of mind has changed from that easy indifference with which I went to receive Communion sacrilegiously, not having been to Confession, when I got married! And I recall that phrase about how anyone who takes Communion sacrilegiously eats his own damnation. What does it mean? How could I have been so free and easy? And when I went to Communion in faith as a child, did I ever feel all they say one feels? No, never.

Time and again I set myself to thinking *rationally* about my condition, and I go back to consider my heritage and the habits formed in childhood and the unconscious and a thousand and one things, but when the hour comes I feel myself drawn to the church, where I go and hear Mass. And I know full well that if reason gets the better of me I will fall back into anguish and suffering and never again know peace in this life. No! I do not want to die altogether.

I have made mock of doubt, and now I am fallen back into it. Doubt! How ridiculous all the lucubrations on doubt have seemed to me! And now I will have to go through yesterday's ridiculousness all over again.

Am I not perhaps a prey to auto-suggestion? Am I not creating a fictitious and insincere state of mind? Am I not creating a fiction in myself by this constant reading of books of devotion, by these Masses and rosaries and prayers? Am I not perhaps to deceive myself in the belief that this illusion will give me peace?

Are these ideas perhaps demoniacal temptations?

People have noticed the change in me. Some newspapers even discuss it. I have created a new position for myself. Is this not some new kind of slavery? If I persist in this change—a matter of divine grace—and return to my childhood faith, won't it be somewhat fictitious? If I return to what I have been all these recent years and let what is happening to me now pass away like a summer cloud, a temporary disturbance, neither one side nor the other will receive me as before: to both sides, I will seem a madman or a hypocrite. I have displayed all my weakness in the light of day, not knowing how to be wary. I have brought all my debilities into the open, not knowing how to be circumspect.

Why do I worry so much about what others think?

The forms pride takes are countless. I have a letter telling me that the writer had gone through what I am going through. I exclaimed: Poor man! Why should I think I'm superior to others even in my capacity for tribulation and strife? I'm truly sick, sick with *I-ism*.

I've lived on the empty vanity of making a spectacle of myself, showing the world my spirit as some sort of example, something worth knowing about. Like those poor people who show off their sores by the roadside there are people, literary people, who show off their wounded souls and present themselves as interesting beings. Like children sporting a bandage on a hurt finger, they make the most of their injury, delighted with themselves, playing at being worse off than they are, thinking how worthy they are of notice.

Still, a certain modesty has saved me. I have not displayed that secret delight in me myself, that *in-me-myself-ism*. I was aware of its evil, of its being an ugly vice and a font of sin, and I kept it to myself. This grace which God has granted me to allow me to keep to myself my secret self-pride is what now allows me to fight against it.

And I have also been saved by the real affection I have been able to show my friends, the sincere love I have felt for those good people.

My anonymous contributions to *La Lucha de Clases*, the continuous propaganda work for that kind of elevated and noble and caring socialism, the campaigns I carried on without thinking of myself, were a blessing for my soul. Amidst all my spiritual misery I found reserves of nobility and abnegation, thanks be to God!

But now I must root out my vice, put an end to my secret self-indulgence and to that spiritual masturbation for whose sake I hid from everyone. It is not enough to keep pride from being seen. It may even be better to let it be seen. The point is to avoid allowing it to get a hold within you, for it is in private that it can be cultivated with greater delectation.

And what numberless forms this childish *I-ism* takes! Even as I wrote certain letters, didn't the thought cross my mind that their recipients would save them? Haven't I dreamed in idle moments that once I was dead my correspondence would be collected and published? The sad vice of the literati! The fatal vanity which sacrifices one's soul to one's fame! Nowhere as much as among the literati are the consequences of sickly self-love so fatal, a funeral procession of envies, presumptions, prides, pufferies, and hypochondrias. Imagine—writing letters for posterity!

Imagine—living for the sake of history! How much simpler and healthier to live for eternity!

Then there is a degree of self-love which is truly sad, when one lives to please oneself and not others and this takes the form of amusing oneself in one's work. This is masturbation of the spirit, onanism of the soul, self-worship. Anything to avoid recognizing our wretchedness, our nothingness, to avoid annihilating ourselves before God so that He will free us from annihilation!

Humiliation, humiliation! Humiliation in order to achieve humility! Crown of thorns, derision, a reed for a scepter, bloody mockery, and grace, Lord, to endure them!

These very notebooks, are they not a form of vanity? Why do I write them? Have I succeeded in keeping them hidden, as was my first intention? But, looking at the matter another way, should I hide away and let die in me what grace has inspired in me? Should I allow the fear of exhibiting myself hinder the publication, Lord, of your grace and favors toward me, stop me from describing the misery of a modern spirit for the instruction of others, and perhaps their consolation? For in all truth, my illness is common, trivial, and ordinary—and the disease of almost all the literati. And now, when God deigns to call me, after permitting me to make a certain literary name for myself in a certain circle, it must be for some reason.

Sincerity, holy sincerity! Let me not think of me

and my glory but of yours, Lord, and let me neither seek nor turn aside from scandal.

———————

Death.

When you are stricken with a fatal disease, your family will avoid telling you that you have only a year or a few months to live. And can you then count on that much time? Is four, five, ten years more than one? Are we not all fatally afflicted?

Few people consider the amount of time left to them. Few face the fact that we are all condemned to death. Yes, condemned to death, all of us.

If men were immortal except for a few, in what despair would that few live! Well now, we might as well assume that other men are immortal but that we are not: for others will die for themselves and if they die after us they will not die for us, not, as far as we know, die at all. As far as you are concerned, all those who die after you are immortal, or as good as immortal, if there is no other life, for once you are dead, what difference does it make whether others follow you or not? Since we all die, we do not fully absorb the significance of death. The idea that "we all must die" obliterates the terror of "I must die." In the measure that the proposition is extended from the individual to the universal scale it seems to become more abstract, more mathematical, more passionless, less tangible and real. "We shall all die" is a statement said as if it were "the three angles of a triangle are equivalent to two right angles," as if it did not impose an overwhelming reality upon our life.

Our imagination helps to deceive us. Since we represent the world to ourselves as continuing to exist after our death, we do not realize that the world we represent as surviving us is only a representation which will die with us. The world, our world, will come to an end when we do. If there is no other life, our end is the end of the world. A sad consolation indeed to think that the world will go on and that our children and our works will live—and we dead! A sad consolation if when we die we die totally and return to nothingness! It is no consolation at all, but disconsolation and despair. But a beautiful idea if we expect another life!

There is only one supreme moral and practical problem, the problem of the beyond, of what lies beyond the tomb. If the world which you imagine surviving you is a nothingness, then it is no more than a piece of your imagination that will die with you.

Would that I could find, not words, but fiery sensations and intuitions to transmit to others the emotion of death.

We already have the experience of death—assuming that there is no other life—in our experience of deep sleep. To die, then, would be to go to sleep forever. When we go to bed, why do we hanker after sleep? Because we expect to wake up. But just try imagining one night, with total concentration, that you will not awaken, and you'll see what becomes of your sleep and what real horror is, however slight your power of imagination.

It must be altogether terrifying to feel life's sleep come upon you like an invasion and to attempt to resist it by striving to keep your eyes open, and then to have your mind wander and nod off while you make desperate efforts to fix your attention on things, exhausting yourself in the effort and surrendering all the more deeply to a total swoon.

Imagine to yourself as vividly as possible that you are suddenly stricken with blindness, and that then, just as you are adjusting to your blindness by making the most of the impressions you receive from your other senses, you go deaf. Progressively you lose your sense of touch and smell and taste and even your sense of movement, so that you become an inert thing for whom not even suicide is possible. You still have your solitary thoughts, your memory. You can still live in the past, in your past. But then even your thoughts begin to abandon you, and, deprived of all senses, you can neither create substitutes for them nor renew them. They begin to liquify and to evaporate and you are left with the mere consciousness of existing. After a while you lose that, too, so that you are left alone, you remain completely alone . . . no, you don't remain, for you no longer are anything. Not even the consciousness of your nothingness remains.

What a gift of grace to believe like the peasant who gets up with the sun to work his fields and with the sun goes in to rest from his labor! His days are serene and he dies as he has lived. In the other life, it must be a glorious spectacle to see the roles reversed and a gradation of glory completely opposite from that of this world: the great of this world, those who live in history, brought low, acting as a support for those who were ignored here, and all in tribute to the Lord.

O the wretchness of literat-ism, of neo-mysticism, romantic religionism, fashionable piety, conformist Catholicism, tasteful faith, gutter-journalism, party dissension, formalist dogmatism, all the petty vileness of narrow souls!

Grant me, Lord, the ability to withdraw into myself, so that my faith will be in me and will be mine!

Notebook 4

✝

DEATH.

Media vita morte sumus: in the midst of life we are in death. That is the beginning of an antiphon of the Lenten collect of the Dominican breviary.

_____

D[eath].

I heard about a man who died in the hospital. When the priest went to anoint him the man did not want to open his right hand, which he had tightly closed. When he died, it turned out that he was keeping a coin in his hand.

Thus do many people act, except instead of their hands their spirits are closed and they want to keep the world in them.

The poor man did not see that once he was dead his hand would not belong to him, but to the earth.

_____

There is no salvation outside the Church. What does that mean? What does *Church* mean here? Does this mean that simple Protestant villagers will not be saved?

In a Catholic country the humble and perfect thing is to be a Catholic. The perfect thing, in principle, is to abide by the religion one inherits.

Perhaps, for the person who thinks that there's no salvation outside his Church, there is none.

Sects are human in the measure in which they deny or oppose others. The most godly sect is that one which strives the most to absorb and embrace all the others,

*70**

the one in which the others best fit. What is the plague of Protestantism? Its anti-Catholicism.

Of all the tortures to which Christ was subjected in His Passion, none was mortal. The wounds were not deadly but painful: the most painful wounds are not the most serious. It was all a matter of inflicting pain. A blow whose eventual consequences are slight may hurt more than a mortal wound. Christ endured whips, the crown of thorns, blows, and then, nailed on the cross, perhaps with bones dislocated, He died of pain, of an excess of physical suffering rather than of an organic failure of his vital organs. It is thought He may have died of tetanus; in any case He died of pain.

Let me die spiritually, Christ, of pain for my sins.

Christ must suffer a new Passion and crucifixion in our souls so that He may rise there and redeem us from eternal death.

Mental prayer eludes me. My bookish habits are such that I can only conceive of pious thoughts and propositions by reading, as a commentary on what I read, and I am forced to crystallize them by writing them down. Study in order to write! Such is the goal of intellectualism: to think in order to produce thoughts. It is the terrible vicious circle of our economy transferred to the world of the spirit. One does not think for the sake of oneself, for one's own salvation; one does not *meditate*, one *thinks*. One thinks to produce thoughts. One thinks while reading; one meditates while praying. To meditate is really to consider with love, through concentration and withdrawal, a mystery, a given mystery, trying to penetrate to its loving essence, to its quickening center. To think is to establish relationships between different ideas. The highest degree of meditation is ecstasy; the highest degree of thought is the construction of a philosophical system. Meditation makes one better and more saintly; thinking, more wise.

In our sad economy one produces to consume and consumes to produce, a vicious circle, as if we were never to die. And in our mental life it's all a matter of producing new ideas or images so that in the process of consuming them aesthetically we may produce still more new ones. Hence our terrible literat-ism.

When by much meditation on a mystery we become more virtuous, our virtue becomes a habit whose foundation lies in the mystery itself.

I have been a great talker because my mind needs to talk, and the material word has always stimulated me. I have thought aloud. I have formulated by own ideas by trying to transmit my thought to others, thus discovering and developing my thinking. Hence, my presumption in always directing the conversation, taking it over, forever interrupting while never suffering anyone else to interrupt, insisting on setting the theme of the discussion and then turning it into a monologue. I thought, but I did not meditate. And so I sought company and avoided solitude. Now I begin to meditate on what I have thought, to examine its roots and very soul. For this reason, I am more drawn to solitude now, although still not very greatly.

Humility.

Christ's greatest humility is demonstrated in His submission to His Father and in seeking the latter's glory, not His own. Jesus rejected all human glory, all that glory which those who would make Him a genius or a superior man would ascribe to Him. He rejected all that exaltation of which He is made object by those who call Him the great revolutionary.

"I receive not honor from men" (John 5:41). "If I honor myself, my honor is nothing" (John 8:54).

I lost my faith *thinking about dogmas*, about the mysteries as dogmas; I recover it *meditating about the mysteries*, about the dogmas as mysteries.

Thy kingdom come.

To ask it is to ask for death, since we will achieve it only through death.

But deliver us from evil.

Deliver us from the evil one, from the Devil.

Our flesh incites us to serve it with concupiscence; the world asks us to serve it, offering us vainglory; the Devil invites us to serve our own selves with the complacency of our own pride.

A Mystery.

St. Catherine of Siena said that the Saviour's actions are so fertile in teachings that by meditating on them steadfastly each person will find in them the nourishment most suitable for the salvation of his own soul, and that it is profitable to see Christ's teachings in various lights so that each person may take from them the most suitable meaning.

Humility.

What is exclusively our own, exclusively true of us, is precisely our nonbeing: it's our only rightful possession. Whatever we have of being we have by divine grace. Whoever humbles himself annihilates his nothingness, and by annihilating his nothingness he exalts

Diary

and purifies his being. Whoever humbles himself before God humbles his nonbeing before Being and thus elevates himself in Being. "He that glorieth, let him glory in the Lord" (I Cor. 1:31).

The most humble of the earth is the most holy, St. Augustine says.

———

History. John 3.

In our deeply restless times, in which a religious sense seems to have awakened, many of us go, like Nicodemus the Pharisee, to visit Christ by night, secretly, when no one may see us, and we say, "Rabbi, we know that thou art a teacher come from God: for no man can do these miracles that thou doest, except God be with him" (John 3:2). No one, in effect, can thus move our hearts; no one can give us this thirst for another life and this longing for faith if God is not with him.

Nicodemus, the Jewish Pharisee, worshipped in secret, and the woman of Samaria, the poor sinner of a despised race, publicly acknowledged Christ in the scorned city of Sychar. The Samaritans, those simple semi-pagans, needed neither signs nor miracles, and believed in Jesus simply by hearing Him. But to the Jews Jesus said bitterly, "Except ye see signs and wonders, ye will not believe" (John 4:48). How fine the faith of the Samaritan woman! Like her, our soul goes for water to the traditional well, the treasury of knowledge and study and human consolation. And then one day we find sweet Jesus beside the well, wearied with the road, "about the sixth hour" (John 4:6), at noon, in the middle of life's bustle. And He appears to us as in tradition asking for our attention and our study. The religious problem tempts and attracts our natural desire for truth, stimulates our thirst.

74*

And Jesus, who exclaimed on the Cross, "I thirst!"—
thirsted for love and adoration and justice—bids us
drink by asking, "Give me to drink." He wishes to be
given our love, have us attend to Him with love, not
as a vain matter of curiosity, but as the principle of a
simple and humble life. And we ask, "How is it that
you, one of the simple men, ask me for love?" He
answers as He did to the Samaritan woman, "If thou
knewest the gift of God, and who it is that saith to
thee, Give me to drink; thou would have asked of him,
and he would have given thee living water" (John
4:10). The thought flashes through our mind to ask
for faith to live in tranquillity like simple souls: it is
Jesus saying these things and offering us the living
water of faith. And still we resist, saying He has no
place whence to draw it. Because the well of our reason
is deep, we can no longer believe, after having been
through rational analysis. Ah! if we could only believe,
we say to ourselves, but no, it is no longer possible.
Pristine simplicity has left us forever. The well is dry.
There are no living waters in our soul and none in
science either. And Jesus tells us that whoever drinks
the waters of worldly wisdom will soon thirst again,
for it is a water of which the more one drinks the more
one thirsts, while whoever drinks the living waters of
faith will no longer thirst, for it shall be "a well of
water springing up into everlasting life" (John 4:14).
And like the Samaritan woman we say, "Sir, give me
this water, that I thirst not, neither come thither to
draw" (John 4:15). And then we are bidden to summon our affections, our idols, the spirits before whom
we have prostrated ourselves, the doctrine to which
we cleave, just as He asked the Samaritan woman,
"Go, call thy husband, and come hither"; to which
"the woman answered and said, I have no husband"

(4:16-17). In the same way we must answer, "We have neither idol nor master." To which Jesus will reply, as he did to the woman, that we have had many, that we have gone from one to another, from one master to others, from doctrine to doctrine, handing ourselves over first to this one and then to the other one, without ever having married any, merely fornicating with each, in search of intellectual pleasure and delight, to satisfy our intellectual lust. Thus I have gone after one doctrine and then another, pursuing delights of the mind.

"I am the one who brings to my divinity those who know their weakness" (*Imit.* Bk. III, Ch. LVII, 3).

He takes into His Being those who recognize their nonbeing.

The development of Christianity was due to the teachings of Christ, aided providentially by Hellenic philosophy. If the prophets of Israel were the announcers of the Messiah, Hellenic philosophy was a human preparation for the sacred mysteries. The climax of Hellenic philosophy was the "Know thyself" on the temple at Delphi.

"Know thyself!" said the inscription, but Carlyle said, "No! You are unknowable. Know your work and carry it out!" But what is my work? There is something more than knowing yourself, than working or knowing your work and carrying it out, and than loving oneself. That is to be oneself. Be yourself, and since you are nothing, be nothing. Let yourself go, be lost in the hands of the Lord.

---

28 May.   Acts 17

"Then Paul stood in the midst of Mars' hill, and said, Ye men of Athens, I perceive that in all things

ye are too superstitious." He meant by "too superstitious" too much devotion to religiosity.

"For as I passed by, and beheld your devotions, I
found an altar with this inscription: to the unknown
God. Whom therefore ye ignorantly worship, him declare I unto you."

He is Spencer's Unknowable, Schopenhauer's Will,
the vague Ideal of our own men of Athens.

It was to the men of Athens that Paul said, "In him
we live, and move, and have our being: as certain also
of your own poets have said. For we are also his offspring" (Acts 17:23). It was to the men of Athens that
St. Paul declared this pantheistic mystery.

"And when they heard of the resurrection of the
dead, some mocked: and others said, We will hear thee
again of this matter."

The doctrine of the resurrection of the dead was the
touchstone of scandal and commotion in Paul's preaching.

Dionysius the Areopagite believed and was converted, and he was the true father of Christian mysticism.

———————

Thy kingdom come.

"It was an axiom of the Jewish schools that any
prayer in which a reminder of the kingdom of God
was not to be found was no prayer at all."

P. Didon, *Jésus-Christ.*

———————

The Social Question.

In the time of Christ there were two great Messianic
currents, one political, the other religious. One group
dreamt, under the name of the Kingdom of God, of
the reestablishment of the kingdom of Israel and of
shaking off the Roman yoke, and they awaited a war-

rior as Messiah. And today there are those who await an earthly Arcadia, the reign of equality, an end to bourgeois domination and Romanism, the promised land here below, and justice here below. These are the people who dream of the triumph of law, of parliaments, and of class war. The doctors of world socialism are the new Talmudic doctors. The kingdom of God is for them their own reign. "They place their ideas in place of God's thought" (Didon). Jesus adopted the then-current phrase "kingdom of God" just as today he would adopt the term "reign of justice and equality and fraternity." But His kingdom is not of this world.

Religious spirits know that the kingdom is spiritual and internal.

Humility.

Withdraw your gaze from the death that awaits you and from the nothingness you merit and fear, and look backwards to consider your past nothingness before you were born. What were you before you were born? Merely an idea of the Divinity. Why are you yourself and not someone else? That is, why are you? In yourself, in your consciousness, you behold the mystery of creation. If you can ponder your birth calmly, why not calmly ponder your dis-birth? And if death terrifies you, why does not your dis-death, that is, your birth, terrify you? How little we think about our birth, our personal origin! I am I and not someone else, that is, I am.

Feelings without concepts to sustain them, without bones, are pulpy and flaccid and lead to sentimentality. Without faith, the religious sense becomes sentimentalism, finally turning the soul into a pulpy mass.

On Our Nothingness.

As we become nothing, that is, as we become accustomed to our nothingness, we shall become all, become our all, become in a certain sense gods.

"The more man gets away from himself and his concern with things, the more God in all his richness comes to man; God lives in you in the measure you die to yourself" (*Das geist. Leben*, p. 321).

Divest yourself of what is human in you in order to remain with what is divine in you, in order to lay bare the divine. What is human in you is that which you call and believe to be your *I*. Below and within your consciousness of yourself there is your consciousness of God, of God in you.

———

D[eath.]

St. Cyril begins his eighteenth Catechesis with these words: "The root of every good action is the hope of resurrection."

———

Sufferings.

"It is possible for man to merit participation in each suffering of the Passion of Our Lord Jesus Christ. Only, in consequence of the fruit of *His* passion we should be more quickened by it than if we had suffered that Passion ourselves; without the fruit of His Passion no suffering of our own could be fruitful."

(P. Denifle, *Das geist. Leben*, p. 235.)

Human wisdom went so far in Stoicism (insofar as it is identifiable with Epicureanism) as to suffer all earthly ills with indifference. To embrace them and revel in them and love them is superhuman.

"Blessed are those who weep, for they shall be comforted." Those who weep, not those who suffer. They weep who suffer with humility. The Holy Spirit is the Comforter.

Notebook 5

+

THY WILL BE DONE.

This cry encompasses all prayer. God is asked for what must be in any case: that His will be done.

"And this is the confidence that we have in him, that, if we ask anything according to his will, he heareth us" (I John 5:14).

———————

That pure shadow surmounting the centuries across the waters of the world without sinking from sight you believe to be a phantom, and yet you ask it that you too may walk the waters of the world without sinking from sight. But you lack faith and you feel yourself sinking and you ask it to save you. And then it asks you: O man of little faith, why do you doubt?

Why do we doubt? Why do we not recognize Jesus to be the true Son of God? We would then surmount time, without sinking into it; we would then surmount our years like a phantom floating above them, and, continuing our progress towards heaven, we would behold the world's current flowing beneath us, the waters of time flowing and carrying away each day's malice.

———————

The colder the soul is, the more it will find itself soaked in the dew of grace when it wakes from its spiritual nights.

———————

How is it that suddenly, today, the 9th of May, 1899, in the midst of my studies, I am overcome by a craving to pray? I have had to lay down my book and retire to my room to say a brief prayer and to read in the *Imitation* the prayer asking for light for the spirit.

———————

Today, the 15th of January, 1902, in the midst of reading Holtzmann's *Leben Jesu*, p. 102, I again take up this diary.

———————

Our Father.   15 January 1902
   Always the Father, always engendering the Ideal in us. I, projected to infinity, and you, who are projected to infinity, meet. Our lives, parallel in infinity, meet, and my infinite I is your I, the collective I, the Universe I, the Universe made person, and it is God. And I, am I not my father? Am I not my son?
   Thy will be done.

End of Diary

Unamuno as a boy

Unamuno as a young man, about 1882

Salamanca, with the Old Bridge over the river Tormes in the foreground

Apse and Cock Tower of the Old Cathedral, Salamanca

(Opposite) A page from the beginning of Notebook 1, Diario íntimo

+

Escepión toda sabiduría terrena, y toda
humana y propia complacencia.

_____

El misterio de la libertad es el
misterio mismo de la conciencia refle
ja y de la razón. El hombre es
la conciencia de la naturaleza,
y por su aspiración á la gracia
consiste la verdadera libertad.
Libre es quien puede recibir la
divina gracia, y por ella salvarse.

_____

Hay que buscar la verdad y no
la razón de las cosas, y la verdad
se busca con la humildad.

_____

Estando en Munitibar cuando el
apuro del parto de Ceferina me

Self-portrait, from Mi vida y otros recuerdos personales

The Irish seminary
in Salamanca

Unamuno on the beach in Hendaye, about 1927

Unamuno reading in bed, his favorite place for working, 1934

Copy of the portrait of
Unamuno by Maurice
Fromke, inscribed by the
artist to Professor
Warner Fite of Princeton
University, who
translated Unamuno's
Niebla (see Letter of 19
November 1928).
Courtesy of George
Liddle Fite.

Unamuno on the balcony
of the Rector's residence,
University of Salamanca,
1934

Unamuno in his study, 1934

Last photograph of Unamuno, May 1936

II

Selected Letters
1890–1936

To Pedro de Mugica   Bilbao,
                                                   26 July 1890

My very dear friend,

I am going to answer your last two letters. I am
busier these days because my fiancée came three days
ago from Tudela to Guernica, and I shall be making
frequent trips there. Yesterday morning, on St. James'
Day (a holiday in Spain), I went to Guernica. I came
back this morning to do my tutoring, and tomorrow,
Sunday, I'll leave here at 7:00 a.m. and arrive there
at 8:30, staying until early Monday. I go to Guernica
every holiday. It's the best sedative, the best way to
soothe my tantrums. My fiancée has a most lovely
character, lovelier even than her eyes. The poor thing
was brought up in the school of hard knocks, having
been orphaned when she was twelve. Later, living with
her grandparents, she was her grandfather's nurse. She
suffered a great deal from the other children in the
family, of which she was the true head. She took everything cheerfully. I have never known her to be in bad
humor. Her good spirits are spontaneous and natural.
Now she has gone to live with a widowed uncle who
has four small children, and the poor fellow was very
much moved when he told me that she brought happiness to his home and that thanks to her he has been
able to manage. Considering the silly and very inad-
equate education received by most of our middle-class
Spanish women [. . .] it would be impossible to find
someone with more insight, penetration, and good taste
than she has. She reads what I bring her, understands

*85**

it, reasons out her opinions, and has the simplest, most honest heart you could find. She's a happy little girl (though not little chronologically), like a canary or a goldfinch, and hasn't one iota of flirtatiousness. She plays with her little cousins, who love her madly. She keeps them entertained and bears the weight of the household.

My work on the war is progressing. I have a collection of *La Guerra*. I'm looking for the *Cuartel Real*, and they're going to give me *Irurac-bat* and *Euskaldune*. The official facts are of no consequence to me [. . .]; the most important thing is the spirit, the inner impulse; a pile of tiny events, a few anecdotes, a few episodes furnish me with more territory than one of Dorregaray's campaigns. My work is a novel about the psychology of an individual, a town, and a race. I investigate the motivations of ex-Carlist soldiers which took them off to the hills. I have a thousand scraps of information on the feud between the country people and the inhabitants of Bilbao, on the influence of the clergy, etc. etc. The work is underway. Some samples—

1. It's a psychological fact that in the throes of death one returns to childhood, forgetting recent things because of a kind of amnesia. This leads me to depict a scene in which Ignacio, my novel's hero, falls mortally wounded at Somorrostro. Deaf and blind from his injury, he sees his childhood years brought back by the automatic functioning of his brain. [. . .]

2. There's a passage about the influence of the clergy and the small-town mind, a sort of philosophy in literary prose, which I can back with data. [. . .] And there are a brief depiction of the bombardment of Bilbao, scenes in the Carlist club before the war, rustic episodes, a Carlist shyster, a dialogue between a Carlist

86*

and a republican, domestic scenes, etc. From time to time I will send you parts and see if you like these samples, even though they are among the least vivid. [. . .]

I'm in a hurry. My respects to your wife, and to you a cordial handshake, from

MIGUEL DE UNAMUNO

To Pedro de Mugica   Bilbao
                                                1 September 1890
My good friend,

I should be ashamed to take up my pen to answer you after the three letters I've gotten from you. If you knew my state of mind these days you would understand and perhaps forgive me. I have been attacked by persistent hypochondria with a tendency toward a laziness I can't quite overcome. I don't do anything, I don't study anything, I work at nothing, and I am consumed by anxiety over a step I can't resolve to take. It's a most terrible thing, this timid and indecisive character of mine. I waste myself in pointless imaginings, in deliberations, in making plans, and in doing nothing. My house seems like a tomb. For some time now I have hardly spoken a word and there's a sad and silent struggle taking place, for which I'm entirely to blame. It's a struggle between my mother and me over who will speak first. She knows what I want, but I can never find the decisiveness to open my mouth.

My poor fiancée, who suffers in everything pertaining to me and endures the worst consequences of my chronic indecision, is in Bermeo, where I've been to see her.

I don't find the energy in myself except to keep

*87**

pursuing my studies of the Carlist War and the character of this town of mine. I alternate this with the obligation of studying Greek. Not a word of philology, which I've forgotten all about for some time. The Carlist War is my salvation. It raises me up out of my apathy, shakes me up a little, and, with my visits to poor Concha, it's the only thing which soothes me.

[. . .]

I live in the Carlist Civil War, and only in it. I give both body and soul to this work of mine. I am at the highest boiling point. I do nothing but collect notes, observations, and abstracts, working with fervor (that's the word).

Give me the details of the rock-throwing contests when you were a child, tell me in what years they took place and everything that you know. You must have known many men who served in the Carlist ranks. If you know the reasons which sent them off to the woods and hills and how they talked about the war after it was over, whatever notes you could send me would be extremely valuable. I say extremely valuable because your natural traits and perhaps the education you have received in philology and the sciences cause you, like me, to be very much given to details, to little events, minute matters, and not to bold syntheses and generalizations. I prefer a hundred anecdotes to a philosophico-historical dissertation on Carlism like those Aparisi wrote. From a hundred bits of town gossip and details and individual cases a quick mind can extract more juice than from the most enlightened dissertation. I take you to be a keenly observant spirit, and the news which you gave me about the rock-throwing contests and your Carlist friends confirms me on this.

I shall gather data and more data, pile it up and give

it order. I will make a scaffolding with which I will build my tower, my novel, and then I will tear down the scaffolding. The details will make the work, but only a few of the most characteristic ones. Out of a great heap of details about the entrance of Don Carlos into towns I have constructed a representative description of such an entrance. I keep the most characteristic and outstanding details, and the rest I mash into the sauce which seasons the dish.

Where did you spend the war? Did you stay here during the bombardment? Were you armed? What did you think *then* about the Carlists? Etc. Do you recall any details of the action at Somorrostro? Do you remember the state of mind of Bilbao during the war? [. . .]

Do me a favor and take some time off from philology, pry into your memories and the depth of your political sentiments and paint for me how the storm built up during the years between 1868 and 1870, something of those turbulent pilgrimages which the Carlists took from their club on Calle de la Torre, provocateurs with white berets and cudgels, singing "Ay, ay, ay, mutillac."

You were a young man then. Do you remember something of the proclamation of the Republic in Bilbao? Something of the Glorious Revolution of '68 here and what happened? Do you remember that illumination which was made on the twenty-fifth anniversary of the pontificate of Pius IX?

On all this I have abundant data, but what you might give me would go in a preferred place to increase my collection, because of the abilities you have as an observer. For my purposes, personal recollections are worth a thousand times more than the official documents with which Pirala has written his heavy-handed and boring book of history, a model of botched patchwork, a storehouse of news items, a collection of proclamations and official documents, of battles and meetings of negotiation, soldered together in the worst style imaginable and with the crudest critical sense possible. That is not a history; it is the material for a history. Pirala deserves praise for his laborious diligence, for the care and energy with which he has collected the stones, timbers, and other materials for the edifice. But from time to time the poor fellow trips up badly because of his desire to set himself up as a critic and a philosopher. God has made him a library mouse, nothing more.

[. . .]

Please forgive my delay. The pleasure and act of writing you and busying myself with my work has given me a little breather from the torments that I am suffering these days. Now that I've finished this chattering letter I will fall once more into my indecisiveness.

Pardon me, and a hug from UNAMUNO

To Juan Arzadun   Bilbao,
                                                                  18 December 1890

Dear Juan,

I wrote you days ago that "I'll write you tomorrow." Today is tomorrow.

Conchita was here. She came on Friday and left last night: that's why I couldn't write you before. The event will take place the 25th or 31st of January. If you were to be here, we would be most pleased to have you attend: she told me not to forget to say so.

I am on tenterhooks these days: spine-tingling prurience: it won't go away until I've got her in my power.

The idea of a formal wedding terrifies me. I can already see myself dressed up like a puppet, lacking in all the informality of my ordinary bearing, deprived of my daily suit, with its wrinkles and baggy knees. I can see myself arriving at the Church with a retinue, abashed, tied up in knots. I see myself involved in a formula-comedy, all of it meaningless today, dead symbols in the eyes of a people pretentious by inheritance—like any people. I see myself being watched, under observation by innocuous malice. I wish there were no such thing as a wedding ceremony, with all its obligatory silliness—and then the rounds of toasts, horror of horrors! I am repelled at their making a comedy, an excuse for a fiesta, out of what is most intimate, most withdrawn, most personal, something which should be the most silent thing in the world.

I am also repelled by the *arras*, the dowry of thirteen coins, a senseless ritual for most people. For me it merely serves to recall its original significance: the time when a man bought a woman from her parents. I can't stand all this pagan dross which has flowed down to us as hollow formula.

There should simply be a public benediction, a public vow before the altar of the God of the People, two signatures in the civil registry—and there's an end to it! That would be simple, serene, free of dead ritual. And then home! Without people, without all that tumult, without all that eating. Unsociable, that's me. Eventually we'll be left alone, free of the gaze of innocuous malice. After the sterile ritual, the fertile mystery.

My unsociability is incurable, the only cause of slight disagreements between the two of us; I, staunch as a Quaker in my ideals, scorning etiquette and formality,

and cut out to stay at home, where she strives to do-
mesticate me.

You can't imagine how happy she is to be told that
she has already polished me up a bit, that previously
I went around like a tramp, while now I am a mite
more presentable. When she hears these things she
expands as if to say: "You see, I've tamed the bear! It
won't be long before he will be jumping through the
hoop and dancing atop the drum, grumbling all the
while, of course, but while he grumbles he'll jump
through the hoop and dance on the drum. You all think
he eats little children? Nothing of the sort! I simply
take him by the ear and he comes along as meek as
meek can be; if I scold him, he licks my hand; I can
make him drool like an ox as I lead him away." I'll
never forget the day when I decided to dance; she came
apart with laughter; my *gaucherie* delighted her. There's
no question but that she has civilized me, but even if
a bear be overcome with culture, a bear he remains,
and I remain a Quaker.

I'd like to pass as well-brought up, but not as a
"gentleman," not a "clubman." Good manners are one
thing, urbanity another. I don't even know how to
dance, nor play any instrument, nor sing, nor do card
tricks or prestidigitation, nor make conversation with
pedestrian people on silly or trivial subjects. How many
times she's scolded me because of my clumsiness! And
how many more times she will! And yet she will come
to see soon enough that I'm not really clumsy, not at
all. But there you are: it's all because I have no parlor
tricks, not a single refinement. I've lived all my life
among men, a man who talks endlessly about the affairs
of men, heavy nonsense, indigestible stuff!

Still, I'm gradually becoming civilized: she has taught
me to greet people, talk to young ladies, and many

other useful and pleasant habits. And she has much more to teach me yet!

Children really love me. They won't leave me alone. And how I like them! I'd challenge anyone to make better birds of folded paper, of the flying or nonflying kind; or better tables, ships, bonnets, caps, bellows, balloons, all out of paper; or to make a dancing doll, or to draw pictures without trim. At her uncle's house in Tudela the place turned into a children's riot whenever I appeared: "Make another!" "One for me too!" "One more for . . ." "A boy at school told me to ask you for one for him . . ." "Make an extra for when this breaks," and so on.

Poor children, so full of life, crammed with passions, all of them usable, all of them serviceable! I believe, along with the Jews, that everything serves some purpose, is good for something; I believe that even the obvious avarice and egotism of children can be of some benefit.

But children are killed with rules: their intelligence is smothered under a crust of foolishness, their imagination buried under faded funeral wreaths, their hearts buried alive in precepts. An awesome burden, the precept!

If I ever have children, they won't be sent to school. I'll teach them all I know and even what I don't know. I'll draw for them; I'll write what they'll read: stories, lessons, explanations, everything.

Children's literature is awful stuff, super-awful, written by schoolteachers and priests—the two main enemies of childhood! The former are people who put up with other people's children by way of gainful employment, the others are men without children of their own.

What a sad time when we are buried under gerunds,

pluperfects, ellipses, the newest names: Jeroboam, Solomon, David, Amsterdam! Luckily we pay no attention [. . .]. But just you try explaining that a language can be taught without a word as to a preterite or pluperfect, or subjunctive, or gerund, and just try teaching it more doctrinally, more scientifically than with grammar, then you will be attacked by the educational breadwinners, that entire plague who, with the best intention in the world, are wreaking an irreparable damage. It's painful to see a school, listen to what is being taught, and how. [. . .]

But enough of pedagogical matters. You will probably reflect on my running on this way about children. What can I do? It is the obsession of the nest.

Besides, I am cured of romantic illusions; I do not believe in ardent, eternal love and I expect much of my passion is for children. If God does not grant me children of my own, it will not matter: I shall create them out of my mind, and after all, isn't *she* a child? A child, a real child, even to her countenance, which is what I like about her. She has the outgoing character of a child, and her character is grafted on to the soul and body of a woman, which is what I desire and shall possess.

Furthermore, I do not believe in what romantic novels call conjugal bliss based on love. I consider marriage a serious thing and my Quaker spirit accepts it as the least of the world's ills, and I am prepared to accept it in all its prosaic character. She is a house plant and I am a domesticated bear: everything shall go well. She will civilize me completely, and I will take refuge in her from the imbecilities of the world.

And then I shall really be able to work: I shall say everything I wish to say and, like it or not, I shall add my note to the general concert. And it may go unnoticed by the immense chorus or the immense jangling, but the supreme harmony is made up of many such lost notes. And if I become a singer of small parts, fine; if I sing a principal role, even if restricted to the national stage, better still; if not, that too is all right.

I think, that in so far as my interests and work are concerned, it is best for me to get married. I remember you once told me that I need a safety valve, and I think that's what it will be: my ideas may be produced with less impetus and violence, but they will be produced in purer state between kisses. It seems unlikely that my ideas and fancies will not be refreshed and purified in my head when I sleep, tamed by happiness, next to her little blond head. I think that just one kiss of hers on my forehead will separate the iron from the slag. And then, it will be a restraint which will oblige me to proceed with greater caution [. . .]!

For a long time a stupid selfishness inspired me with fear over taking this step, and I used to say to myself "Is it all over if I get married? All the spiritual energies I would devote to her would be lost for my work!"

But I'm all over that. I used to agree with those monsters of ambition and selfishness that all those men worthy of emulation, were celibate. This sounds like a confession. Let's go further: I have on more than one occasion been so stupid as to think that if I have children, I shall have to supervise them and love them, and this will take away from the concentration I owe to my ideas.

If I had a child today and the house were to catch fire, which would I try to rescue first? Would I save my child, or save my notes, the children of my mind, the children of protracted enthusiastic, incandescent work?

But such thoughts are simply the bestial orgies of an imagination poisoned by pride and ambition; my heart, which thank God I have kept pure, has forcibly suppressed these mad fantasies. Everything I have said is cruel nonsense, and I shall never repent of them sufficiently.

Now, I do believe that to form a man is the most delicate and glorious work of art. It's not a matter of engendering a child and then leaving it just like that, handing it over to idiot teachers in an unknown world.

You can't imagine how I'd like to bring up a child my own way, from birth, without any interference whatever, do it all myself: teach him to care, to feel, to think. Parents who do not form their own children have no right to complain later about them no matter what they do or whatever the eventuality. Education today is the worst possible, so detestable it horrifies.
[. . .]

Once in Madrid I encountered one of those savages who consider women to be fancy furniture, or something worse; I told him the story of how a mother in Guipuzcoa received the news that the *Guiris* had killed her eldest son: she called the second son and told him: "You must be off now, perhaps to get killed by the *Guiris*, while I stay here to pray, along with your brother in heaven, for our triumph." When the savage from Madrid heard this, he exclaimed, "That was no woman."

She was no less than a heroic woman, she was larger than life! In the mind of the savage, some sentimental kitchen-maid would strike him as more sublime, and more noble if she was of the type who'd swallow phosphorous matches if a boyfriend jilted her and left her dishonored. [. . .]

I had promised you a narrative, but I haven't finished it yet. I have three in progress; the one for you, another one, and one for children. I outlined the first one to you hurriedly. The next one is about a man who marries, in the belief that he is wildly enamored, a woman most beautiful in the eyes of all. He escorts her around triumphantly, he enjoys her deliriously, he is ecstatic in the contemplation of all her perfections (not a single perfection of those demanded by the traditional canon is missing in her).

But it turns out that his love for his wife grows cold, it is snuffed out, and he falls madly in love with the maid, a raw young thing with the little face of a monkey, an ugly duckling in official eyes, but of whom they are forced to say: "She's homely, but there's something attractive about her . . ." In the end he leaves his wife and goes off to live with the maid and stays with her for the rest of his life.

It concludes with a dialogue between the hero and a friend of his, a dialogue in which I state my own aesthetic, my aversion toward the prescribed ideal woman, the woman who come out of books, all that foolish rubbish which calls on an "ideal" woman to be equipped with a tiny thin mouth, a straight nose, a delicate neck, and so on; and against all those imbecilic preceptives which have made beauties of hollow bland absurdities like the famed Castejon sisters with their dead faces, emblems of bourgeois stupidity. I knew a girl in Madrid who sold eggs, and she was snub-nosed, dark, scarred by smallpox, wide-mouthed and thick-lipped, and she was truly beautiful; and, according to what I was told, was much sought out. I'm sure you know that passage in Diderot in which he tells of a most aesthetic eunuch who could not pick out a girl pleasing to the Sultan; he chanced to meet a man from Marseilles who pointed out a desirable girl to him; the Sultan was quite taken with her. The eunuch returned to consult the man from Marseilles and find the formula (Diderot tells the story and I simply translate his beautiful vulgarity), and the man from Marseilles told him: "I desired her from the moment I saw her; if I had had any money, she wouldn't have gone to the Sultan's harem." And the poor eunuch realized he'd never be a connoisseur.

I belong to the school of the man from Marseilles: as regards physical beauty, there is no better test than the spasm which shakes one, jolts the nerves; as regards spiritual beauty, the only measure is in the dealing; and there is no other formula than these two together. And each one of these reactions may be so strong as to cover the other.

It's because women lack the precious discernment of the man from Marseilles as concerns others of their sex (as with us) that they judge feminine beauty so poorly themselves: women's taste in respect of their own sex is horrifying. Whenever I hear a woman say that another woman is lovely, I am on my guard. Concha tells me I have bad taste, which is funny; I wouldn't dare tell her anything as hypocritical.

Well now, I'll leave off the subject, so that there be some paper left.

MIGUEL

To Juan Arzadun   Salamanca,
                                                    17 June 1892
Dear Juan,

From *El Nervión* I have learned of your transfer to Santona, which delights me, since you are closer to Bermeo—and to Bilbao. I spent the month of June harassed with the farce of examinations. I am inclined from now on to fail provisionally everyone who has been recommended to me and to put him on the list of bad ones, in the absence of proof to the contrary. I warn you in case someone you know should ask for a recommendation.

It's been a time of letters, cards, and visits to this house, which has bored me to death. Half of Bilbao showed up, just as the students from Deusto arrived here to be examined. I examined law students in metaphysics, and there was much jubilation when the rumor got out that I and not the assistant teacher who had taught the subject was doing the questioning and marking the papers.

Of course the rigorous thing would have been to fail almost everyone, since the Jesuits have poisoned their minds by inculcating them with meaningless statements full of foolishness which the young are supposed to carry around learned by heart. There you would have seen the thought of Kant or Hegel expounded in a minute or two, or that of Spencer or John Stuart Mill or Darwin, and then refuted in another minute or two. It's nauseating to see what the *wise* Jesuits do to their students. They put in their heads an endless quantity of logomachies, games with words, slanders, calumnies, and atrocities—all the pseudo-scientific trash and debris of bloodless orthodox Scholasticism.

These pedants (you can't call the Jesuits anything else) think that knowledge is reduced to solutions and formulas. They believe that they know Hegelianism, to take one example, when they have learned its letter without being able to absorb its spirit. It doesn't occur to them that a man who reads a book and forgets everything it says can derive from it more advantage than someone who learns it from memory. They lack, to put it most simply, a scientific spirit. Blind in not distinguishing pure speculative knowledge from knowledge dedicated to a practical end, they do not know that while a machinist or an engineer needs *solutions*, someone who thinks about mechanics or a mathematician needs *method* and spirit, whether he arrives at a solution or not. This work is never lost— it's as sweet to chase a hare as it is to eat it. Thus it happens that metaphysics, which ought to be the school for freedom of thought and the gymnastics of reason, is reduced by them to a collection of merely verbal solutions meant to save the young from the supposed baneful consequences of one thing or another.

Nothing will be right so long as we have not convinced ourselves that the Jesuits' knowledge and wisdom are nonsense, empty pedantry, a hodgepodge of useless erudition, of feigned, make-believe profundity, and that they only manage to make their students turn away in disgust from study. [. . .] I hope that people, who are now being disillusioned, will finally become convinced that there's nothing to this business about stupid people never getting into the Society of Jesus. There is a great deal of stupidity in it, especially since it's almost entirely composed of very so-so mediocrities and very pompous people who think they understand something because they have read it and who believe that knowledge consists of quotations, dates, and discussions of worthless and insignificant opinions.

I'm indignant with those people, so don't be surprised at my annoyance. Without any spirit of hostility, I assure you that the Society of Jesus is a refuge for all manner of foolishness, of all modern teachings poorly understood and served up diluted in a broth of orthodoxy in order to give the unfortunate students they educate all the fake flowers, all the commonplaces, all the husks of cheap ideas, all the dead leaves left behind

100

by the living forest of living knowledge, all the intellectual excrement of the living organism of human
knowledge.

People who think that two systems differ according
to the solutions they offer and not the methods they
employ, those who think that positivism is a collection
of dogmas, those who fix their sights only on the practical consequences which they imagine will flow from
some doctrine or another—understood as they understand it, not as it is in itself—all these people neither
have nor will ever have a scientific spirit.

You can't have any idea of the destructive effects of
our official instruction. As if the Spanish people were
not already sufficiently stupefied and brutalized, as if
ignorance was not great enough in our country, the
universities carry out a mission of perverting the intelligence, thus completing the poisonous work of the
secondary schools. Imagine for yourself a professor of
Greek literature who doesn't know Greek and has
never read the classics except in translation, and—well,
there you have it all!

When I said to a professor of Spanish literature that
if I were teaching the subject I would spend each
course making the students read works chosen from
only two or three or four authors—possibly only one—
and then to comment upon and criticize them, he was
scandalized. To him it seemed better to tell them that
Calderón was born in such-and-such a year, that he
wrote such and such works, that he had a style with
such and such characteristics, that he had these defects
or those, and to tell the plots of one or two of his works,
and then to do the same thing with another writer.
But can one take up in a single course all the major
writers? The problem is to cover a given amount of

material in such-and-so many classes, dividing each into three or four or five parts, which includes this period, that, and the other—and finally literature becomes bibliography. The students must know what style each author used and what defects the professor finds in him, even if the student has never read him.

Enough of that. Perhaps you may see these notions developed later on in my "Old Times and Middle Times." At the same time I have in preparation a work which I may call "New Discourse on Method," if such a title isn't too presumptuous. It is the quintessence of my studies and philological meditations.

This is my second work, still unformed and embryonic. The first, which after long gestation is coming along well, is the novel. It is now complete and rounded out. [. . .]

When my novel is finished I will begin to put my philosophical notes in order. I aspire to write a work which will be accessible to any *cultured* and *educated* reader, even if he is not familiar with philosophical studies. I want it to be lively and agreeable—to do, in short, serious philosophy, but philosophy combining the greatest depth that I can reach with the greatest beauty of form and agreeableness of exposition, something resembling the work of Renan, Taine, and even Spencer. This business of writing philosophical books crammed with technical phraseology and obscure references and quotations should be left to people who think that a new name for something explains it and that merely verbal distinctions (between irritability and sensitivity, for example) are real distinctions—left, that is, to the Jesuits and the whole gaggle of orthodox Catholic "thinkers."

How much Spain needs to recover the pleasure of

philosophical study! Here philosophy is taken to be something arid, abstruse, and complicated, so it isn't comprehended that certain kinds of thought may exert the attraction of a poem, that many people consider Hegel's *Logic* an amazing epic of abstraction, and that Goethe found sublimity in Spinoza's *Ethics*. Between Fr. Zeferino González, F. Mendine, Ortí y Lara, Roy y Heredia, and my friend González Serrano, they have made philosophy into something that turns the stomach. Good González Serrano is another of these unfortunates who *knows* things but doesn't think. He knows the words but not their music. His writing would put a man to sleep even in the middle of an attack of kidney stones. He is heaviness, aridity, and dryness personified. He lacks flesh.

I do not know if I shall fail in my effort, but I will try. I do know that in a country where the tone is set by the Castilian—an essentially comicotragic and formal beast, a species of half-civilized Bedouin brought up on theology and words—a style that is free and easy, a style more suggestive than pedagogical, and a series of spiritual exercises for reason may not seem to merit the name of philosophy to those who think philosophy is the science that tells us whence we came, where we are going, and who we are. These people live in the hope of setting up penalties and punishments to make thinkers come to agreement on, for example, the problem of free will, because they believe that if people stop believing in the doctrine of the freedom of the will they would let themselves rob and kill others. I also know that these people call Kant a philosopher because he wrote poorly and Schopenhauer a humanist because he wrote agreeably. (Still, I can't deny it, Kant thinks more than Schopenhauer.)

Strauss is a wise man, to the orthodox, because he can be read only by the initiated, but Renan they consider a superficial rhetorician, because everyone has read him.

So that you may have some notion of these people I will tell you that an acquaintance of mine was amazed that I used my time and my intelligence in writing [. . .] a novel, and when I told him that I hoped to write a philosophical work, he asked me what parts of philosophy I planned to undertake, if I divided the subject into ontology, cosmology, and theology, and what my definition of philosophy might be. He probably took me for a crazy man when I told him that giving definitions leaves me cold and that if he read my work he would—perhaps—see what I understood by philosophy.

To sum it up, this business about some *intellectual exercises*, a guide for meditation, doesn't fit in the heads of these people who want readymade answers from you, so they'll be able to say, "Unamuno offers such and such a theory to explain this matter or that," just so they can have one more theory to add to their collection of intellectual knickknacks.

I tell you it makes me sick at my stomach, and I believe it is a duty of conscience to work for the culture of this poor country, the victim of dogmatism and pedantic nonsense, each of us in the measure of his strength.

If this summer we can see each other, I would read to you a part or all of my work in gestation—the plan, program, spirit, and scaffolding of my "Intellectual Exercises." A part of it I mean to explain what speculation is, how it differs from applied knowledge, and what value it has. A part will combat the notion that reason governs man, that he conducts himself according to the abstract doctrines which he professes; here I mean to hold reflective consciousness in less esteem, in favor of the unconscious. Another part will establish what scientific method is and how it ought to proceed. Another part will show that purely speculative scientific inquiry is artistic, and very substantially so. I begin with a lively and *picturesque* report about our universities, about the eagerness of parents for their sons to get a degree at the right age for having a career, about the road to Calvary on which anyone with the rare vocation for science will suffer (a vocation confused with the oratorical one), and about the desire to learn not for its own sake but in order to show off. It will be, in short, a study of the terrible mental torment which we subject our students to.

[. . .]

And what pleases me the most about this work will be what I will put at its end. I shall pour out my soul, my indignation, and my mental sorrows by attacking the universities and the professors (an association of executioners of intellect). I will gather up my bile and curse the *teacher* (who deserves his bad luck), agreeing with the government and the people who way down deep hold the teacher and the professor in disdain. In this sad and rude philippic I mean to present these educators as models of ignorance and an obstacle to progress. And then at the end I will place these words: *by Miguel de Unamuno, Professor of the University of Salamanca.* And I shall stand fast and await the avalanche, if it comes. Already see how I've hardly finished one work before starting another.

The 25th I leave for Bilbao where I will be all of

July and August and most of September. I tell you this in case you write me or come through Bilbao.

Concha is very well and we await what will come.

. . .

  [. . .]

You know that I love you.

MIGUEL

To Juan Arzadun   Bilbao,
3 August 1892

Dear Juan,

Now I am a father.

This morning Concha gave me my first child, and they are both very well.

  [. . .]

About my first impression at seeing that doll which seemed to be made of wax I can tell you very little. It was curiosity I felt above all—curiosity against a background of great indifference. The true feeling of fatherhood came when I saw him suckle at the breast of his mother.

Now, what will come of all this? Because those eyes which open not to see do not say anything clear. When he makes little faces in his sleep you would say that he is dreaming of the unknowable: poor little thing!

In short, as someone said to me some days ago, the die is cast and I am avenged.

I would be very pleased to attend your wedding if I can and if there's a chance. Your sister told me that your fiancée was there with her mother, looking for a house.

I have read *La Débâcle*. I am not satisfied. That

106[*]

enumeration of the battle of Sedan without any plan tires me. Fleguieux, Illy, Bazeilles, etc., etc. . . . endless, endless talk! The ending is what I liked best. The whole thing seems very much a lie; it exaggerates the carnage and the horror and the bloodshed, and I think, with Enrique Areilza, that the depiction of the ambulance is not true to life. I cannot forget Tolstoy in *War and Peace*. Tolstoy, who took part in the Crimean campaign, is less bloody and less given to depicting horror, and above all less carnal, and he kills his character with more naturalness. His soldiers are not absorbed in the battle itself. This compares with my own *documents*.

Areilza is right when he says that death is a natural thing, that it is not those who are dying but their families who play out the drama of the deathbed scene, and that in the hospital most people die as if going to sleep (especially those who are wounded), without thinking about death itself, serenely, letting out a few weak moans of pain. One must give back to death calm, serenity, and naturalness above all.

I am working more than ever and with greater success than ever on my spiritual child. While my child of the flesh was struggling to be born, I was mentally working on the gestation of the other "child." I hope to God that these two children can help one another and protect one another, like brothers, and that my child of the flesh may take pride in being the brother of the child of my mind. Poor little things! Both of them will wander through the world exposed to the insults of man.

I have spent some days in Somorrostro, very fruitful days. I have seen everything with complete clarity, I

have *felt* much, and I have reconstructed a good bit
. . . the work is going well.

I have collections of my articles in *El Nervión*. If you
like, I will send you my "Old Times and Middle Times."

I am going to see now what my little one is doing.
The poor little thing has a good nose. He's not very
fat, but he's long and has very beautiful eyes—his
mother's.

Since as yet he has no history, there's very little to
say about him. Today I have not had a single irregular
heartbeat, and I am happy about it; the fact is that I
am sound in spirit and in body, since I am taking
natural things in a natural way.

The day before yesterday I scandalized a bourgeois
by telling him that the pain caused by the death of a
beloved person is a matter of exaggeration. Grief doesn't
last very long. It is usually more painful to be ruined
or to ruin oneself than to lose a loved one. In my novel
I reflect on this.

Have you heard about *Martín Fierro*, the gaucho
poem of the Argentinian José Hernández? When I
have the pleasure of seeing you I shall lend it to you.
It's a great thing. It is written in the gaucho dialect
in stanzas of ten verses to be sung to guitar accom-
paniment. It has sold 58,000 copies in Buenos Aires.
He is the number one poet in the Castilian language
(or something like it) who is alive today, as I see it.
He is amazing in his primitive strength.

I didn't realize that I was writing such a long letter,
that it would go beyond two pages. The fact is that
my son is sleeping. Tomorrow he will be baptized,
and I still don't know what his name will be. I haven't
even thought about it. Also, I didn't care whether the

child would be a boy or a girl. I am sound, thanks to God.

You know I love you.

MIGUEL

To Pedro de Mugica   Salamanca,
                                                28 May 1893
Dear friend,

[. . .]

[. . .] Every day I am firmer in my intention to read only classical works; the rest are a sheer waste of time. Now I'm devoting myself to English literature. Shelley has me enchanted—excellent stuff. Do you know anything about the German poet Hölderlin, of whose poetry Lange says in his fine "History of Materialism" (*Geschichte d. Materialismus*) that he is "grandiose and wild"?

I have said little to you about Ibsen because I know little about him. I've read three of his plays. One, *Ghosts*, struck me as a monstrosity, crammed with falsities and hardly reasonable. Another, *Hedda Gabler*, left me cold, but I liked *A Doll's House* very much indeed. I've also read an extract and some fragments of his poem "Brand," and it pleases me enormously. Do you know why I haven't read more Ibsen? I'm putting it off until I can read him in Norwegian.

[. . .]

You tell me that there's one German genius I haven't given the study he deserves—Wagner—and that in my remarks on the decadence of the German genius I haven't taken music into account. [. . .] Now that you bring the matter up I'm going to make a confession:

109*

I am deaf to music. Asking me my opinion of Wagner is like asking someone who is colorblind and very weak of vision what he thinks about Raphael or Titian. Don't bring music up with me, for I don't understand it. It's a pity, there's no doubt about it, a source of spiritual pleasure is closed off to me, but what can I do? I'm just built this way and it troubles me no more than darkness troubles a mole. For this reason I take refuge in literature and painting.

How much does Münsterberg's *Psychology* cost? Find out and let me know. From what I've heard it's quite good.

It doesn't seem strange at all to me that Tolstoy, Ibsen, and Amicis are moving toward socialism. All of us whose souls are open to true reality go that way. And socialism will advance further as soon as the traces of that pedantic and insufferable Karl Marx are erased and the prattle of Bebel is dissipated. Socialism is before all else a great *moral* and *religious* reform, more than an economic one. It is a completely new ideal to take the place of that of the placid and harmful middle class, who busy themselves with futile pursuits and idle diversions.

I'm getting back to work on my novel, and with great zeal.

With the wholesome and noble candor which I want to exist between us [. . .] I'm going to ask you to economize as far as you can in sending me German books I haven't asked you for, because, although I want to remain abreast of German literature and science, our differences of taste, education, and intellectual orientation work in such a way that you are sending me very fine books which would please me more if they were something else. For this reason, I haven't sent

110*

any to you, hoping that you would tell me what you prefer. [. . .]

[. . .]

Another time I'll write at greater length.

Your friend UNAMUNO

To Pedro de Mugica   [Salamanca,
                                    Spring 1893]

Dear Friend,

[. . .]

Now I'm involved in an election campaign. From here I send articles to *El Nervión* concerning the new municipal elections—articles against politics. There is no politics there, but only business. It's a question of Echevarrieta, Chávarri, Solaegui, and Company taking over Bilbao in the name of political ideals.

Ideals? Not unless there is faith, Mugica my friend, faith, true faith.

Question: What is faith?

Answer: Believing what we have not seen.

No, no, no, that's not faith. Faith is the force of the soul which engenders dogma, not that which believes in dogma and maintains it. Faith isn't a receptive power but a creative force. Faith, true faith, is the enormous drive of the soul which engenders dogma, a living, moving, flexible dogma, a dogma that evolves, not that poor dead scrap of flesh, that mummified corpse which is handed down by tradition. Do you know what I base my opinion on when I say that those who today take themselves to be Christians don't have faith? On the fact that if they hadn't received through tradition the dogma of Christ's divinity, it wouldn't occur to them when they read the Gospel to say: "This man is

*111**

God!" No, there's no true faith like that of the first Christians, who in the work of centuries made of Christ a God by leaping over the antinomies of reason and struggling against cold logic. That, that was faith: a divine breath which engenders dogma.

It's the same with politics. Political opinion is not the flower of the soul, the flower of all the faculties, no. Republicanism or Carlism don't spring up out of the depths, out of the bedrock of the soul and out of its innermost folds. Political opinion is merely opinion, something false, a cold idea. It doesn't come from the marrow, from one's intimate being. Political opinions are like those insects pinned up in boxes, in boxes of political entomology, with labels alongside saying: such-and-such genus, such-and-such species. How wretched! These things are dead, but despite being dead they stir about, they excite themselves, they infect the atmosphere. How right Hamlet was to say: "to die, to sleep; to sleep, perchance, to dream . . . !"

If you could see what a beautiful child I have! How he opens his eyes to look at God's trees, which have already leafed out, what cries he gives when he gets out into the open air, under the sky of the free earth! Those cries are a prayer, a true prayer, a poetic hymn! And to think that this human soul—because he is a true human soul—might be able to be maimed and crippled by these so-called schoolteachers and school-masters. Believe me, he isn't going to go to elementary or secondary school, not at all. I will teach him every-thing, learning it all again myself. The trouble is that he would thus be deprived of a social education, of the things gained through give and take with his com-panions. One must be especially careful of these first years, which I believe have an enormous effect on life. I have little belief in the psychological inheritance of merely individual qualities, [. . .] but I believe very strongly in the effects of the first torrent of impressions of the senses when the brain and the mind are being formed [. . .]. What we see when we are children of one, two, three, or four years of age and then forget— this lives on, lives and breathes. Even though it doesn't take on any definite form in our consciousness, it has a greater impact than clear ideas. One must be very careful with the first three or four years. There's no greater misfortune than to carry, as so many people do, some repugnant bogeyman in the uttermost depths of one's being!

Forgive me. I've already rambled on twice, about faith and about bringing up children. I forget that I'm writing you, so I launched forth on this matter with full lyricism. No doubt it seemed to me that I was pouring my soul into my novel, where I put so much into telling about my hero's childhood and into describing true faith.

[. . .]

I hope your daughter is well. My good wishes to your wife.

And you know what affection is felt for you by
　　　　　your friend MIGUEL DE UNAMUNO

To Valentín Hernández　　　　　Salamanca,
　　　　　　　　　　　　　　11 October 1894

My esteemed comrade,

I have received the first number of *La Lucha de Clases*, which you have been kind enough to send me, and I am deeply appreciative, delighted to know that the Socialists of Bilbao can count on an organ which I truly desire may prosper.

113[*]

For some time now, along with all those who make some effort to take life seriously, I have been concerned with what has come to be called the social question. I observed the march of socialism, which I scarce knew anything about except from the absurd and malevolent explanations preferred by those who fight it desperately. However, even through the medium of the calumnies and the stupid arguments in which ignorance and bad faith feed each other, even through all the lies, I glimpsed the only forceful and vigorous ideal which can unite and revive our nations. I took up the study of the political economy of capitalism and of scientific socialism at the same time, and I have come to the conclusion that socialism, clear and pure, without masks, the socialism initiated by Karl Marx with the celebrated workers' international, and now joined by currents from elsewhere, is the only ideal truly alive today and that it is the religion of humanity.

The task of propagating it in our Spain is a hard one. Bourgeois capitalism—which is beginning to sink under its own weight, fatally crushed by the very laws of liberty proclaimed by its defenders—bourgeois capitalism defends itself till the death by means of protectionist measures, with monopolies, with armed peace and extravagant armies, with threats and promises and lies, with sham welfare, sometimes denouncing socialism and at other times emulating it under false labels in order to deceive others and even deceive itself. This last tactic yields some results: many people are deceived by State socialism, by ex-cathedra socialism, and so on. And there are people who paint a picture of certain of the mighty as Messiahs and benefactors of the working class. And daily we hear that socialism is something imposed, the death of liberty and of the individual, the stagnation of progress.

It must also be made clear that bourgeois socialists are enemies of true socialism or they are deceiving sophists. Confusion and error must be dissipated. The struggle, it must be repeated endlessly, is between those who work so that all may eat and live and nourish their spirit and those more or less concealed vagrants who live off the work of others. It must be proclaimed that each one, and he alone, should enjoy the fruits of his labor, for that is the measure of the emancipation of the proletariat and the destruction of bourgeois capitalism, and it should be most especially repeated at all hours that socialism means liberty, liberty, true liberty—the *free man* on the *free earth* with *free capital*. We must encourage the holy sense of solidarity in the face of the brutal egotistic individualism of the satiated, of the exploiting caste which, though it trembles before anarchist bombs, regards anarchism with a secret sympathy (since in the last analysis it is its own doctrine!): they speak of anarchism as more *logical* than socialism, and they hope, as their only hope, that the barbarism of the maddened desperados will quench the ideal of the workers who are spiritually sound.

It should be pointed out that there is no question of eating little children alive, nor of *eliminating* the rich, but merely a matter of making those work who can work, under penalty of suffering hunger and degradation if they do not. An endeavor must be made to show that socialism is not revolutionary from a mere fondness and inclination for riot, since in truth it is only the idle rich who live riotously; that revolution may come to be a painful necessity; and that it depends on the exploiting class whether or not the final phase is as smooth and non-violent as possible. Revolution for revolution's sake is a sentiment proper to souls steeped in the disguised anarchism of the bourgeoisie, who are intent on stirring up rivers so as to fish at their greatest ease, living without work, while they amuse themselves at the bullring. The social revolution is a means, probably and unfortunately inevitable, for the triumph of true peace, not of the armed peace which devours Europe's strength much more than a revolution would do.

And then the cobwebs in the heads of the intellectual workers must be swept away, for these intellectuals have served, until today, as a Civil Guard for bourgeois capitalism. In Spain the most appropriate place for active propaganda is among people in the intellectual professions (even though all professions are intellectual, and it would be impossible even to plow the ground without intelligence), who are still convinced that their interests coincide with those of their masters. I know many people who in their hearts and minds are socialists, but who are held back from declaring themselves and joining with the humble and disdained from a shameful fear, the result of an adulterated education, a caste education, one handed down to them, and who are inhibited by reason of a false, all-too-human prudence, by cowardice, spiritual consumption, and a good deal of more or less conscious hauteur.

This shameful shame, this chain of false concerns, is something that inhibits many and stifles their spirit. If only those in my own circumstances would take the last step and break that chain!

I hope that you will grant me the use, from time to time, of your weekly columns, so that from them I might do something towards the diffusion of our common ideal. My native city, Bilbao, is admirably suited for the task: the plague of bourgeois capitalism is quite nakedly evident there and, like much of what seems to be sound corpulence, is mere tumefaction. I have

endless notes on the condition of that city, and from
them I would be able to give form to worthwhile reflections.

In order to work for the triumph of the emancipation
of labor, of the working class and of the proletariat, in
favor of a socialist peace, you can count always on
having at your side

your comrade MIGUEL DE UNAMUNO

To Leopoldo Alas ("Clarín")   Salamanca,
                                        31 May 1895

My very esteemed friend,

There is so much to say that I don't know where to
begin. I have been one of your most assiduous readers,
and many a work of yours has been the subject of
discussion as my friends and I walked these plains. I
have often thought of writing you my impressions, but
it always seemed that it might be a bit presumptuous
on my part to do so—until the discussion of *adolescence*
came about, and, because of its very unimportance, it
has seemed to me a good pretext for addressing you.
Like you, I have felt the void around us and am aware
of the small number of people with whom we can
commune. I believe the solitude in which I live is a
source of strength; but it is so by virtue of impover-
ishing me, sharpening all that is exclusive and dis-
criminative in me, at the expense of the human quality
which gives life to relations among men.

First, a few words regarding the pretext for my letter, this word *adolescent*. [. . .] And now I will speak
to you of my own endeavors with the simplicity proper
in such matters. I have put into the articles which add
up to "On Authentic Tradition" a great deal of spirit

and work; though I have been writing for some time in my own Bilbao, I am altogether a novice in the *national* press, and I have a great desire to work, to do everything I can for the culture of my country, and to create a place for myself in belles-lettres, in addition to my place in the university. It is hard to begin in any case, and since here almost no one reads a new writer, without a recommendation to back him up, one has great difficulty in making headway . . . I knew that you had read my writing, for I thought to detect that fact in some details of your own recent work, and therein my principal reason for seizing on the word *adolescence*. A few critical remarks from your pen could only increase the number of those reading my works. My letter was, as you of course understood, an opportunity to say to you: "Have you read me? Do you know me? What is your opinion of my work? Do you think it worthy of calling the public's attention to it?" Your answer satisfies and encourages me, and I am grateful to you, and I only want you to judge me with complete freedom.

I think, however, I should tell you something. What an enormous difference between the red-hot boil of concepts and ideas taking place in one's mind and the hard stone into which they are transformed when they are exposed to the air! Every time I correct proofs and I see my ideas agglomerated and my intricate, rather incoherent style and expression, I go through hell.

I put as much effort into each article of mine as if I were about to die; I avoid weakening the argument for the sake of consistency or in order to tie up loose ends; I have no use for connective tissue. I sacrifice the thread of the rosary for the sake of the beads; others do the opposite. The first draft of each one of these articles was three times longer than the definitive version. My work really consists in condensing what I have written first. . . . My style, more graphic than picturesque, must surely produce a certain weariness, even a kind of stupor induced by the electrical discharges of successive shocks, whereas a continuous current is more easily endured. I strive to force the reader to collaborate with me (and you know better than I what our readers are like), and thus I furnish only points of view and a text for meditation, my intention being to be more suggestive than instructive. As·soon as I set down an idea and prepare to develop it, another one, associated with the first, appears, and I leap from one to another.

Without any presumption whatsoever I can aver, as regards my remarks on the mystics, that everything I have said is the direct result of my immediate reading of their texts. As I said to my teacher Menéndez Pelayo the other day, I will not resign myself to writing criticism of criticism . . . to being a resonance, a harmonizer of the average opinions of cultured, serious critics concerning a given point.

I have closely and carefully followed your latest course, a tendency towards a mysticism of sorts, and your obituary piece on F. Zeferino as well as . . . other works of yours have inspired a thousand ideas in me, and doubtless they will give rise to still others which will be made clear to you.

I have my own tendencies toward mysticism, for not in vain did I attend daily Mass and receive Communion monthly with true fervor and without formalistic profession until I was twenty-two, when, from sheer religiosity, I left off doing so. I have my mystical tendencies, but they are embodied in the socialist ideal, such as I hold it. I dream that socialism will constitute a true religious reformation once Marxist dogmatism withers and something more than what is purely economic becomes patent. How sad to contemplate what is called socialism! What lack of faith in progress, and what a lack of *humanity!*

I can well understand the period through which you are passing. For some time I have been planning to write a story which can be reduced to the following outline: A youth arrives in Madrid bearing within him a profoundly religious education and fine religious sensibilities; beneath this protective covering, which serves to isolate him to a certain extent, his deeply serious moral sentiments regarding life grow even stronger, and the day arrives when he no longer needs the covering, and this cape, which proves too small, is rent. Then, from sheer desire to rationalize his faith, he loses it (which is what happened to me). Inasmuch as he bears God in the marrow of his soul, he has no need to believe in Him, for his belief is already a reflex act. His entire being is the result of an inner travail; he is deeply religious, and does not need to be a believer. But he goes into the world, enters into collision with one and then another. He must do battle, and in the course of his battles his energies and moral sentiments begin to flag, and he grows weary and senses that the world is devouring his soul. One day he enters a church to hear Mass and the very place itself—the lights and the children around him and the multitude which *hears* something silent in silence, and the atmosphere as a whole—transports him back to his innocent years, and draws from the depths of his soul states of consciousness buried in his subconscious, takes him back to a past age, evokes by association a world of *adolescent* purity, and he feels his moral sentiments burgeon under the old cape still warm with the old warmth. His moral energies are strengthened as they are wrapped in his infant's clouts, and he returns to the earth which covered his roots. He takes on new faith and hears Mass without being an official believer, bathed in his primitive purity. Until a man bears Christianity in his marrow he has no recourse but to conserve its forms: without *form* there can be no consciousness, and whatever is to be organized in the depths of his spirit must go through the forms.

[. . .]

I have a high respect for every individual, every person, most especially for those to whom I owe something—and I owe you a great deal. I don't believe I can pay my debt by contributing indirectly to the value given your signature by forming part of the public which calls for your work; I have another idea of how the debt we owe someone who has taught us something should be paid. Let it be clear then that I have done no more than comply with a precept of my own moral code.

In my soul I rejoice in the fact that we have entered into contact. You will find in me, always and in all things, a sincere appreciator of the value of your work, which I esteem most highly (among the best in our culture), and an attentive colleague, even a friend, if the occasion should arise. I offer you a spirit genuinely Basque (such is my proud boast, despite my *anti-casticismo*, my anti-caste-ism), a spirit both open and simple.

Your most devoted correspondent, with the utmost respect

MIGUEL DE UNAMUNO

To Juan Arzadun   Salamanca,
                                     30 October 1897
My beloved friend,

Your two children are very handsome, and I hope that everything comes out well with the third. My own children improve all the time, except for the sick one, who keeps getting worse. My fourth and latest child, the little girl, is very cute and strong and happy.

Thanks to my family, to my not living alone, I have not fallen into despair and into an inner life as tragic and terrible as that of poor Pascal, who was ruled by dread and not by the holy fear of the Lord [. . .].

How much I have to tell you about the terrible self-consumption of intellectualism! There is a disease, a terrible disease of the stomach in which, the stomach lining having been damaged or destroyed, it begins to destroy and digest itself. Within consciousness, intellectualism is precisely the same sort of thing. I will write about it when the truce that I have imposed upon myself is over. [. . .]

But all of this is very involved, and it takes too long to tell. Perhaps one day I'll give you the notebooks in which for the past seven months I've been writing everything that comes to mind, everything that I feel and think and discover inside myself.

I work from within and from outside in more than ever, but I believe it's my duty to hold back my most intimate thoughts, to avoid all show and fashionable gesture, to keep my distance from curiosity-seekers, so as not to let the most precious things evaporate in publicity. This damned literary profession fills us with vanity and steals our true inner being. Always on stage!

When I look back and see the road I have travelled, it seems clear to me that what I am feeling and thinking today is the fulfilment, completion, and vivification of my former inner life, its purification. I can well say that it is not the destruction but the fulfilment of my tendencies. Thus it happens—and here I'm answering a point you raised in your letter—that I feel myself to

*122**

be more of a socialist than before and in the same way as before. Present-day Marxist socialism sins only in what it leaves out. . . .

The bad thing about the socialism of today is that it proclaims itself as a single and complete system, forgetting that after the problem of life comes the problem of death. What is there beyond this life? If when I die I die totally and if other men die as I do, then to make life easier, more enjoyable and pleasant, is, since it increases the sorrow at having to lose it one day, to bring men to the unhappiness of their happiness, to the terrible *noia* of poor Leopardi, to devouring spleen, to the dark despair which cast a pall over the decadence of Rome in its age of stoicism and of suicide. If when we die our consciousness returns to the nothingness from which it sprang, then the only salvation that is left is to preach the collective suicide of Schopenhauer and Hartmann. From the very depths of the social problem arises the religious problem: is life worth living?

Socialism has strength because it has substituted tangible things for vague ones, but its weakness lies in making the economic factor the only basic one, in ignoring the fact that there are two hinges of human history: the economic motive and the religious one.

[. . .]

I have so many things to tell you! I have passed through such internal anguish! It has revealed to me the very depths of the eternal problems, especially the problem of one's own eternal salvation. I have felt myself at the edge of nothingness without end, and I have come to feel that there are other ways of entering into relation with reality than merely reason, that there is grace and there is faith, the faith which in the last analysis is a matter of wanting to believe. Do I really believe, or is it only that I want to believe? I do not know. I am disoriented, but I have greater peace inside.

May God give you peace, health, and true happiness. This is the wish of your friend who embraces you,

MIGUEL DE UNAMUNO

To Pedro de Mugica   Salamanca,
                                              2 January 1898
Dear friend,

Before anything else I must express my wish that you and your family get off to a good start in the new year and that you get through it safe and sound and happy.

[. . .]

I'm up to my neck in endless work. I want to publish in book form my articles "On Authentic Tradition." I have finished three essays ("The Evil of the Century," "Jesus and the Samaritan Woman," and "Nicodemus"), which will form part of some "Evangelical Meditations." I've done four articles for a collection which I'll call "Skyscapes and Landscapes," and I'm working on a revision and extensive expansion of the articles about my memories of my childhood and school years that I published in *El Nervión*—articles which will make a book called "Childhood and Youth," and I have not stopped working on my "Life of the Castilian Language."

[. . .]

You're not doing yourself any good in not getting close to people and in absorbing yourself in such an exclusive and single-minded way in the historical dictionary. Life is something more than just family and science.

And I must say it: why that mania about the Jews which shows itself so clearly in your letters from time to time. I'll be frank with you: I admire that people for a number of reasons, among others, for their spirit of anti-militarism and cosmopolitanism, for their disdain for the stupid virtues of "gentlemen" (the remnants of barbaric customs), for their lack of patriotism, for their opposition, in short, to everything symbolized by that unbearable Kaiser. The Englishman and the Jew are the two types of men who are the most agreeable to my taste. They are the most active workers for a future international society—diligent, anti-militaristic, without stupid notions of pride. I understand the ill will that many people there have toward the Jews, but the reason is that they are the most active and effective element there in dissolving the dregs of barbarism which the German still carries within himself. In England there are Jews, but there is no antipathy against them. I sincerely admire the science and the deep feeling of the nation of Hegel, Goethe, Schiller, Fichte, Schleiermacher, Schopenhauer, Uhland, and so on, but I can't admire the insufferable conquerors of Sedan, or those who admire Bismarck and Moltke (two utterly repulsive creatures), or the Junkers, or the "protectors" of the Transvaal, or, in short, the Prussianized Germany of the present day. And this sentiment of mine I can see to be now widespread in Europe, thanks to that wretched excuse for a human being, the great Wilhelm.

Forgive and pardon this outburst at New Year's from your friend who wishes you true health, light, and peace,

MIGUEL DE UNAMUNO

Letters

To Pedro Jiménez Ilundain   Salamanca,
                                     3 January 1898

My dear friend,

How pleased I am to receive your letter! Also in front of me, on my desk, is the letter your wrote me from Gallarta.

From the state of my own spirit I understand yours. What a shame that we can't talk together for a while, face to face in free and unrestricted conversation!

What you tell me of your state of mind, combined with my own state of mind, demonstrates that today's youth almost generally *feels* as much as it thinks. It's a result of weariness with agnostic rationalism, it is the postulate of practical reason which surges up forcibly from the piled-up ruins of pure reason (in Kant's terminology), it is truth superimposing itself upon reason and, in short, it is the voice of St. Paul resounding in our souls, as when, addressing the Athenians before the altar they had raised TO THE UNKNOWN GOD (Our Unknowable), he said: "Whom therefore ye ignorantly worship, him declare I unto you."

The generation before our own could live in intellectual positivism, because, brought up in the Christian faith, they carried it with them as a substratum of their positivism, and it supported them without their knowing it. But a generation raised on positivism, finds it must necessarily return to search for the hidden source which their fathers kept from them.

I am preparing some "Evangelical Meditations" and among them there is one, "The Evil of This Century," in which I develop the fact that nowadays our souls are borne down by nihilism, the devastating prospect of a nothingness beyond this world. If we are all condemned to return to nothingness, if humanity is a

126*

procession of specters who come forth out of nothingness only to return to it, then the process of alleviating
miseries and bettering the temporal human condition
is merely a matter of making life easier and more "com-
fortable," and the prospect of losing it all more somber;
it is the unhappiness of happiness. We have become
obsessed with reason, as if personal goodness were not
a means of bringing us to truth, more powerful perhaps
than reason, which does not go beyond the mere relations of things. . . .

Few convictions have been as deeply rooted in me
as my belief in volitional determinism. But this as-
sumes that all reality can be rationalized, that our science can determine anything. If, in mathematics, which
is considered the most exact of sciences, we find imaginary quantities and indeterminable functions and in-
commensurable relationships for our mode of counting, why would there not be a similar condition as
regards psychology? If there is no final meaning to
creation, then all of it is a total absurdity.

[. . .]

How terrible to make one's way across the steppes
of intellectualism only to find ourselves, one day, face
to face with the image of death and total annihilation
come to pay a warning visit. If you only knew the
nights of anguish and the days when spiritual things
have no savor! The worst thing about a stomach ulcer
is that the stomach begins to digest itself to the point
of self-destruction. The same thing happens with the
ulcer of intellectualism: awareness devours itself by
dint of sheer analysis. The cure is said to be in dis-
tractions, which means dissipations, sinking into the
vice-ridden obsession with life. It's useless. When we
are called, we must respond, and when the image of
death rises before us, we must stare back steadily until

we can look at it with rose-colored glasses and see through it.

The crisis came upon me with sudden violence, although today I can see the development of it all in my writings. What surprised me was the sudden explosion. I took refuge then in the childhood of my soul, and I took refuge in retreat, when my wife, seeing me weep, impulsively called out "My child!" She called me her child, her son. I took refuge in practices called back from the days of my childhood, which had been somewhat melancholy, but serene enough. Today I find myself disoriented in large measure, but a Christian who asks God for strength and light so that I may find consolation in the truth.

What I long for most is freedom, true freedom, which means being master and not a slave to myself, being what I happen to be and not what others want me to be. For the damnation of a public figure comes when the world forms a crust around the nucleus of his inner being and sets up another being for him, weighing him down with excess baggage: these public figures build up a second self, an external and inauthentic one, foreign to what they really are. How well St. Paul described the struggle between these two beings, those two men that we all carry within us!

[. . .]

Reason supplies us the relationships of things, their exterior, but as for the quintessence of anything, its spirit, can we possibly reach and penetrate it, except through love? And love is faith. And faith is a fact, a true fact, and therefore irreducible. To attempt to rationalize facts is to attempt to demonstrate axioms, to reduce them, turn them into the dust of facts, and thus to end in nihilism. A fact is a concrete axiom, and an axiom is an abstract fact. And faith is a fact. How does it come about that the most logical of all spirits—John

Stuart Mill, Claude Bernard, Littré—ended in the faith of their childhood? The life of the spirit is not to be smothered by abstract reason, for life is essence, and reason is pure form.

We must learn to *be* good, and not merely to *do* good.

[. . .]

You can rest assured, friend Ilundain, that from your very first letter I have kept my eye on you and—I *awaited you, I hoped for you.* And I have not been deceived. Our friendship will remain firm.

I desire health, light, and true peace for you.

Your friend, MIGUEL DE UNAMUNO

To Pedro Jiménez Ilundain   Salamanca,
                                                                25 May 1898

My dear friend,

It's been some time since I've had any news of you. When you acknowledged the copy I sent of my "Meditations," on whose final form I am now working, you agreed to write me. Of myself, what shall I tell you? Worldly preoccupations and family affairs have served to calm, to a great degree, my mental agitation. This is all to the good, for it allows me to get back to my ultimate self and allows the fruits of my experience and disappointments to jell, protected by those concerns as if by a cape. [. . .]

I want to write "The Social Kingdom of Jesus" with an easy mind, from my heart and from my life. The central thesis is that the same morality which is called for between individuals should be applied to relations between nations. I mean to condemn war and militarism and all the barbarous feelings brought into being by exclusivistic nationalism. We still do not have Christianity in the marrow of our bones, and until evangelical truth becomes the spirit of our spirit and the substance of our soul, there can be no true peace. The superman of whom poor Nietzsche dreamed, the new man, is none other than the Christian, who is not yet made but is still in the making.

The entire point of civilization is to protect the evolution of the Christian soul, to help it loosen the impure bond to the pagan past; if civilization does not serve this end, why then it serves no human end at all. The Christian soul must rid itself of the warlike impulses of military heroism, of narrow patriotism, and of all earthly attachments. Heroism must give way to sanctity, and patriotism to brotherly compassion.

God is the true fatherland of the soul, and man should be master of the earth, not its slave. Here you have, in a highly compressed form, the central ideas of my "The Social Kingdom of Jesus," an essay which will strike some people as Utopian Christianism, and others as Anarchism. As against law, justice; and in place of legalism and duty, grace and sacrifice. Law, duty, legality, and the categories of Roman Law, this crude way of thinking which continues to be the real gospel of all those countries that call themselves Christian, must be transcended or abandoned.

All those Roman ways of thinking born of war and based on private property, the entire juridical construct of a citizenry of slaveowners, have infiltrated modern souls and even Christian doctrine itself. The Catholic Church in large measure is only a compromise between two ways of thinking which are mutually destructive: Roman Law and the Gospel, the Twelve Tables of the Law and the Sermon on the Mount. The entire goal of our work must be to make the human soul ever more Christian.

And if this outline of a Christian society, a pro-

foundly and radically Christian society, seems an un-
realizable dream, if the City of God seems Utopian,
the answer to that is to be found in the words of Christ:
"Be ye therefore perfect, even as your Father which is
in heaven is perfect." These words are the most solemn
consecration of Utopia. Divine perfection is unattainable. Nevertheless, unattainable divine perfection gives
us Christ as goal. Only by aspiring to the unattainable
does one attain the attainable. Only by striving for the
impossible is all the possible achieved. Only those nations which—like individuals—set their sights on the
ideal nation, on the kingdom of God and His justice,
on the social reign of Jesus, only those will prosper
and live in peace. At this time, however, pagan heroism, racial hatred, worldly honor, and militaristic patriotism are exalted—and in the name of religion. Here
you have, I repeat, along very general lines and without
the flesh that will fill out these ideas, my essay on "The
Social Kingdom of Jesus."

The other two essays I am writing are "St. Paul on
the Areopagus," which attacks dilettantism, literatism,
aestheticism, and so on, and "The Prayer of Dimas,"
which deals with the gap between high intentions and
actual deeds.

Where does it all lead me? I don't know. I only
know that for the time being I think I have found my
way. I also think that I am fulfilling a spiritual need
and duty. Many years ago, when I was still scarcely
more than a boy and most deeply imbued with religious fervor, it occurred to me one day, after I returned
from Communion, to open the Gospels at random, at
any page, and place my finger by chance on some
passage. And my finger chanced on: "Go ye therefore,
and teach all nations [. . .]" (Matthew 28:19). I was
profoundly moved: I took it as a mandate to become
a priest.

But since I was already courting the girl who was to become my wife (I was fifteen or sixteen), I decided to try again and clarify the matter further. I went to receive Communion again on another day, and when I got home I opened the book again and found my finger pointing to John 9:27 . . . "He answered them, I have told you already, and ye did not hear: wherefore would ye hear it again?" I can't tell you what an impression this made on me.

Sixteen or seventeen years later I still recalled that morning. I was alone in my study. The sentence kept recurring and resounding in my mind and the memory of those words remained with me always. I have told the story to my friends many times, explaining it in different ways, but the impression has always remained engraved on my soul. And when, a year ago, I was prey to those relentless spiritual shocks, that strange experience of my youth returned with renewed force.

Now that I have entered upon a period of relative calm, I think I am re-making myself upon the basis of *practical reason*, re-forming myself on the ruins left by *theoretical reason*.

[. . .]

Don't forget to write me, for I would like to hear from you. I promise you another longer letter. You already know what good I wish you and how I pray for your attaining peace, light, and life.

Your friend, MIGUEL DE UNAMUNO

To Leopoldo Alas ("Clarín")   Salamanca,
                                  9 May 1900

My dear friend,

Yesterday I read the article in *El Imparcial* which you devote to my "Three Essays"; my first impulse was to write you at once. But I contained myself; I allowed my thoughts to settle overnight, and will write you now instead; and what I write now will be a confession, in which I strip myself and even strip the concept I had formed of you. I will let my pen flow *ex abundantia cordis*. You and I and others have always called for sincerity—perhaps in response to a general longing for it which now animates the moral atmosphere. And yet, despite our efforts, are we not perhaps unable to achieve our aim? You have been, in great measure, one of my mind's educators; you have brought certain things to my attention, certain authors and ideas, and you have made a strong impression on me with many of your narratives. How often did you and your work figure in our discussions when I was between twenty and twenty-five, up there in Bilbao! I owe you, then, gratitude for all that. And there is more to it: because of similarities in our temperaments and education, perhaps, I have thought to intuit in your work certain sorrows, an inner struggle, the battle we all of us wage against our carnal selves. In Madrid, I have heard people speak of you more than once with obvious fear or admiration, rarely with affection. And I, who have suffered not a little because of those who praise me but have no affection for me, felt I could understand this profoundly unjust attitude. A thousand times I have heard people say, and I have said so myself, more than once going too far, that you are over-zealous in praising the senilities of most of the established writers (though not all of them) while maintaining an attitude of reserve towards up-and-coming youth. Those of us who have delighted in all that was truly good in Valera have lamented what you had to say of *Morsamor*, as we have lamented the scant value you have assigned the lively and highly original Ganivet, and mourned

133*

that you were silent about the work of Campión, so noble, robust and fine, and that you did not stop to consider as it deserved Blasco Ibáñez's *The Cabin*, a novel superior, for my taste, to any by Galdós or Pereda. (This is my own very personal judgment, of course: the right judgment must lie somewhere between yours and mine, no doubt.) On the other hand, it has also been pointed out that you have exerted yourself in furthering works of pedestrian quality, possessing some simple nobility perhaps, doubtless appealing, but lacking in all strength. In any case, we all doubted that you could personally have given them the importance you assigned them in your criticism. The upshot seemed to be: what a shame that a man of such talent, so clear-headed, does not operate with complete disinterest and put his prejudices to one side when he makes a judgment! You will recall what happened to you when the unjust campaign was waged against your *Teresa*; you will remember that Maeztu, echoing others, denied your *bona fides*; and you must have suffered in the face of all these attacks. For who is not sensitive to such? And you could have heard one of the most conspicuous persons of our literature say: Why, that man knows every type of martyrdom! He knows how to wound even while praising! And I, when I heard this kind of talk, either kept quiet, or echoed the observation (why deny it?); or I defended you, and did so for what I considered a weakness on your part.

But a letter is such a poor thing! What I wouldn't give to be able to meet and talk face to face, so that this Unamuno, who is, good or bad, quite another person than you think, might reveal himself to you! If we could only talk with souls bared!

And now I come to your criticism of my "Three

Essays," and, inasmuch as I wish to be totally sincere, you will allow me to make use of an artifice, an infantile one perhaps, and that is to permit me to speak of myself in the third person. But first I want to tell you that I am grateful to you for your piece as regards its overall effect on the large public which follows you and is guided by your opinions, for it will increase the circulation and sale of my little book, an eventuality of great importance to me.

There would be no point in my sketching my autobiography here. If you have read *Peace in War*, or if you are going to read it, you will find it all there. Unamuno is a victim of himself, a *Heautontimorumenos*. He spends his life battling to be what he is not—without achieving it. Most of the things which seem to vouch for others he vouches for himself. How sad it is, after a childhood and youth of simple faith, to have lost all faith in an "other-worldly" life, and to hanker after name and fame and vainglory, a mere mockery and pale imitation of immortality! When Unamuno states and restates that one must live for eternity and for history it is only because he suffers from wanting to live in history; and, even when his better side shows him the vanity of it all, his worse side draws him on. As St. Paul said: "For the good that I would I do not: but the evil which I would not, that I do." While he is thought to seek fame and notoriety impelled only by the one anguished motive, he undergoes drastic changes of heart. And from his heart he wrote his "Nicodemus," intimate confessions unwisely made public, and then people said his motives were improper. When he first began to write, you took notice, but thought his name a pseudonym; later, when he was launched on his "On Authentic Tradition," you wrote him that his work was "strong, new, original"; and he was filled with pride! What encouragement these words gave him, words written by a man who had worked upon his spirit in youth! And then, about that time, in the *Heraldo*, you wrote an encomium which was probably excessive, though he did not see it that way. But Unamuno is aggressive, and he has the unfortunate habit of deprecating too many things (less now than before). In the last essay of "On Authentic Tradition" he alluded to you, judged you severely, repeated the allusion elsewhere, and you said nothing. In an article later you called his work on tradition "circumspect" and said he was a disciple of Menéndez Pelayo. Recalling the words "strong, new, original," Unamuno now found something wrong with "circumspect," and also with his being called a disciple of Don Marcelino Menéndez Pelayo, when he knows he is not a disciple of this one or that one, but of everyone. And thus matters stood. He published his novel, a novel into which he put ten years of meditation, of study, of contemplation, his life as a child, the dramatic siege of Bilbao, to which he was a young witness, his mountains, his Basque race. He sent you the book, and you answered that you would not be able to read it for the moment, but that when you did you would give him your opinion, and the poor man said to himself: he won't. And he waited and waited and waited in vain. And he continued trying to provoke you with more or less veiled hints and references. And, in your own writing he noted highly transparent references and allusions to himself; one day you would point out that there are things which are discussed and praised and then purposely let pass: another day, that there are writers who are undeniably good, but who, like lobsters, give you indigestion. Meanwhile poor Unamuno strove to be what he was not and dreamt only of furthering his novel (which, *inter nos*, is in my judgment—of little value in this case—vastly superior to everything else he has done). And one day—Unamuno himself admits it—partly to break down your silence, and partly because he suffered from his ambiguous attitude towards someone like you to whom he was deeply indebted (as mentioned at the beginning of this letter), he wrote you, and in doing so tried to be sincere and clearly to explain what had happened. And you wrote him a kindly letter, yes, but, as is the common vulgar practice, you tried to wipe out the allusive insinuations provoked in you by those of Unamuno, denying them, and claiming you could not recall them. Some other course would have been preferable, the more so since you had been justified in your actions.

Meanwhile, Unamuno was gaining a following in Spain (especially in Catalonia), as well as in Spanish America; he was quoted with relative frequency; he was acquiring prestige and renown—not without serving as a target for attacks, which is only natural, all the more so when one is aggressive oneself. The notion that he was changeable, volatile, disoriented, a victim of literary indigestion from overreading, was already becoming established, as was the suspicion that he hungered after notoriety and sought it out down crooked paths, or that he was a savant striving to be an artist, or even that he was brilliant, original, and independent. Many avoided his writings, thinking them intricate and sibylline (a belief which greatly harmed him). In America it was said that he did not seem like a Spaniard: it was said by way of praise, but it is perhaps his misfortune to be "uprooted," as Barrès might say. And he, the intellectual, and intellectual first and foremost, aware he was victimized by this very intellectualism, took up the cudgels against it—and

*137**

his anti-intellectualism turned out to be thoroughly intellectual. And he went on suffering. There followed a crisis in which he more than once broke down; his life would have been a hell had he been without a wife and children. And then he began to believe he had really returned to the faith of his childhood and, even though he did not truly believe, he began to practice, burying himself in the most routine devotions, in order to bring back his youth. There was rejoicing in his house, he saw his mother happy (she is the only restraint on his setting down much more of what he thinks); his sister, having come out of the convent because of illness, stayed with him until, recovered, she could take her vows. But he was aware that what he was doing was false, and once again he found himself disoriented, once again a prey to the longing for glory, to the anguish to live on in history. And he, who well knows how harshly everyone judges the ups and downs of conscience, saw how superficially they judged your own attitude in religious matters.

And then of a sudden you gradually began to break your silence in regard to him, and now here and now there, you began to quote him, *en passant*, but with deference. You gave an account of his translation of Schopenhauer, you spoke of an article of his on teaching, and—now we come to the "Three Essays." Allow me to take up your critique.

It is a very-well-done critique, but most of all, clever, most clever. You have shown yourself a consummate master of saying one thing to the mass of the public and another to those who know how to read. The opening, where you speak of Unamuno's reluctance to be called a scholar is all right, yes, you're quite right. But then: what is to be said about Unamuno? That his language is intricate, ingenious, studiously con-

densed, and incorrect. I see an obvious exaggeration
in all this, for at the same time you speak of my "clear
transparent Castilian, most elegant, oftentimes elo-
quent and inspired." But what is said by way of en-
dorsement of Unamuno? That he is original. Well now—
it would be best not to overdo it. That kind of literature
abounds in France, although here in Spain, amid all
this un-mature writing, Unamuno's book might well
play some decent role. For your part, you bring up a
whole raft of writers—not as some people will assume
(and have on occasion so assumed) merely to show
you read studiously, but rather so that the reader, when
he sees Unamuno's name shuffled with the others, will
exclaim: This Unamuno is a cultured man all right,
learned enough, who erases his tracks with a whopping
big noise and repeats in a new way what A or B or C
or D have already said; a useful writer, in short, intelligent, instructive, but—original? You grant him
"the obvious and capital originality of saying things
on his own account, of having thought them through
himself, though he may have heard or read something
similar—though not the same" and so on. Your own
reasoning is that Unamuno unloads his short work "of
citations and references to authors and doctrines which
in one way or other may agree with his own theories
and lend the force of authority." Herein is the pivot in
your clever argument; "*He does not quote anyone; he
speaks as if what he says, novelties for many people, had
occurred to him alone, or as if he did not know that others
have already held to such notions. Still, one must not
believe that he is being vain, or that he wishes his concepts
to be thought unheard of . . .*" and so on. Now really,
friend Alas, in all sincerity is this not a mortal thrust?
Why does Unamuno not quote his sources? First of
all, because if these *novelties* are not exactly his own,

neither do they belong to A or B or C, but rather permeate the contemporary intellectual ambiance, and he does not recall reading them here or there, for they have emerged in the course of all his reading. Unamuno is no scholar, even if he is learned, and he does not read very much (that is the truth) though he has read widely. Unamuno could not foresee anything *"without relation to anyone."* According to that criterion, no one is original. Shakespeare, perhaps the most original genius of all, borrowed all his themes and arguments, all his thoughts, everything, from others. Why speak of originality, which can never be a creation out of nothing? Unamuno reads a bit (not much now), he meditates more, reflects, and allows what he has made his own to grow, to sprout. What is its source? Man is a social product, every day more so. "Go Within Yourself," the best of the "Three Essays" in my own judgment, has come from his soul—and therein lies the originality, in spontaneity, even though it may seem forced. There are theories more radical than those sustained by Unamuno, of course, there are concepts more *protagoric*, but is it not your purpose to suggest to the canny reader that Unamuno strives to be radical and *protagoric* to an unheard of degree, just as on other occasions he has seemed to be a neo-mystic? This is a confessional letter, an unburdening, absolutely sincere and, friend Alas, I happen to believe that the Unamuno you found "strong, new, original" in "On Authentic Tradition" is so, not because he thinks up new thoughts (no one does), but because he thinks them up with all his body and soul. And his originality lies in the way he says them. And the poor man holds his originality so highly! And, in all truth, you, you yourself, friend Alas, think the same, you believe the same. Is it not a bit strange that you should apply that criterion of

*140**

the *absolute*—with a certain canny reserve—and, because absolute, impossible originality, when not long
ago you found that Rodó "demonstrates an astonishing
originality" (!!!) in his explanation of classic *leisure*?
Now here, between ourselves, as we share confidences
which I long to be of a noble and holy sincerity, I
would ask you, do you really believe, with or without
"astonishment," in that "originality" of Rodó, an originality you begrudge Unamuno? Because in all truth
you, who study and read, must have seen that doctrine
of classic *leisure*, not in this one's work or the other's,
but in a hundred places. And I am sorry to bring into
the argument a person so *circumspect* (and I deliberately underline that adjective), so likeable, so modest,
so noble, as the *American* Rodó. He sent me his *Ariel*,
a book which you recommended to me by letter as
"very sound," and it is. You advised me to "speak of
him," and I will, but, frankly, it was only your recommendation that got me to finish reading his book.
For he is sound enough, he is likeable—but I have
already read all he has to say in countless French authors! He struck me as the very echo of the *Mercure*.
Compare the manner in which you treat Rodó, compare the manner in which you treat that noble spirit
Ochoa (small matter as a writer), compare the way
you tried to get us to swallow the *Horizontes*, by the
man who wrote such tender pages in *Dolores*; recall
how extra-indulgent you were with our friend Martínez Ruiz; recall how you did not let go by in silence
the senile abortion *Morsamor*, by a man who was once
great; compare all that with your utter silence regarding Campión, your unjust treatment of Doña Emilia,
your coolness toward *The Cabin*, and toward Ganivet,
and with your emphatic reserve and double ulterior
motives dealing with poor Unamuno. (There is no

*141**

shadow of irony in all this, my good friend: I am pouring out my heart in these pages.) Once again, one more
time I say: you were one of those who nourished my
mind, and I WANT to be your friend and to talk to
you truly, apart from and beyond all the wretchedness
of our literary careers, and there is no solid relation
possible unless it is based on truth and sincerity. . . .

Speaking of the "Three Essays" you say that "whoever
in this country is capable of writing anything of such
forcefulness—and they are few in number—do not usually have the courage to do so." And why do you think
Unamuno has not set himself up as a critic? (And he
is urged, incited, to do so by some of the *new people*,
who tell him "the post is vacant" and, when they say
that, they are thinking of you.) Precisely because he
hasn't the courage, because he lacks the courage you
lack to tell the truth about our consecrated literary
heroes; because, having been a pupil of Don Marcelino
and having learned a great deal from him, he does not
dare say what he really thinks of him (he drops indirect
hints, as in that "Joaquín Rodríquez Janssen," which
you ordered not to be published in *La vida literaria*);
because, being a friend of Galdós, and he, being one
of those who most regard and encourage him (I was
on the point of writing "admire him") in his work,
will not declare how superficial and rhapsodical and
hack-like he seems; because, since he is not on good
terms with Echegaray, he would not have it thought,
if he were to say what he really thinks, that he did so
for wrong motives. Unamuno does not go in for criticism because he has no courage and because, since he
is a writer himself, he does not want it said, as is said
of you, that he seeks allies, or that in attacking, praising, or keeping quiet, he is merely defending himself,

that he judges everything *subjectively*, in the sense that he judges in external relation to himself as writer. . . .
[. . .]

Why be falsely modest? When you consider yourself and consider others and judge your own work, you do not deceive yourself, you do not practice deception on yourself. The same is true of me. And I firmly believe I could count on a public ten, twelve, a hundred times larger, if people simply made up their minds to read me and put aside the legend of my learned and sibylline intricacy. And, what's more, I believe that I would achieve a certain popularity—something for which I yearn. If you knew the hopeful anticipation that led me on during the writing of my *Peace in War*, into which I poured all my childhood and youth! With its defects and all (greater than in any other work of mine), it is, alongside my "Landscapes," which I will soon publish, my favorite child. I think now of your *Regenta*, and of the reaction it provoked. You were accused with sovereign injustice of plagiarizing Flaubert. What I saw in the work was the flower of your experiences and reflections as a youth, the naturally freshest part of you, torn from reality itself, deeply felt and intuited. And in this work you were original, truly original— and there is no reason for anyone to cite Flaubert, no more reason than for me to cite those with whom my thought coincides. (I am again pleading *pro domo mea*). But I do not wish to appear a flatterer, something I am not, nor have I ever been. On the contrary, I am unfortunately inclined to censuring those I most love, because since I love them, I would like them to be as they should be, in accordance with their inner beings.

I again beg you to read the poor fruits of my endeavors, my favorite, and to let me know whether I am mistaken in my love. A writer who produces a little

143*

book of seventy pages which "makes you think," and about which you intend to speak in many periodicals and perhaps make of your analysis the theme for the first pamphlet you write (and how very grateful is this restless spirit of mine, thirsty for attention, avid to be heard!), such a writer, does he not deserve that a professional critic should try to read a work into which he has poured his entire youth and ten years of meditation about the pages of history and the peaks of his native mountains? If I am mistaken, if it is not what I think, if without polish and cutting it will not be a novel superior to all those others so carelessly written, then do not spare me. Is it a defective child of my spirit? I have before my eyes a defective child of my body, a poor hydrocephalic son, and so I can tolerate another torment. Because my poor sick little boy, the idiot, when I examine his features deformed by illness, seems to me more handsome than my other four children, and the latter are truly handsome and lively and cheerful.

I know that this letter thus far is part confession, part complaint, part gratitude, part recrimination, and part (why not say so?) advice; my only hope is that it all results in a *true* friendship. For you and I, friend Alas, have called each other friends, but let us put our hands on our hearts and ask, have we really been friends? If we look deeply, no, we have not been, and looking even more deeply yet, yes. Yes, at least in so far as I am concerned, because you had a great deal to do with the education of my mind, and all those who contributed to the formation of my spirit are my friends.

After all, what does it matter what they say about us, if beneath it all we sense what they think about us?

Do you know what some of my most profound satisfactions have been? To have seen without any room for doubt some sign of my influence in the work of others; to have seen, before anyone could point it out to me, the influence of my novel on Galdós' *Luchana* and in other volumes of the later *Episodios*, to see it in Guimerá's last drama, to see it spread here and there, to have first nourished Maeztu, and in large degree Arzadun, and Campión himself (all three of them fellow countrymen of mine), to have given them spirit and have had them take it.

Enough of this. What a shame, what a shame we can't talk face to face, alone, at length, with no one around! What agreeable periods I have spent with some people, working at getting them to know me truly and care for me! Yes, friend Alas, care for me. It's my obsession, and, even greater is the obsession to be able to love: for my hide is so thick and I am so damned aggressive! In my drama (which is a confession, in manuscript now with Galdós; if you would care to see it, I will write him to send it on to you), in my drama I have confessed myself even more thoroughly than in "Nicodemus."

Enough, I say. And now, before I regret having written you, without rereading this or correcting it, I'll put it in the post, this very minute, on my way to class to translate and comment on Aristotle. I yearn for a friendship to come of it.

Your friend MIGUEL DE UNAMUNO

To Leopoldo Alas ("Clarín")   Salamanca,
                                     10 May 1900

Dear friend,

I have just received the clipping from *El Imparcial*—with errata corrected—sent along with your note. But what am I to add to what I wrote in the most lengthy

letter which somehow got off to you yesterday? Last
night I would have taken it back (I always feel the
same about any letter after mailing) but I told myself
by way of justification that I had been sincere in all
ways. [. . .] And yet, should I have not withheld my
first impressions? No, I think I did the right thing.
Let us know each other's weak points. Even though
for some time I have had them on my *adquirenda*, I
do not know Recejac, nor Gourd, nor Gibson, nor
Marillier, nor the Abbé Mercier. (But William James,
the intellectual progenitor of Bergson, I do know.) I
do little reading because I have read much. Only Hegel
has nourished me for any length of time. The nucleus
of my essay "Faith" is formed by works of Lutheran
theology: Herrmann, Harnack, Ritschl. But as is my
usual practice I read without taking notes; later I re-
think the thoughts and allow them to settle, and after
a while I allow them to well up in my writing without
recalling the form in which I read them. I wish only
to give my own form to ideas which *do not belong to
anyone but to everyone*. What we know we know among
us all; no one today can say, "This is mine." The
surprise of originality can merely be to embody, to
make into one's own flesh and blood, what already is
in the air. Unfortunately, what is to be seen is mere
juxtaposition, conglomeration. That is why I cannot
stand writers like our friend González Serrano, whom
I like as a person. The same question was brought up
in regard to old Campoamor, that most original poet.
But how small is mankind! And you may well say to
yourself: "This fellow defends his originality to the
farthest limit, he won't abide correspondences nor co-
incidences!" If I could but explain myself, if I could
only tell everything I think about myself and others!
When I read Schopenhauer's letters: what a swarm of

associations! Herein you will surely discover my deepest weakness. But is it really that? I don't know. I have the temperament of a battler, and am as stubborn as any Basque, striving to prevent the greed in me from smothering ambition and striving also against caring more about what is said of me than what is thought of me or what I think of myself. I wait, working, and wish to see only if my novelties within Spain will some day be considered banalities (what a good word!) outside Spain. Presumption? I do not think so. Of the three essays, you prefer "Faith," which is obviously the one most in tone with your own ideas and feelings. For my part, I prefer the first one, "Go Within Yourself!" which is the one preferred by those of my friends, the so-called *gente nueva*, the new wave, who have written me. It is the one most my own, the one into which I have put most spirit, and, whether it be highly original or very little original, it is the most original of the three. This first piece sprang from my heart, the other two from my head. You say that the thesis of "Ideocracy" is dangerously erroneous, by reason of the false *idea* which I have of ideas. I do not believe I have any such false idea of ideas, and as proof, I am willing to refute my essay, expounding against my own thesis by using all the arguments others might expound. I care very little whether the thesis is or is not erroneous, for the thesis is the least of the matter in a work of this type. It is an occasion to pour out one's soul. Still, I believe my thesis more lively than the opposing one, for I believe that an idea is an epiphenomenon, a reflection, a mere shadow. In my essay "Faith," I like best my description of the little church of Alzola. I agree with Nietzsche, I posit ideas merely to unload myself of them, and then go on to give birth to others, even if they contradict the first notions, and

147*

set down whatever freely occurs to me. Am I striving to be novel for the sake of novelty, to *épater le bourgeois?* No. It is merely my way.

[. . .]

Yes, yesterday's letter may have been impertinent, but it was dictated by my thirst for sincerity (and I would want that sincerity to be what it cannot be: absolute). I was grateful for your article, I was pleased, but, in all truth, your cleverness hurt me profoundly. God spare me from cleverness! If I have ever been clever or canny I regret it now.

Another notion disquieted me last night: I told myself that I had handed myself over, lowered all my defenses, and that the letter I had written you could serve as a rock quarry from which to stone me. But then I justified myself by asking if I hadn't written it from the heart, with all sincerity? [. . .]

Was it a severe letter? I don't think so. [. . .] For I am deeply convinced that you have suffered all the hurt to your self-esteem mentioned in my letter to you, who I believe (perhaps I am mistaken) find yourself in a state of mind analogous to mine. You have doubtless endured, suffered in your soul, clever praises and yet been gratified at hard attacks made without pretense.

I have read again the article which has roused such a storm in this poor unquiet spirit of mine. In effect, doubtless, it will contribute to the possibility of more people being able to judge me on their own; it will increase for me this damned prestige we all seek, it will increase it in the majority of your readers. And so I should limit myself to giving you my thanks, without reserve. All this would be the worldly thing to do, and it would be prudent, and it would be clever of me. But, I am not downcast for having bared myself before you. Whatever the result, your grateful friend will breath more easily.

MIGUEL DE UNAMUNO

To Miguel Gayarre   Salamanca,
27 September 1900

Dear friend,

Harnack's *What Is Christianity?* was on my list of books to buy. A thousand thanks, then, for sending it. It is of great interest to me. Every day I get more involved in such studies.

I know his *History of Dogma*, that enormous work, and it is one of the most solid and suggestive works that I know. No gibberish about it, that I can see, though I am not surprised that you think there is. The same might be said about a manual of histology, for that matter.

There can be no doubt that the existence of Christian beliefs, dogmas, and so forth is as real as the existence of cells, myelin, or neurons, and that the former are as subject to laws as the latter. The dogma of the divinity of Christ has its embryology, as much as the brain does. The point is to know how to trace it, and Harnack, to my mind, is one of those who have done it best. For all of which reasons I cannot get over my astonishment at your telling me that you do not understand the evolution of dogma, for I don't believe you suppose that the immediate disciples of Jesus had a theology like St. Thomas's *Summa*. Nor do I understand what you mean when you say the Greeks were right on this point. Do you know the *Esquisse d'une philosophie de la religion au point de vue psychologique* of Sabatier? It is the book in which I see best

*149**

and most clearly the position of the so-called liberal Protestants (almost my own position), who have thrown overboard all dogma, not only the dogma of the divinity of Christ but practically the dogma of a personal God as well.

For me, God is not a rational necessity; I have no need of Him to explain the universe: what I cannot explain without God I cannot explain with Him. But He can become a need of the heart, the revelation of the Father. I realize that all this will strike you as a kind of jumble, like everything that happens when one attempts to reason with one's heart, which is as bad as trying to feel with one's head (in the everyday sense).

Inasmuch as I don't expect God to explain anything, I do not make a dogma of my own out of Him, nor even an ideal. God is continuously evolving in me, in my consciousness. Does this correspond with outer reality? I don't know.

I am also surprised that you say "the Gospel is demonstrably bedevilled with lies . . ." Not at all: it is not demonstrable, as far as I know, and not insofar as I understand what a lie is. And I believe that, shorn of its miracle-tales, the Gospel is just what it is, all that it is. A miracle? Everything is a miracle. What is unacceptable is that some things should be miracles and others not.

I see you as—I don't know how to say it—*Sabbathish*, mutinyish, simplistic, *tranchant*—I can't find the word. Your letter reads as if it were written by an eighteenth-century French *philosophe*: it smells of Jacobinism. Of course, in the old Germany of Kant, Goethe, Hegel, and Schleiermacher, following the hegemony of Prussia and the invasion by chemists, industrialists, and military men, the air is full of what they call positivism.

What is it you want? For my part, even though I am more and more convinced of the worth and efficacy of science, I dislike it more every day. I no longer consider it anything more than a narcotic, an opium with which to overcome the pain of longing for an eternity of effective consciousness. Besides, science is turning into a superstition: the microbe will become a teleological entity. "Science tells us . . ." And so on, and so on. At the time of the eclipse (I watched it in Plasencia) no one was terrified at the phenomenon, already forecast; there was even a round of applause for the management of the enterprise: but people spoke with awe about the *wise men* who could predict such things.

When I saw that no one was frightened, I recollected the phrase *primus in orbe terror fecit deos*, and I asked myself: will the gods be eclipsed? But then, when I heard the talk about the "wise men" and about science, I said: No, they will only be transformed! Science is only one of many superstitions. From time to time I plunge into my philological inquiries [. . .], and I have gotten myself into "Lautphysiologie" and even into acoustical studies. You should see what a muddle one can get into following the change of the *o* (of *porto*, for example) to *ue* (our *puerta*)! But all that is like taking opium, or like playing cards. My soul never follows the game.

The old idealist is reborn in me. If we have no God, we'll invent Him. A reason for life must be found, for life cannot be an end in itself for us.

You people work to lengthen life and make it healthier—Bah! Every doctor must deal with the dilemma of either letting the patient die from fear of killing him or killing him from fear of letting him die. And the same thing happens on the spiritual plane.

*151**

Yes, I am dedicated to the noble exercise, not of rhyming, but of versified poetry. Rhyming strikes me as outrageous: an artifice suitable for Stone Age ears. Our Spanish verse is more cadenced and sonorous than melodic and flowing; the beat drowns out the rhythm; it can be accompanied by a drum; it has the cadence of a tribe of chanting Brazilians. It is a dangerous sport if taken seriously? Why? And I take it seriously. Do you really believe that Goethe, Victor Hugo, or Leopardi have not done as much good for humanity with their verses as Copernicus or Newton or Spallanzani or Pasteur with their discoveries? If verse helps me pass some good hours of my existence—could I ask for more? Yes, I take it seriously. As of today it is exactly what I take most seriously. I am not very diffident, don't forget that. I write verses, and I will publish them before my "Life of the Castilian Vernacular: An Essay on Linguistic Biology."

I see you going to the dogs, friend Gayarre, negativized rather more than positivized, in a bad way.

Mugica is an excellent friend, but he is sunk in the muck of Berlin life and in the minutiae of linguistic entomology. His fanaticism for that ape Caligula is incomprehensible.

[. . .]

Enough.

An embrace from your friend

MIGUEL DE UNAMUNO

To Pedro Jiménez Ilundain Salamanca
19 October 1900

My very dear friend, you should not be surprised that I do not write you more frequently, but every day

I am more and more busy and preoccupied. Among my preoccupations, the practical problems are more important than the theoretical ones.

I sent to Barco three copies of my speech opening the school year, one of them autographed for you. If you have not received it, let me know by postcard, and I'll send you another copy. This speech took on a certain resonance, not because of its intrinsic worth (it was one of the weakest things I've done), but because of its occasion and setting. Many are surprised that I decided to preach such things on the occasion of the solemn opening of the school year, to professors wearing their academic robes.

And now comes the most astounding thing. Today in Madrid the retirement papers of all professors over seventy will be signed, and among these is the Rector of the University. The rectorate becomes vacant. They have written me from Madrid to ask if I would accept the post. After thinking carefully I answered that yes, I would, and the Minister offered to appoint me. Even so, I cannot be sure of the appointment. People have found out here, and the news fell like a bomb. Imagine! A conservative government appointing a Socialist, a heterodox, an advocate of dangerous ideas, who is less than thirty-six years old, has been a professor only nine years, and who does not even come from Salamanca— and appointing him after he gave a speech such as the one I gave!

Those who were candidates for the position are upset, because they never thought of me as a likely choice. The matter is more complicated than you would think, but once I'm involved I like to win—and above all to win to prevent Sr. Peña from winning. His appointment would be a scandal. He is personally and very closely connected to the royal family, who made him professor and dean. His appointment would be the greatest calamity we could suffer! I have already been involved in this mess for three or four days. I am tense, I sleep poorly, and I am impatient. I know I shouldn't be that way, but I can't help it.

With regard to my literary work, my contributions to *La Nación* in Buenos Aires are keeping me very busy. But that's where the money is, and that's where I can write with the fewest limitations and the greatest freedom. I am gaining a public in Latin America, and I'm very careful about the whole thing. They have probably already published the last piece I sent them, "Art and Cosmopolitanism," and I'm now busy with an article they solicited from me for their issue of January 1, an article about the social movement of the 19th century. Aside from the contribution and my other journalism for *El Imparcial* and for *La Ilustración española y americana*, I have neglected all my other works, letting them sit on a shelf while I devote myself to a novel on a pedagogical subject entitled *Completely a Man*.

I'm going to try a humorous genre. It is a novel lying somewhere between the tragic and the grotesque, and nearly all the characters are caricatures. One of them spouts absurd aphorisms. The novel is about a man who gets married *deductively*—by deductive reason—in order to have a child and educate him to be a genius, out of his love for pedagogy. He puts his system into practice. The son's life is a dark ruin, and he ends up shooting himself. I hope that it will have more content than my *Peace in War*, without being any longer. I am making an effort to say everything in a minor key, but wish everything to come out emphatically.

The fundamental concept is that the world is a theater, and that in the theater everyone thinks only of the gallery, but that while he thinks he is acting only for his own account he is really reciting a role which he was taught in eternity. (Such is the interpretation which a grotesque philosopher who appears in the novel gives to the Platonic doctrine of recollection.) When his young hero is about to shoot himself, he thinks only about what to say in his suicide note.

In this novel I am departing somewhat from my usual procedures, returning to earlier work in which I made fun of transcendental propositions. I want to write something derisive and to combine—not merely juxtapose—the tragic, the grotesque, and the sentimental. I don't know how it will come out. "The universe was made to be explained." That is the fundamental aphorism of my philosopher, who also says that "if men did not exist, we would have to invent them." Both of these aphorisms are the sharp formulas of intellectualism and of anthropomorphism.

Reading the study *From Kant to Nietzsche* (in the *Mercure*) has increased my horror of intellectualism. At the same time, its opposite, anti-intellectualism, seems to me to be unfitting today. "What is the universe good for? To be catalogued according to science."

I cannot agree with you about religion. Religion seems to me more immortal even than science and so much so that for many people science is becoming a religion, with all the good and the bad of religion. I would like for us to discuss religion at greater length, for I suspect we give the name to very different things. In my judgment, nothing is more wretched than not to be preoccupied with the life beyond death. The fact that the religious problem is again of concern is simply one phase in the rhythm of spiritual progress, in which simple intelligence and the will to live and to live beyond death come into play successively. It is absolutely necessary for the spiritual life of the human species that these preoccupations keep arising.

The definitive triumph of the scientific element is impossible, but if it were not, it would be a great misfortune: humanity would end up in boredom. The definitive triumph of the religious element is equally impossible. Industrialism and an exclusive preoccupation with this life would be as fatal as asceticism. The prototypical scholar is as inhuman as the monk! The man who does not give himself over to the play of contradiction becomes ossified.

No, friend Ilundain, no, the religious question does not preoccupy me more than it should, but much less than it should. To avoid it leads to intellectualist dilettantism, of which I know a fine example, an example who, slightly disguised, I have put in my novel "Completely a Man." He is Verdes Montenegro, a doctor, whose slogan is "What's the use?" He is a kind of Petronius Sienkiewicz. I am forcing his doctrines into often ridiculous paradoxes (and don't forget, my intention is to write a humorous work).

Some months ago I read, in Italian, *Quo Vadis?* It is a stagey book, of value and very vivid, as energetic and as pleasurable as one needs for a best-seller. If it were more profound, it wouldn't have so much success, nor if it were more pedantic. It owes its popularity to church people. It is a second and improved version of *Fabiola*. Everything is clear, everything is well-outlined, everything is superficial and theatrical. It's all line and color, but not substantial. But it is well done, and it deserves its success, although a dozen years hence it will have hardly any readers. Jules Verne also had great success and, here in Spain, Pérez Escrich.

May God give you health (translate this formula as you wish) to raise your three children. [. . .] I have five children, going on six. I owe them, among much else, the diversions they give me from transcendental things, bringing me back to the prose of life, as you say. Having to wade in the prose of life is what suggests to me translating the transcendental into the grotesque, because it is the role that we play when we descend to daily life. "If the gods had to live with men they would be the most grotesque of all beings. It's only one step from the sublime to the ridiculous—and it's a step upward, the step taken by the sublime when it becomes even more sublime." That's the idea which my philosopher, the author of the *Ars Magna Combinatoria*, an essay of rhythmic, superhumanish philosophy, has about comedy.

All my affection, MIGUEL DE UNAMUNO

To Juan Arzadun   Salamanca,
                                                   12 December 1900

Dear Juan,

You're more than right to complain about my lateness and carelessness in not answering you. I intone the *mea culpa* and vow to mend my ways, but . . . if you saw the whirlwind in which I live, and it's not all official either. I've been working some four or five hours daily for over a month now at translating the third and final volume of the *History of the French Revolution* by Carlyle, as I was intent on finishing it before Christmas.

And this very morning I've finished my version of Maese Pedro. Maese Pedro is my name for Carlyle, because of his way of "making" history. Taine has

*157**

drawn a silhouette of Carlyle: it is both systematic and false, like almost everything by the great French falsifier. Maese Pedro sets up his puppet stage, steps forward, makes his speech—filled with interjections and verbal exclamation marks, and periods for silence, to indicate suspense, and "Now, ladies and gentlemen, you will see." He draws back the curtain, takes out his puppets, forces them to speak, react, and work for him. He scolds them, urges them on, insults them, forces them to a dialogue with him; he tells Petion: I already prophesied how you'd end up! And he asks Robespierre things like: What are you up to now, Seagreen Incorruptible? He gives them all nicknames, speaks in the first person, he climbs onto the stage with his puppets, breaks off the play in order to make a speech, and then says: We must get back to our story. And all this amid metaphoric lightning-bolts, a hail of inventiveness and striking descriptions dripping with life: Danton on his way to the guillotine, the Insurrection of Women, the Feast of the *Être Suprême*. Just imagine, if you can, a puritan Victor Hugo, with fancy unbridled. He's a prodigy of the imagination, that Maese Pedro; perhaps not much more than imagination— dazzling, fascinating, and, in the end, dizzying. Some passages are worth remembering forever. He wrote an entire library-full of books to recommend silence (oral silence, doubtless). But his *History of the French Revolution* deserves your reading. [. . .]

And now I am asked to go to Vigo to give, during the second half of January, six lectures, for which they will give me a thousand pesetas and my expenses; they are to be the first lectures in a series which will include Doña Emilia, Echegaray, Cajal, Maeztu, and others. Of course the invitation is troublesome, for as you know, I never like to take the easy way out, to comply merely. These six lectures on *The Social Ethic* will serve me, then, to state the terms of a program which for some time has been maturing in me, and the theme of it is that we European Spaniards should not unfurl the banner of freedom, but rather the flag of culture. Freedom is an abstraction, a mere negative condition. Freedom of conscience, when we haven't yet made a conscience which might be free? It would be like giving fish the right to fly. No, freedom, no. Our people neither deserve it, nor need it, nor would it suit them; culture, culture, culture. An imposed culture, and in the sense that we Europeans, who should constitute ourselves the directors by holy divine right, understand it. As against Catholic reaction (we should call things by their right names) which demands freedom, we should proclaim a *Kulturkampf*, and repeat with Calvin at Geneva: "I do not preach in the name of Freedom, but in the name of Truth." On this head, this essential theme, I will develop at Vigo other themes, as well as speak of the duties of men towards the fatherland; and I will touch on the matter of regionalism, and on almost all the other burning questions. The individual is as great an abstraction as the atom, Natorp says, and I will gloss that thought. And a society independent of individuals is another abstraction. Joaquín Costa has done fearful damage by his adulation of the Spanish people, which always has better government than it deserves, however bad the governments are. We must convince them that they are indeed brute matter and that to avoid falling under the sway of the clergy, which would make them all the more brutish, they must allow themselves to be guided by us, and they will be won over. . . . You'll see how they are! For my part, I have such faith in myself, and am so profoundly convinced of my providential pedagogic or demagogic (taking the word etymologically) mission in Spain, that I will convince them. And I will touch on the religious problem, not the clerical one, and will put the question. God knows that when they say that propitious occasions come to me easily, they are wrong: the point is that I never let the opportunity go by. The opening address devolved on me by inexorable chance: and instead of merely complying, which is normal practice, I put my soul into the speech. I was asked to go to Bilbao, and I realized that the most opportune course to follow would be exactly the one the prudent of the world consider the most inopportune—and I was proved right. I am asked to go to Vigo, and, in place of giving forth with six lectures on political economy or linguistics, I will deliver a compact series of six lay sermons, with a Protestant tinge. And I'll speak to them also of the cult of life, in this poor country which has lived with the cult of death, and of the grandeur of *pro patria vivere*, which means not so much to die as to continue living, when one gives one's life for one's country. And of moral value, of the need to extirpate our most beloved sentiments (as the Basque sentiment), when these hinder us in the march toward progress, and the necessity to look the Sphinx in the face. The lectures will have resonance, I can tell you, because for some time now Providence has supplied a sounding board for the words which come from my soul. Onward! I have a mission to fulfill and I will fulfill it. And I want to subject myself to something higher than myself, in the service of an ideal, so as to have the right to subject other

*160**

things to myself, and not have to pause on my road because of one or two stumbling blocks.

I speak to you of myself with entire abandon, with total frankness. I believe that I am today one of the most representative men of our Basque race—begging pardon of those unfortunates who now call me a traitor, unfaithful son, and renegade. And if they persist in their blindness and insist on sticking to their pettiness, in singing the *Guernicaco* and going on about their feudal *fueros*, their local rights, I believe our race will go along with me towards another destiny and other work.

Years ago Doña Emilia told me I reminded her of St. Ignatius, and I've never forgotten it. I ask God, my God, only to sustain me and to prevent my pride from blinding me.

Catalanism strikes me as something vulgar, vile, petty, low, proper only to a nation of egotists. "We will save ourselves with Spain or without her!" No, no, no! It should be: "We will save Spain, whether she wants to be saved or not." We Basques should ask for something altogether different: not ask that we be allowed to govern ourselves, but for the right to govern the others, since we are the most capable of doing so. We must do as in Italy, where the North has pronounced itself, alone, against the South, declaring Neapolitans unworthy of governing themselves.

Yes, we must proclaim the inferiority of the Andalusians and the others, as well as our fraternal duty to govern them. Málaga should be declared a colony, and we must sweep out all Bedouinism. [. . .] I will proclaim it and if I am left alone, alone I will remain. Do not thousands of Spaniards think the same as I? Then some of those who hear me will say so. All this

161*

will resound in Vigo with sacred sincerity. The Castilian has the advantage over the Catalan of possessing an inquisitor's soul.

At first I tolerate more easily whoever comes to me with samples than I do the person who comes at me with a Credo and a sword and announces: "Believe or die!" That's at first. But after reflection, I realize that the person with the samples takes me for a client, and the other man considers me a man. The tissue of political lies envenoms me. [. . .] And as concerns my part, I will break down the mesh of lies, and, as I said in Bilbao, I will speak the truth, where, when, and in a way to create the greatest effect; where, when, and however most inopportune, that is, most opportune [. . .].

Have a good Christmas

[. . .] Affectionately MIGUEL DE UNAMUNO

To Federico Urales [1901]

Dear sir and esteemed friend,

The truth is that your two questions place me in a great quandary. In order to answer properly I would have to outline an autobiography for you, something both tiresome and perilous. Besides, there would be the added inconvenience of having to make a number of circumlocutions to explain certain things, for I know very well where you stand, and if your ideas strike me as quite reasonable as regards what you affirm, they do not as regards what you deny. On Christianity, for example, I think you are quite wrong when you judge it on the basis of its medieval asceticism, or on the basis of Catholicism, both of which are essentially at odds with it. But that is not the question at the moment. And so I will answer you as God best allows me.

I was a frail child (though never sick), taciturn and melancholic and with a vast reserve of romanticism; I was raised in the bosom of a Basque family of the most austere habits and with a certain Quaker tint. I never knew my father: he died when I was six. It was my mother's influence, then, which counted. As a lad I was devout in the highest degree, with a devoutness which bordered on what is often called (wrongly so) mysticism. At the same time, I was given to reading both controversial books and books of religious apologetics, in an attempt to rationalize my inherited and imposed faith. I have written a good deal of my own life into that of Pachico in my novel *Peace in War*. What I say in a couple of pages of that book [. . .] is strictly true and gives the fairest picture of my spiritual state at that time. When I arrived in Madrid to study in 1880 at the age of sixteen, I was still in that same state of spirit and remained so throughout my first two years of school. I persisted in the attempt to rationalize my faith and, naturally, dogma fell apart in my mind. By this I mean to say that my religious conversion (such is its name) was a matter of slow evolution: having been a fervent practicing Catholic, I gradually stopped being one, by dint of rationalizing and getting to know my faith, from seeking the Christian spirit beneath the Catholic words. And so one day, during Carnival (I remember it well), I suddenly stopped attending Mass. Next I set off on a dizzy chase through philosophy. I learned German from Hegel, that stupendous Hegel, one of the thinkers who have left the deepest imprint on me. Even today I believe that the essence of my thought is Hegelian. Next I fell in love with Spencer, but always interpreting him in a Hegelian manner. Though a man of vast culture, Spencer is, as a metaphysician, very crude. And I always returned to my initial preoccupation: my reading on the religious problem, which is what has always concerned me the most. A good while later, I read Schopenhauer, who grew on me and who has always been one of the two, along with Hegel, who have made the greatest impression on me. On another level: Carlyle, not for his ideas, which strike me as very sparse and not at all original, but for his exposition of them, his impetuous style. It was Carlyle who perhaps contributed most to my finding my own style.

But as much or more than philosophers or thinkers I have been moved and affected by poets: the great Leopardi (I know him almost by heart) above all, and the English lyric poets (Wordsworth, Coleridge, Burns, and others), who wrote my favorite verse.

It would be most difficult to detail the origins of my thought, because during a period of ten or twelve years, from 1880 to 1892, I read vastly, read everything that fell into my hands, especially in psychology (physiological psychology: Wundt, James, Bain, Ribot, and others, I tried out for a professorship in that field), and in philosophy (I have sat for other career examinations in metaphysics), not counting my regular philological studies. But I have always read in all fields: physics, chemistry, physiology, biology, even mathematics. Not long ago I studied pure projective geometry.

About four years ago, I underwent a severe inner crisis, which would be endless in the telling. It was a period of terrible anguish, which is reflected in my "Nicodemus" (an essay which does not reveal my pres-

ent state of spirit, but rather my state at the time).
Under the impact of that inner blow I returned, or
tried to return, to the ancient faith of my childhood.
Impossible! What I have returned to is a certain Christian sentiment, rather vague, the Christianity called
Liberal Protestantism, that of Baur, Harnack, Ritschl,
and the highly attractive French school of Renan, Réville, the two Sabatiers, Stapfer, Menegoz, and so on—
the road pointed out by Schleiermacher.

In another order of things, my readings in economics
(more than in sociology) made me a socialist, but I
soon understood that my background was, and above
all is, anarchist.

But what I do detest is the sectarian and dogmatic
sense given to socialism. Dynamite-ism repels me, as
does the propaganda of violence and its rhetoric. A
Bakunin strikes me as a dangerous madman. It is the
anarchism of an Ibsen I find attractive, and, even more,
that of a Kierkegaard, the powerful Danish thinker
from whom Ibsen and Tolstoy, most especially, have
taken sustenance. Tolstoy has been one of those souls
who has most profoundly shaken my own soul; his
works have left a deep impression.

I believe myself to be, whether rightly or not I don't
know, a fairly complex spirit. But I can point to Hegel,
Spencer, Schopenhauer, Carlyle, Leopardi, Tolstoy,
as my main teachers, and along with them the thinkers
with religious concern, and the English lyric poets.
But, I repeat, it is very difficult for me to point out,
in the torrent of my reading, what influences there
have been. As regards Spaniards, I can affirm, for sure:
none, nobody. I have scarcely been influenced by any
Spanish writer at all. My soul is not very Spanish.

Every day my repugnance for sectarianism is more

deeply rooted, my rejection of exclusivist ideas, of affirmative dogmatists—of those who consider anyone who does not think like themselves to be ignorant, cracked, weak—grows apace. From my master Hegel I learned to seek the ground wherein contraries harmonize. People who see everything clearly tend to be dark spirits, the great Portuguese poet Guerra Junqueiro said to me a few days ago. And I will not read affirmative, aggressive, cutting, combatant writers. They fulfill a function, but it is an ephemeral function. And, since I do not consider myself an advance-guard, nor a propagandist, I remain here in this retreat. I'd give over all my work as a socialist propagandist, work which in some sense was anarchistic (when I wrote for *La Ciencia Social*), in exchange for my *Peace in War*, a novel into which I put my whole soul. Intellectual dryness, with no background of feeling, gives me pause: I fear it. And the "art" of teaching, as well as the service of an economic or political ideal, fill me with suspicion: I find them suspect. Though I am in no part an aesthete, and in fact detest aestheticism, I detest anti-aestheticism even more. I love the inner life above all (Maeterlinck's *Trésor des humbles* delighted me). My "Go within yourself!" expresses this attitude of mine.

I am sure I have made myself clear to you, for even though we differ *ex toto diametro*, we are not without a strong common ground and neither of us lacks *bona fides*. I do protest, however, that I should be thought a spiritual weakling or a victim of neurasthenia. My health these days is bomb-proof, and I count on a first-rate physical vigor. I'd place myself among the best as regards running and jumping, or merely breathing and digesting. All those explanations for certain states of

166*

mind based on physiological unbalance or weakness strike me as crashing superficialities. It's as if I were to explain certain dogmatisms or sectarianisms (there is the dogmatism of anti-dogmatism, too) by calling it hardening of the brain.

You know you have a friend in

MIGUEL DE UNAMUNO

To Pedro de Mugica   Salamanca,
                                        11 February 1903

My very dear friend,

You are right; although I resist it, I am getting old, and I notice that I've lost something of my dash and even my aggressiveness of times past.

Six children! And all that that means!

I'm now involved in the project of collecting for publication in book form the things I've written and published in various scattered periodicals. And in the meantime I keep at my works without stopping, working on "The Life of the Castilian Language" and on "Religion and Science." But I'm doomed to plan some things and then do others.

[. . .]

You tell me that you want to take a look at your old letters to me.

I can send them because I keep them all, without having mislaid any—for the common collection of friends' letters. Some people tell me that the best thing I will have left behind when I die will be my correspondence. Doña Emilia told me so some time ago, and yesterday Dr. Bunge, an Argentinian, said the same thing.

*167**

[. . .]
An embrace from your friend,

MIGUEL DE UNAMUNO

To Antonio Machado   August 1903

My dear friend,

I am much taken with your letter, in which you answer the points I raised with your brother Manuel regarding your little book of verse. So much so that I think it would be well to answer it publicly, and to make use of you as intermediary between me and the public.

Your reactions to your two-year stay in Paris reach me in the course of my reading Léon Bazalgette's *Le Problème de l'avenir latin*, on which I plan to write two or three short pieces.

You say the French "are masters of the art of conversation, which consists in always telling one's interlocutor that he is right, while at the same time maintaining a contrary opinion oneself. We Spanish on the other hand are masters of the art of dispute, which consists in always lacing into one's interlocutor even if we agree with him. The fact is that for a Frenchman any discussion, whatever the topic, is simply a pretext for downing a few absinthes, while for a Spaniard an opinion is like a fighting cock with sharpened talons ever ready for a fight. The French know how to drink and the Spanish do not know how to converse." And you say that to me, a tireless disputant who drinks only water.

Next you comment on my telling your brother, in connection with your book, that we must force our own way through the Spanish jungle, which is mostly

168*

virgin terrain, and you deal with one of my own favorite points, when you say that you agreed with Rubén
Darío and Gómez Carrillo, those idolators of the French
soul, who held that life in Paris is not very conducive
to art because there life is art—not always good art—
so that art itself is redundant, as it were, an almost
useless ornament. And you add: "The contrary is the
case in Spain, where, apart from some provincial cap-
itals with artificial souls, life is unaware of itself and
flows more spontaneously and authentically and more
attractively for art." And further: "I am beginning to
believe, even at the risk of falling into paradoxes, which
are not to my taste, that the artist should love life and
hate art. That is, the opposite of what I believed up
until now."

Let us leave the French de-Latinize themselves, to
be whatever they are or to seek whatever they should
be, and let us be what we in ourselves are, seeking our
permanent essence and ground, de-Latinizing ourselves, too, until we get back to our Iberian, Moorish,
Berber, or whatever, inmost beings. I pass over your
declaration that you are not fond of paradox, the most
perfect form for expounding living truth—a fact of
which Christ was well aware, for he scattered them
throughout his Glad Tidings—and come to your proposition that the artist should love life and hate art.

I have lost count of the number of times I have
written or spoken of the theatrical theater, the novelistic novel, the narrative narrative, and so on. I almost
never go to the theater, since I cannot stand it: all those
gesticulating characters chatting away on the boards
strike me as so many abstracts from other dramas and
comedies, all adding up to a world totally apart from
this world. Most playwrights are formed by reading
other playwrights and seeing plays staged. I must con-

fess I know nothing of Tamayo and that my reluctance to read him or see his plays stems from the fact that he was the son of actors and was raised among them. I would go to the theater only if I heard that some *barbarian* had entered that realm, someone alien to the boards. I have as much aversion to the theater as I have to those who speak like a book, inasmuch as the man who speaks like a book is incapable of making a book which speaks like a man. I cannot stand those professional pedants who chant a refrain on something's being a theatrical piece; the worst of it is that they manage to influence the sheep-like public whose herd instinct tells them that the Venus de Milo is more beautiful than a lively young woman with a turned-up nose and piquant eyes.

And of novelistic novels let us not even speak.

I know we will be told that art is something concrete and specific, with its own laws and rules, and that there are eternal norms of taste, and other such gibberish put forth in learned manuals of aesthetics; but I stick to my own taste, a preference for any fierce cry or wild utterance which comes from the entrails of life, rather than all the tuning-up that leads to the sonnets of Hérédia or the atrocities of Baudelaire.

Nor do I agree that art for art's sake is superior even as regards form. The day will come when, in the name of Beauty, they will set fire to every scrap of printed paper bearing "impeccable" phrases, all of them varnished vacuities. We should not allow anemic spirits to impose their aesthetics on us; nor allow those who are pustulent of body and envious of soul to pass off their dreary singsongs as some kind of perfection.

I heard tell of a famous French composer who when he heard some melodies of a very popular Spanish musician, said: "That is not music; but insofar as it resembles music, it is one of the most agreeable things I've heard." The Spaniard should say: "Let us not quarrel over names; it may be music or whatever; but whatever it is, if it has soul and communicates that soul, it is a thousand times more beautiful than all those cleverly constructed sonatas."

Which is what I do when I speak in public, and they listen to me attentively and even with pleasure, and then say: "of course it is a pleasure to listen to him, but he is not an orator." And I say: "the real non-orators are all liars abounding in adjectives, jabberers who gesticulate and deal in long, rounded paragraphs."

The main concern of our orators is to avoid upsetting the stomachs of the well-fed, to avoid disquieting the hearts of the smug people who accept whatever happens. Art must be, for them, an aid to digestion, a kind of drug, which in the end ruins one's stomach.

Just look at our language, and consider the havoc wrought by stylists intent on getting rid of assonance and bent on other farfetched tasks. In the end we are stuck with the horrible, squalid language used in Parliament and in the press. From time to time some unhappy man strives to weave a language for himself out of his own sweat.

I think of how a legion of stenographers might be well employed if they were sent into the cafés and marketplaces and fairs and small-town taverns to take down everything said there. It could all be published, and many people would be amazed to learn how different the spoken language is—especially in syntax—from the written one. [. . .]

The best thing to do, then, is to travel around the virgin Spanish jungle, get beneath its outer crust, break through its cover, and find the living water which runs there, flowing out of subterranean wells. Flee from the Art of Art, the art of artists made by them for themselves alone; for they act like a pianist who performs only pieces of prestidigitation, exercises in difficult virtuosity, an insult to the public, in short. [. . .]

Remember how Plato, that sovereign artist and poet, barred from his Republic "all those skilful in imitating everything and able to assume a thousand different forms"; the kind of artists who are but for admiration. After rendering homage to them as divine beings worth admiration, Plato tells them they are not allowed in his Republic; and he takes leave of them by pouring perfume over their heads; he contents himself with poets and narrators less agreeable and more austere, that is, truer poets than the first lot.

Best to seek art in life, in life devoid of reflective art; best to affirm your own aesthetic and accept the challenge on your own terrain [. . .].

You know what a friend you have in

MIGUEL DE UNAMUNO

To Pedro de Mugica   Salamanca,
                                                          2 December 1903

My dear friend,

I need to unburden myself. With the winter, I entered a period of inner activity and agitation, which coincides with the peak of a campaign directed against me by the Catholic elements (let's be quite open about it) of this city, and the veiled threat of open hostilities from the bishop. The day may yet come when I shall have to reveal my thoughts entirely and say quite openly that Catholicism—especially the way it is understood here—is de-Christianizing us. Instead of offering the people a light so they can make their own way, they have put them in a wagon and are hauling them through the darkness. And the worst of it is that most of us Spaniards are living a lie, an enormous lie. We live with lies and die with lies. It is not error that kills, but lies. He who preaches the truth without believing in it, even despising it, may enlighten the mind, but he poisons the heart; while he who preaches error in the belief that it is truth and with complete faith in it, although he may temporarily lead people astray, elevates and fortifies the heart. And in the long run the heart corrects the head.

With respect to the paragraph beginning "for me God is not a rational requirement, I do not need Him in order to explain the Universe to myself," I really don't know where I wrote it, but I know that I did write it, and probably more than once, for it expresses my thoughts perfectly. God does not come to us through reason but through the heart; neither His existence nor His nonexistence can be proved through logical arguments. You either feel He is there or you do not; you either experience Him personally—and for us Christians it is through the Gospels, as in John—or you do not. The person who experiences Him doesn't need any proofs, and neither does the person who doesn't experience Him.

And now permit me, in the name of the bonds of friendship that unite us, to broach a subject which I usually keep to myself and which I entrust to your discretion. I know to whom I address myself and that you will not think my words are the ravings of a semi-madman. For some time now, since I experienced a certain deep spiritual crisis, I have felt that I am an instrument in the hands of God, an instrument that will contribute to the spiritual regeneration of Spain.

For some time now my entire existence, my triumphs, the popularity which I am achieving, my elevation to the post of Rector of this university, all seem predetermined to place me in a position of such authority and prestige that my work will be made more fruitful. Everything that I have written or said in public thus far is simply a preparation for my true work, which may begin the day I move to Madrid. Events are accelerating. When I was a little boy—no more than twelve—a strange thing happened to me which left a very deep impression. I don't know whether I have told you this before, but what occurred was that when I returned from Communion one day I went to my room and opened the Gospel and put my finger where it said: "Go ye therefore, and teach all nations . . ." (Matthew 28:19). I thought on this and concluded that I was being told to become a priest or monk, and since I was already involved with the girl who is today my wife, I refused to accept it and decided to investigate further. A month after the communion, I again opened the book and my finger fell on the passage: "I have told you already, and ye did not hear: wherefore would you hear it again?" (John 9:27). Just imagine the effect this had on me; I was crushed. Then my thoughts—not my feelings—changed, I lost God because I sought Him out in the Catholic way, rationally and with arguments and liturgies and externals. I got married and a few years later, six years ago, when I suffered the crisis which seemed to carry me back to my childhood beliefs, what had happened as a child came back with new force. The shock was a call not to the dead beliefs of my childhood, but to their eternal core, their base, to Christian faith pure and simple without ecclesiastical dogmas, a call to sincerity, in a word, and to God. Now I understand the course my life has taken and the importance of those texts, and I see the task that lies ahead of me. Outer circumstances are driving me towards that task, including the deplorable state of this poor Spain where beneath what they call the religious problem, which is really ecclesiastical-political, there throbs the true religious problem, the need for sincerity, freedom, and faith. And so long as we do not undergo something similar to what the Reformation was for the Germanic peoples, we are lost. Because in those countries even the Catholics—whether they know it or not—are more or less reformed. These are the intimate confessions which I entrust to your friendship.

And I deeply sense what I must do, I feel it, I see the path I must follow, and I am drawn to it by a conscious, personal force which is above me. And thus I believe in God, whom I do not need in order to construct a purely logical system of the world of phenomena.

If I were insincere and were possessed of the pride of modesty, I would say that what you said about me in your last letter overwhelms me. Now you tell me that you are sending a study of me to *La Nación*. Thank you. It all fits into my work, to which I give myself over. I must resign myself to praise as I do to censure, without glossing over the feeling and ambition and *amour-propre* which may be part of it. So that humanity might propagate itself, men and women were imbued with mutual attraction and the delight of sex, and so we were given vainglory; if we know how to use, but not abuse, both one and the other, it shall all be for the greater glory of God. I try to make vainglory into a legitimate and fertile wife, not a sterile concubine. [. . .]

You say I should travel to Berlin. Sooner or later,

on one excuse or another, I shall certainly do so. If I have not done so until now, it is only because of lack of money. And it seems to me that even that has been arranged by providence to keep me in this sad Spain, for—why not say so, since I think it?—she needs me. [. . .]

And now I must get to work, I who seem so un-Spanish, for the sake of this Spain. The more decadent and fallen she is, the more she deserves that her sons raise her up. And you can make your contribution from where you are.

A strong embrace from MIGUEL DE UNAMUNO

To Pedro de Mugica   Salamanca,
                                   19 October 1904

My dear friend Mugica,

The King came and went, and then that unfortunate thing happened to him that you know about. I took advantage of the days that he was here and especially of the trip to Zamora, since I went there with him and came back with him and we could talk on the train. He is an agreeable young man, but he seems to be bashful and perhaps afraid in front of the public. Out of fear over his health, they educated him in athletics and in military drill, so he has had little experience with society. Furthermore, he is extremely military-minded, something the people mumble about a great deal and don't like very much. People don't take it at all well that he always goes about in the uniform of a captain-general. The truth is that if there's anything that can incline those of us who are neither republicans nor monarchists toward a Republic it's that a Republic is more a matter of civilians and that those military

*176**

barbarians, who are a thousand times worse than the priests and monks, will have to straighten out and surrender their weapons to a civilian.

The matter of the Pikman-Paredes challenge, forced now by General Luque, and all of the present consequences, again demonstrate the insolent barbarism of those animals in uniform who want to settle everything by brute force. The duel is, in itself, a piece of stupid savagery, but a duel that is organized and codified by military men—whose honor is the most stupid thing I've ever heard of—is indeed something intolerable. With every day I feel more loathing for militarism [. . .]. And what's more, militarism is neither order nor discipline, but the deepest disorder and indiscipline. These brutes should be limited everywhere to be the servants of the intelligentsia, without laying claim to any intelligence.

Here's where this King is running into danger and how he will end by making himself unpopular—today he's not, he still awakens sympathies—if he begins to try to imitate that wretched excuse for a human being, Kaiser Caligula.

[. . .]

I'm getting back to my *Quixote*, which is what preoccupies me now.

How much I'd like to pay you a visit there! I will probably die without having visited that Germany which I like so much (but without Prussian military beasts and without Kaiser Caligula).

[. . .]

An embrace from your friend

MIGUEL DE UNAMUNO

And what about that packet of your letters which I sent you? Don't you intend to return it?

To D. Pedro Jiménez Ilundain   Salamanca,
                                   9 May 1905

My dear friend:

The handiest way for me (to answer your question about what I mean by the word "God") would be to send you my *Treatise on the Love of God*, which I am now writing. But I prefer to tell you plainly and simply that by "God" I mean the same thing as most Christians: a personal, conscious, infinite, and eternal Being who governs the universe. He is the Consciousness of the universe. And I am surprised that you should ask me this. You might be surprised that I should believe in God, in the personal God of Christian theology, but you should not ask what I mean by the word. God, in my writings, means the same thing as it means in the writings of Christian writers. I am neither an atheist nor a pantheist. The positions taken by a Büchner or a Haeckel seem to me to be superficial. I believe that the universe has meaning—spiritual and ethical meaning and purpose.

What I indeed will tell you, and my "Treatise on the Love of God" starts out with this point, is that logical arguments arrive only at the idea of God, not at God Himself. And that idea is a hypothesis, and a very mediocre one, since what cannot be explained without God cannot be explained with Him either— God is needed neither in science nor in metaphysics. But I believe in Him because I have a personal *experience* of Him, because I feel Him working and living in me. And don't ask me more about this. It isn't a question of reasoning, and I don't enjoy polemics. I keep to my God, and I ask Him to show Himself to others.

My *Life of Don Quixote* keeps opening up a road to me, little by little, despite the more or less silent hostility on the part of writers of the old school. And it's not the Catholics who are scandalized the most, but the partisans of Science (with a capital letter), the people who are now giving us that infamous garbage in books that sell for four *reales*. They are taking over Spain and we must put a stop to their kind. Our salvation is to return, with true modern knowledge and not phony Science [. . .] to our mystics, and to bring down all the physiologists, doctors, and engineers meddling in philosophy. You will see in my *Treatise*.

To the struggle! Others, to Europeanize Spain. I, to see if one day I can Hispanize Europe. God give me strength. But you will ask yourself, "Will this man go mad?"

A warm embrace, MIGUEL DE UNAMUNO

To Pedro de Mugica   Salamanca,
                                   10 November 1905

Dear Mugica,

Young José Ortega y Gasset, the son of Ortega Munilla, the editor of *El Imparcial*, will introduce himself to you with my calling card. He is in Berlin now, at the Central Hotel. He is an extraordinarily agreeable young man, very cultivated and intelligent, much superior, for that matter, to his father, who, although a nice fellow, is rather frivolous [. . .]. The boy is studious, and he wants to meet you. Please guide and assist him, but don't, for God's sake, push him into philological studies, which I believe don't interest him. What he wants is to learn German and then philosophy and aesthetics. Considering all those French influences which are unchecked and doing so much harm today, one must help out a young man who goes to Germany but not—as most of them do—to study engineering.

Ortega is, to my mind, one of our most valuable young intellects, and he needs and deserves help. Introduce him to people of influence [. . .].

Until later, an embrace from

MIGUEL DE UNAMUNO

To José Ortega y Gasset   Salamanca,
                                              17 May 1906

My very dear friend,

[. . .]

Every day, friend Ortega, I feel more and more impelled to make gratuitous assertions, more given to arbitrary statements, to the passionate stance, and every day I am more rooted in my own form of anarchism, which is the true form. And thus I become more and more isolated. I don't fit in anywhere, not even in myself.

Every day I am less interested in ideas and things: every day I am more interested in feelings and people. I am not interested in what you say, I am interested in you.

You write: "The subjective interpretation of a fact scientifically inexplicable. . . ." Scientifically? My long distrust of science is turning into hatred. I hate science, and miss wisdom.

> For nothing worth proving can be proven
> nor yet disproven

as Tennyson says.

If you only knew, my dear Ortega, the travail I undergo to give birth to what they call paradoxes! If you knew of the suppressed tears that go into my latest writing! And why, I ask myself, when I am merely a man of passion trying to take hold of himself and find consolation in despair (my life is resigned despair), why is everyone so intent in making me into a sage, a pedagogue, an educator, and other nonsensical things?

Enough of that.

When it occurs to me to write a book review, whenever that may be, I'll let you know.

And I don't know when I'll go to see you. I don't feel any desire to leave here. I want to cultivate my solitude. But I really would like it if you would come to spend a few days here.

These days, beside working on my "Treatise on the Love of God," I am writing verse. So far this year I have written more verse than in all the rest of my life put together. . . .

By next Monday you will have an article from me, and I expect you to look at it as you would a piece by anyone else. It will be full of arbitrary opinions and gratuitous assertions. I will assert myself, and I am, just as you and all of us are, gratuitous. I cannot prove myself logically.

You know how loyal and true a friend—which is what counts—you have in

MIGUEL DE UNAMUNO

To José Ortega y Gasset   Salamanca,
                                             30 May 1906
My very dear friend,

I don't wish to remain silent a single day longer in answering your justified reproach regarding the tone of my last letter to you. I believe and confess you are right. After all, you are in no way responsible, neither in part nor by art, neither from afar nor nearby, for the lusty gale sweeping my soul, my poor little soul. And you can't know how my intimate solitude grows

181*

and deepens. I grow ever more solitary. And now I scarcely enjoy any company but that of other recluses like myself. I am not interested in anything that interests most men, and they are not interested in anything that may interest me. When I come to explain the talk I gave at the Zarzuela—and I would do and say the same again—I will be saying things incomprehensible to the majority.

But you are right: I was unjust. I chose to see in the ideas you were unfolding in your letter only what was opposite to my own feelings (I won't say ideas) and something you have taken from the learned *Germania*. And I am growing furiously anti-European. So they invent things? Let them invent! Electric light works just as well here as it does where it was invented. (I congratulate myself for having thought up such an ingenious aphorism.) Science makes life easier in its applications and it is one door to wisdom. But aren't other doors? Don't we have another door in ourselves?

When we meet face to face, I'll have more to say. For the present I beg you to forgive the tone of my letter. I live amid continual change, and I write not to gain glory nor *pour épater le bourgeois*, but to get the better of my passions, to subdue my impulses. Who knows?—perhaps Spinoza's *Ethics* or Newton's *Principia* have the same psychic source as Goethe's *Werther*. [. . .]

Pay no attention to the idiosyncrasies of
your loyal friend MIGUEL DE UNAMUNO

To Juan Maragall   4 January 1907

A good year to you, my dear friend, a good year! I don't know how it will work out for me. I begin it under what people call the sign of a lucky star, but I think there is nothing more terrifying than happiness. I have my health. So do my wife and my children. I ended the year with a better balance sheet than in other years. I meet with more respect around me . . . and I am afraid of it all. Happiness more than adversity makes it easy to see the emptiness of life, *L'infinita vanità del tutto*. Once we've gained temporal happiness, we may lose it; it's like fire in water or ice in fire.

The state of things in Spain drags me down. I don't know if you chanced to read a piece I published in *El Imparcial* at year's end, wherein I spoke of you with the affection and truth you deserve. The article reflected my state of mind. I'm stifled by the vulgarity around me. There may be ideas, but there's no idealism, and ideas are just the degeneration of idealism. And there's no real feeling here. I find people neither love nor hate, neither admire nor despise anything.

You said I was like the last combatant in a lost cause. And I fight them, the *Africans*. Because it is precisely the "Africans" who least understand or feel my Africanism. To turn against European culture, when—and *because*—I know and feel it, is to enter into it, penetrate it. One of the most intimate relationships is the one we call opposition. One of the closest of solidarities is that of combatants. This fact will explain much about me. When I was a child, my mother, who had studied in France, had me learn French; I read German at twenty, English at twenty-five, and I've scarcely read in Spanish. I have lived outside Spain in spirit—and that is what has made me Spanish. And I am so Spanish, so Castilian, if you will, because Castile has come to me, not through its literature, but through itself, its fields, its sky, its fruits, its people. I have come to know Castile not through her writers, but in herself, with *immediacy*. And that is so, despite my being from a region where the sea reflects the mountains, the mountains where I was born and grew up, as did all my forefathers.

And such is fate that here I am considered a bad Spaniard, too foreign.

I know that if there were a strong desire to sustain and impose one's own culture, alien cultures could be assimilated. I know that if people were capable of turning against the directing principles of Western civilization, they would enter fully into that civilization. But—they are not interested. They parrot the latest philosophical, scientific, literary, or artistic novelty from Europe and continue on—the same. Just listen to the talk in Madrid from the adorers of Nietzsche: he serves as a pretext for them to become followers of Maura.

All this makes me sad and weary. But I will find in this very sadness and weariness the strength to fight on. I will have my fill of calling this nation vulgar and maudlin.

God grant you your serenity and me my disquiet! An embrace from your friend

MIGUEL DE UNAMUNO

To Juan Maragall   Salamanca,
                                      15 February 1907

My dear friend,

For some days now I have been wanting to write you, when it happened that I read your "This Is My Faith." I'm happy to see you writing for a newspaper in Madrid, and I hope that I have had something to do with that. [. . .] The article is very good. What you say about youth consisting principally in the condition of not having a past left me with a very deep impression. It is one of those fruitful discoveries of self-evident things, and you don't know what horizons this equation of youth and not having a past is opening for me. Very good, very good.

Your remarks about the sun are also very good. I'm translating with my students in class a portion of the Odyssey, and I again see what light meant to the Greeks. But to us? What a contrast! Light saddens us and fills us with worries. We are always seeking ourselves, and in the street, in the light, we lose ourselves.

And how right you are in what you so vividly say about the hypochondria that arises from a shooting pain. Here I am, healthy and strong, and yet I have gone through that hypochondria, through worry over angina, over a heart ailment. I know all about imaginary illness. My wife cured me of that.

In your last letter you spoke to me about my "campaign tent." Yes. In my life of struggle and fighting, in my life as a Bedouin of the spirit, I have placed my campaign tent in the middle of the spirit. There I retire, there I reforge myself, and there the glance of my wife restores me and brings back the breezes of my childhood. We met, almost as children, in Bilbao. At the age of twelve, she returned to her native town of Guernica, and there I used to go at every opportunity to walk with her in the shade of the old and symbolic oak tree. And there we were married. The good nature in my wife's heart shows through in her eyes, and in her presence I am ashamed to be sad. One day years ago when I was worried about my heart, she saw me weep, overtaken by pain, and she uttered a

185

"My son!" which still echoes within me. And that is my campaign tent.

[. . .]

Until next time, embraces from your friend,

MIGUEL DE UNAMUNO

To Alberto Nin Frías   Salamanca,
                                         19 July 1907

My esteemed friend,

I am in agreement with you in almost all you write: your admiration for Taine, for Goethe, for Gladstone. We part company only in that I suffer from Franco-phobia or miso-Gallicism, and I say "I suffer" from it, because I cannot justify my mania. I accept all that may be said in praise of France, but my heart is not won over. I do not have a Latin soul. Of France I care only for the bold minority of Huguenots; the Sabatiers, Réville, and such. Rousseau and Amiel are in no sense French. I am repelled by the spirit of Voltaire, Montaigne, Racine, Zola, and company, though I grant their greatness. They achieve clarity by shutting their eyes to the mystery. What most attracts me in your own book is your preoccupation with religious problems and interests. You do well to cite Taine's phrase: only those lack religion who do not concern themselves with it. Religion is my own supreme concern. . . . Religion necessarily takes on a different face in different countries, and each must be true to its own nature. Take a Spanish Catholic or anti-Catholic: the content of their beliefs is entirely different, but they hold them in the same way, as you will see if you examine them microscopically. In contrast, the difference between a Spanish Catholic and a Yankee Catholic, or between

*186**

a Spanish freethinker and a Norwegian one—even
though their beliefs are the same—is quite profound.
[. . .] It seems to me that you are wrong when you say
that Spain "is the most Catholic country in the world";
it is an error into which one easily falls if one judges
Spain in accord with her history rather than her infra-
history. France is much more Catholic than Spain. In
France, even the atheists have Catholic souls. By Catholicism I mean a religious conception which is *social*,
not individual, and which is moreover intellectualist,
Scholastic, not of the heart, a religious conception in
which ideas are given primacy over feelings and faith
is a matter of rational adherence to abstract principles.
And the Frenchman is much more logical, more in-
tellectualistic, less moved by feeling than is the Spaniard: he is more Catholic. Compare St. Teresa or St.
John of the Cross with Bossuet. We have great mystics
and bad theologians: the French have great theologians
and no mystics.

"The monarchy should live on in Spain," you say,
and you are right. Monarchy is stronger than a republic to carry out a *Kulturkampf*. Hildebrand proclaimed the superiority of the Church over the Empire,
while our Liberals proclaim a free Church in a free
State. In Spain this is an absurdity. [. . .]

Do you know Ganivet? He represented the strongest
force Spain produced at the end of the last century.
He died quite young and is thought to have committed
suicide in Riga. Beneath the enormous composition of
the *Trabajos de Pío Cid* lies genuine gold. He is a great
man not only for Spain, but for any nation. He seems
to me grander than the idols of the Francophiles over
there. [. . .]

Your friend MIGUEL DE UNAMUNO

187*

To Rubén Darío   Salamanca,
                                              26 September 1907

It is always the same, my dear friend: you have been
told everything disagreeable I may have said about
you, but no one has bothered to mention the rest. If I
were someone else I would set about explaining the
business of the "feathers" and justify everything by
citing, as relative praise, a very similar phrase written
about you by our friend Rodó. And yes: I will say that
I prefer in you whatever is native, whatever has line-
age, whatever can be traced to indigenous sources, over
whatever you may have taken from France, a country
I find disagreeable, and even over whatever you may
have taken from my beloved Spain. But: enough of
that.

I accept your letter as a lesson, and add that I think
you are right. Now that I begin to see that I will
actually grow old—and I ask God for a long old age—
I have set about probing the spiritual gains accorded
my nature, which is not so much severe as it is hard
and withdrawn. With the years, the Calvinist inquisitor which I have always borne within, harsh and ever
dissatisfied, has somewhat toned down.

There is a good deal of talk about you—and about
me—and almost always, I believe, it is pure blather,
always within the framework of wild praise or wild
blame. Either you are exalted or you are denigrated
without merit or justice—not a bad thing in itself. You
once inscribed a book to me "With sincere but restrained admiration"; and I commented: All admiration, if it be sincere, is restrained, and if it is not restrained, it is either insincere or unintelligent.

I would like to write about you and your work with
equanimity, most especially about your influence, which

has certainly been enormous on Hispanic-American and Spanish letters. I would need all my serenity and would attempt to say something both doctrinal and poetic. But with the coming of success—and I do consider myself a success—the instinct for battle has waned.

If I have not sent you my *Poesías* before, it is simply because I did not know your whereabouts. I am a man of fixed place and abode and you are a nomad. But now that I know where you are stopping, my poems go out after you [. . .] and I need say nothing of them.

I have just finished reading in *La Nación* your piece on the legend of Verlaine. I know scarcely anything of him beyond his verse. Your appraisal seems fair to me; the legends of artists are for the most part sheer fantasy.

I have your latest works, but neither *Prosas profanas* nor *Azul*.

Enough for today. It would be nice for me to hear from you more often. I think more highly of your poetic genius than you could know, even though it is the opposite of my own bent; but perhaps I think even more highly of your character, since your poetry most likely is a result of your character. In short, I'm not sure what I'm talking about here.

I offer you the loyal and unreserved handclasps of a cordial friend,

MIGUEL DE UNAMUNO

To Rubén Darío   Salamanca,
                                              10 November 1907

Sometimes, my dear Darío, I don't answer letters for months on end and sometimes I answer them by return

189*

mail. It all depends on my mood. Letters are my delight and my great outlet; that's why I hate any regularity where they are concerned.

Your news that you are going to your Nicaragua moves me deeply. You are going to the place where you first opened your eyes to the light and your lungs to the air, to the land of your childhood. I have always believed that a poet is one who preserves, not only eternal youth, but eternal childhood, in his soul. I mistrust men who do not keep memories of their youth floating on the very surface of their souls.

There is no consolation like that of revisiting the places which were the site of the first vision of life; there, virginal impressions are reborn. You cannot imagine how I am recreated among the mountains which ringed my cradle, when I visit them on lovely afternoons toward the end of September.

[. . .]

You, a poet, and as such a grown child, are returning to the land of your childhood. I expect that this voyage will give you a new source of inspiration. You once told me about an ox you saw in Nicaragua: you will find the same ox right there again, a sphinx representing eternity, in the same field, and as it salutes you its eyes will bid you welcome.

Be proud of Nicaragua, just as she, I am sure, will be proud of you. [. . .] I expect some sort of gift from your trip. Speak to us of your country and raise it up in your arms. It is lovely to watch a mother pick up her child in her arms for everyone to admire and bless it; but it is even more beautiful to watch a robust, sinewy son raise his mother high and carry her over the mud, to save her from being splashed and for everyone to bless her. [. . .]

You, now in your prime, and with more memories

than hopes, consecrated by the young, admired and loved, are returning to your homeland, like Ulysses to Ithaca after roaming the seas. From your return to your homeland we can all gain something.

Let Nicaragua be for you like a mother's knee where you can make silent confession, without violating any sense of restraint—because a mother can sense things—and let her give you new life. That is what your loyal, good friend wishes you.

Your heartfelt friend extends to you a frank loyal hand,

MIGUEL DE UNAMUNO

To Luis Ross   Salamanca,
16 December 1907

How happy I am, my good friend, that you are now in our Spain. And what pleasure I would feel to have you here! Yes, sometime in the next two weeks would be a good time for me, for I will be free, on vacation. I assure you that here, in this old city of Salamanca, you can spend two or three days very nicely, and not just one.

Until then, when I can clasp your hand, I am
          your friend MIGUEL DE UNAMUNO

To Pedro Jiménez Ilundain   Salamanca,
16 January 1908

My dear friend,

I did not expect to write you until I could send, a month from now, my *Memoirs of Childhood and Youth* whose final proofs I shall correct tomorrow. I don't think it is my best book, but I do imagine that it will have the greatest success. It is the clearest and most pleasant thing I have written, and has a certain wit and grace.

What I do continue selling, and very well, is my *Quixote*. A certain M. René Johannet is now translating it for me into French. I will give you his address in case you want to meet him. He has already sent me one chapter, the last one. He has also translated some of my poetry, but I don't know when he will publish it. This poetry is also being translated into German.

Aside from that I am only reading—more than ever—and writing articles for Latin America. *La Nación*, which last year published forty of my articles, has given me almost 5,000 pesetas. And now I have also *Caras y Caretas*, and shortly there will be a Chilean newspaper. Thanks to all this and to the fact that I got a raise last year, I got a little bit ahead for the first time. This year promises to be even better. I expect to earn between three and four thousand duros. Given the modest way I live, even though I have seven children, that's enough for me. What does not happen, unfortunately, is what you indicate. What happened to El Greco is happening to me, and that is that as I get older, I become angrier, more intransigent and personal. As I acquire more authority over the public I use it with greater and greater boldness. The publication of my *Poems* has been thus far the greatest scandal but I expect to produce a greater one with my *Treatise on the Love of God*.

I am generally contented with my career. If I have improved my lot economically, I have gained even more in authority and prestige. They already fear me here, and they hardly discuss me (which is not good).

And outside of Spain—and outside of Spain is what matters most to me now—I am gaining more ground with every passing day. In Latin America I am perhaps the Spaniard with the most authority. In Italy the number of my correspondents is growing, and also in other places. Now I am waiting only for the translations which are being made of my work.

And in the midst of all of this my deep love for Bilbao grows daily, and the faith I place in it, if it ever manages to shake off the spirit [of the Jesuits] and to overcome Basque stupidity. On this matter I have sent an article to be published soon in a newspaper in Bilbao, *El Coitao*. What is necessary there is to raise the spirit of the liberal element, which is slightly depressed. . . .

I have interrupted this letter to receive two Argentinian visitors, a sister and brother. We talked a great deal about Argentina. I continue to play with the hope of making a trip to Spanish America.

And I will end now so that this letter may get off today. You ask me why I don't ask you for books. I will do so soon. Right now I have a great deal to read, mainly in English. I shall probably go to Bilbao for Holy Week.

Embraces from your friend,

MIGUEL DE UNAMUNO

To Luis Ross   Salamanca,
                                  1 October 1908

My very dear friend,

When on my return to my home in Salamanca after the death of my saintly mother (May God grant her His Grace) I was just getting ready to write you, the

193

postcard from Matilde to Concha informed me of your
condition. What can I say to you? What I want is for
Matilde to try, in the midst of her worries, to keep us
informed about your condition and about the state of
your illness, as often as possible. I especially want to
know the results of the operation.

For now, get better and later we shall speak of many
things. Would you perhaps be able to come here after
the operation in order to recuperate in this calm and
tranquil Salamanca, which you already know and which
in the autumn is really delightful? You'll see. I don't
think there's any other place where you would be surrounded by friends so devoted as the ones you left here.

[. . .]

Your friend who embraces you,

MIGUEL DE UNAMUNO

To Matilde Brandau de Ross Salamanca,
23 October 1908

My unhappy friend,

At this moment I learn by telegram the terrible,
irreparable misfortune which afflicts you. I don't know
what to say, can't find the words. Although I have
been fearful for some days past, the news struck me
like a bolt from the blue. I don't know what to do.
Poor Luis! So young, so full of hopes, of talent and
good will, so strong, so affectionate and loyal and open!
God will have rewarded him for his virtues: this I
believe and pray. But—what about you? You, our good
friend? I ask that God give you whatever strength you
need.

And I don't know what more to say.

See if there's any way we can help you more than

*194**

with our condolences, our sharing in your sorrow, if there's anything we can do to help you in your sad situation. Depend on us as you would depend on your oldest and most intimate friend. For you to be here alone, widowed, afflicted, and so far from your country and your parents—in everything I am at your disposal.

Adiós. With my hand trembling in sorrow I reach out for yours to steady it.

Your friend, MIGUEL DE UNAMUNO

To Pedro de Mugica   Salamanca,
                                        13 April 1909
My dear friend,

"The time has come and he's written me!" you'll exclaim when you get this letter. But as the proverb has it—but I don't know what proverb to apply here. The last letter I have from you is more than two years ago. In two years I have forgotten many things, but as a matter of fact I have forgotten nothing. The only sure thing is that I feel more and more the passing of time. We are getting old; that is, I am getting old.

I saw what you wrote in that Augustinian periodical about my *Memoirs of Childhood and Youth*. Thanks, many thanks, but I don't think it matters very much to the public whether or not this book coincides with the articles I published ages ago in *El Nervión*. For God's sake, and for God's sake again, my friend, less bibliography!

I've plunged again into theological muddles. I'm reading the *Dogmatics* of Julius Kaftan, a professor there in Berlin, and it interests me greatly. I keep getting more and more interested in these matters, and less and less interested in philology. Of course I can't

195*

quite quench this continuous torment, this perpetual preoccupation with what must become of us after death.

Some two months ago in Las Palmas de Canarias my drama *The Sphinx* was produced for the first time. Now the Oliver-Cobeña company will tour other parts of Spain with it. It's a play written more than twelve years ago. They say it had a good success, something I can't quite get used to believing. It is three deadly acts of tedium; I wrote it during a month of dejection.

I keep working on my "Treatise on the Love of God," into which I've been pouring all my inquietudes and sorrows for the last three years now.

I don't know whether you've heard that my poor mother died this past summer, on the first of August. She would have remained a paralytic. She died almost without notice. I was in Portugal for about a month, in Espinho, where I went with my wife and my smaller children. When I arrived in Bilbao, she had already been buried. Now I have my older sister with me— the other one is in a convent—but we have not cleared out the house in Bilbao except to maintain it, in order to be able to go there in the summers.

Every day I grow fonder of my nation. After a period of indifference, I have returned to loyalty toward it, and today it is the Spanish nation which satisfies me the most. It is the only one where I find a half-dozen people with whom I can talk about anything and everything.

Our little corner of the world has changed much, but I believe for the good. If you came back here you wouldn't know it in many respects.

I continue to think about taking a trip through Spanish America, where I have more and more readers and friends, but I don't know when it will be.

I'd also like to return to Italy, where I have made

some acquaintances and where my writings have echoed somewhat. And I keep wanting to see England.

But as far as Germany is concerned, the truth is that it interests me less and less. The barbarity of its erudition and its mercantilism begin to scare me. I am more of a Germanophobe than ever. And I am the more so when I see the baneful effects Germany has on the young Spanish men who go there. Fortunately, I believe that in the Latin countries a reaction is starting against scientific Germanism—in Italy, at least. The lack of comprehension of these people among whom you live frightens me; they strike me as deformed by intellectualism and by music.

And you, what are you doing?

You already know what a fond friend you have in

MIGUEL DE UNAMUNO

To Teixeira de Pascoaes   Salamanca,
                                                    4 March 1909

My dear friend,

It is high time I wrote you and acknowledged receipt of your *Senhora da Noite*. I was hoping to do so after having read your book with a certain calm, but, my friend, they push me around from one place to another, and I have an enormous pile of books to read. I was in Valencia for about a week; I took your book with me to read but I wasn't given a minute's rest. I want to do something about this last poem of yours, but I read it too quickly to do so.

I am preparing my book on Portugal on the basis of the article I sent to *La Nación* of Buenos Aires (the last articles I sent were from Lisbon, Alcobaça, and Guarda, where I was last November). In the chapter

197*

dedicated to your *As Sombras* and to my visit to the charming and unforgettable Amarante, I shall add my impressions of your last poem. I should like the book to come out this fall, and it will be called *Souls and Things of Portugal*.

You can't imagine the dizzying whirl of things in which I am involved and in which people involve me. They force me to parade my lay apostolate throughout all of Spain. And now I am busy in the production of a play.

I don't know how I stand up under all of this. Just imagine: two and a half hours of teaching per day, administrative duties in my capacity as rector of the university, my regular newspaper columns for America, and there is so much to read! And to see! And to live! And a private correspondence which grows larger every day, even as my time grows less and less! (By the way, I don't remember whether I answered the very moving letter I was so grateful to receive from your mother when my own mother died. If I didn't answer her, please apologize for me and tell her how warmly I thank her for her kindness.)

But it's better this way. Vertigo, vertigo, vertigo! Struggle! Work! Peace and quiet are terrible things. The din of combat drowns out the murmur of the deep eternal waters which say "All is vanity." Struggle and work give rise to mutual compassion, which is love; peace only gives rise to envy.

I also have with me the *Elogio de los sentidos* of Corrêa d'Oliveira, although I haven't read it yet. The fact is that for some time now Portuguese subjects are among those that interest me most, and I would like to arouse the same kind of interest here and in Spanish America.

And that is all for the moment, although I take my leave of you with regret.

*198**

To your father, your mother, and the rest of your family, my sincerest greetings.
An embrace from your friend,

MIGUEL DE UNAMUNO

To Casimiro González Trilla
Salamanca,
2 October 1909

My dear friend,

Today is the first day of classes, and I am writing this letter with a certain discouragement and dismay. Following an absence of two months in my native region, I returned here to find a stack of letters to answer and nearly a yard-high pile of pamphlets and books, half of them Argentinian. And all of them request a judgment, a letter, some advice and counsel. After two hours and a half in class, office work, literary articles for magazines and newspapers, prologues to other people's books, walks, and such, there is scarcely time left to read the books I seek out for myself, let alone those which seek me out. And those South Americans are implacable: one could spend a lifetime taking care of them, and each one wants personal attention. What horrendous vanity!

I turned forty-five three days ago. I've gone beyond the midway mark in the journey of my life. With the death of my mother a little over a year ago, the preceding generation vanished from our family. Now, I, my brothers and sisters and cousins are the vanguard, the older generation. And I remember now how I laughed at a poor seventy-year-old woman who used plaintively to lament that she was an orphan! Yes, the old are orphans: they have no paternal protection but God's. Our children do not protect us. It's now that I know solitude. And I ask myself: "What have you done, Miguel, in forty-five years?" Others think I've done a great deal, but I think I haven't even got started. [. . .]

Contemporary European civilization, as it is aped everywhere, repels me. I find scientism and progressivism equally repugnant. They're both attempts to hide deep spiritual despair, to evade the only essential problem: the immortality of the soul. Making money, activity for its own sake, and science are all opiates.

And I want to provoke and promote the tragic position, the authentically Spanish position, that of *La vida es sueño*, of life as a dream. I am going to write four articles on the subject for an English journal called *The Englishman*. I believe we are destined to die as a people with a character of its own, but we should die fighting, affirming the ideal for which we die, the ideal which makes us unadaptable to modern civilization. We should die protesting against modern civilization, cursing it and damning it.

Adiós.

An embrace from MIGUEL DE UNAMUNO

To Casimiro González Trilla   Salamanca,
                                   12 November 1909

Yes, my friend, it was indeed Spain, the legitimate Spain, which put Ferrer up against a firing-squad. And they did well to shoot him. Ferrer was a malicious imbecile, and not a restless spirit, no mere disturber of the peace. His schools were a living horror, pedagogically monstrous, detestable. His teaching was of a notorious vapidity and bad faith. The stupidity of his textbooks horrifies one. And his schools were closed down, not as atheistic, but as anarchistic.

If a school teaches heretical doctrine, let the Church

condemn it; if it preach against liberty, let liberty have it out with the school; if the school be atheist, let God close it down; but if it conspires against the existence of the State, the State should close it.

Ferrer's schools preached the lawfulness of pillage. And you are wrong, friend Trilla, with regard to Ferrer. He was not a disquieter. His schools were heavy-handed, anarchistically and atheistically ham-handed. To teach physics so as to demonstrate that there is no God is as stupid as to teach it so as to demonstrate that there is. This kind of thinking is gaining ground.

I don't wish for my country a species of Argentinian liberalism, and even less, of French liberalism, that horrendous and tyranical atheistic Jacobinism which persecutes every Christian feeling and which conspires to uproot from the soul of the people any faith in another life.

At the rate we are going, we must soon divide up, not into good and bad, nor into Liberals and Catholics, but into those who long for another life, whether or not we are sure of its existence, and those who, renouncing it out of hand, are satisfied with the present life: into transcendentalists and terrestrialites.

Once Ferrer had been condemned by the tribunal, not as instigator but as a participant in the burnings, there was no reason for him to be pardoned. What was at stake was the spiritual independence of Spain: the government could not succumb to the pressure of European "knavery"—anarchists, masons, Jews, scientists, and dolts—who wished to impose their will and who even *before the verdict* and even *before the sentence*, were already trying to pervert the ends of justice. They had declared Ferrer innocent a priori.

Now, if the Liberals had been in power, the true Liberals, they would have had Ferrer before a firing squad with as much and more reason than Maura had, so that they might not be confused with that horde of workers and scarecrows. No, it was no sacristan-mentality that was responsible, even though their kind takes advantage of such an act.

The entire vacuity of Europe, that is, of France, has raised its voice in protest over Ferrer. Even down in Argentina! And I like that. It strikes me as just right that the arch-folly of Creole *Enlightenment* should raise its voice in protest. And if the heart of liberalism continues to beat, it is not, as you suggest, "despite the vacuity," but because of that vacuity itself, of which that liberalism is the offspring. Argentina worships the name of Luther or of Voltaire, but that is only because those names don't mean anything to them.

Although I hate official, dogmatic, ecclesiastical Catholicism, I am quite in conformity with the essential Catholicism of the Spanish populace. [. . .]

And I will write to Argentina, yes, to *La Nación*, on this point and in the spirit of this letter. I will thus reinforce the truth and scandalize the simplistic rationalists who are legion there.

Our essential legacy, our life's well-spring, is our faith in another life. We should maintain it at all costs, with reason, without reason, or against reason.

No more for today. Everyone is well here.

An embrace from MIGUEL DE UNAMUNO

To Pedro de Mugica   Salamanca,
                                        7 June 1911
My dear friend,

I'm sure that when you see this letter you'll say, "But what's happened to the man?" We'll leave this aside for the time when I finally write you in another mode. Today my dear friend and companion Don Agustín del Cañizo is leaving to pay you a visit on my behalf. He's a professor of medical pathology here who is going to spend several months there on a fellowship. I gave him some lessons in German—written German—and now he wants to learn to speak it a bit while he carries out his research. Please take care of him as you would take care of me, even though I don't know if by my silence I have lost some of my right to ask favors of you. I don't think that's the case.

Your friend embraces you, MIGUEL DE
UNAMUNO

To José Ortega y Gasset   Salamanca,
                                   21 November 1912

Dear Ortega,

[. . .]

Let us agree to overlook our petty differences: you and I are above them. I will endeavor to limit my use of paradox (what?) and my insinuations, while you weigh the value of your words, such as, for instance, "impertinent," "humbug," and such. But, enough of that, for we are both agreed on the fundamentals and we respect and care for each other. Yes, yes, I realize that some actions of mine could wound you—because people I despise might use them against other people whom I esteem not only fundamentally but on the surface as well. Let us move on to other matters.

While our good friend de Onís, the neophyte, roundly affirms that there is no University in Spain, I am committed to the task of remaking the Spanish University. I do not care to be the one to render an account of the task of moral sanitation on which I am embarked. . . .

We sally forth upon weekly lectures, without the noise of publicity, appearing before workmen's circles and even going to the countryside. Last Sunday I managed to shake this sleeping city awake, and we are now beginning to make use of the general enthusiasm. We have already saved a building here from being made a barracks forever. It will become a student residence instead. The students seem to be waking up. And I have begun proceedings against a professor whom the students accuse, with good reason, of ineptitude. (He's a surgeon who murders the hospitalized poor.) But the worst of it is the situation in the countryside.

It's an outrage: a dozen absentee landlords (dukes, marquises, and counts, among them) are depopulating the land. The people do not move away, they are thrown out. And they are thrown out in order to make room for bulls, sheep, and hogs. The landowner is better served by two tenant farmers with 98 head of cattle than by four tenants with 96 head. More people could live here, and not altogether poorly, but they would add up to less rent. However, the technical side of the question, of which I believe I have some knowledge, is no matter for a letter. It's enough to say that the interests of society and the interests of the landowners are opposed. And now that we have set about preaching the holy crusade of agrarian associationism, you can't imagine the state the absentee landlorders are in.

[. . .]

Canalejas was assassinated by the supposed Liberal democratic party—"supposed," inasmuch as it does not exist. Just as a Liberal conscience does not exist. And that poor weak voluble man, will-less and inconstant, found himself alone, and was forced to swallow absentee landlordism. Having it in his power to be a Lloyd George, he became just one more politician.

And I don't think he found his great obstacle in the Royal Palace, no, but rather in that awful Liberal agglomeration, which is just as oligarchic and bourgeois as the conservative mob made up of the rich and their servants and lawyers. He was assassinated by republicans—shopkeepers, petit bourgeois, works-foremen, publicans—who run amok on Revolutionism without content, or on that stupid Ferrerian anarchism, or on more formal radicalism. Apparently there are people who would rather die of hunger, biting monks and the military, than eat, believing in another life. The case of Nakens, that monster anticleric and antisocialist, is typical. Just as deplorable is the case of our friend Simarro, and even that of Besteiro and Morente, according to what I hear. No, no, that is not the way. Even Catholicism must be used and made democratic and socialist.

Some sectors now cry out for Maura, for La Cierva, requiring them to lance boils without purifying the blood. No, it is not surgery which is wanted, but internal medicine, a diet, a regimen. Maura will come, if he does come, and he will begin to pull the levers of power (not bad in itself), and we will be back at the shyster-solution of all things through the law of local administration, with which he wanted to make the revolution from above!!! A monstrous concept, and only a simple-minded lawyer, a litigious attorney for the rich, could think up such an absurdity. Even now, in the face of everything, those pedantic Catalans are threatening to block the administration if their Associationism ("Mancomunidades") is not brought forward, another bit of shysterism with a basis in infantile vanity. Meanwhile people are being dislodged, entire towns reduced to one inhabitant, and pasture-lands go without renting; there is a return to cattle-raising, and

*205**

everything possible is done to prevent the intensifi-
cation of farming from adding to the national territory,
and—competition sends the income from rents down.
But I will avoid discussing technical matters. The whole
thing is a maneuver. If we legislated in the manner of
Lloyd George, or something like it, the endemic wrong
would be reduced. But then, since some duke with
seven automobiles would have to be satisfied with three
. . . I'll talk about this later. It is all painful, painful,
painful. When I spoke at La Fuente de San Esteban
(Elorrieta will tell you about it), with the emotion
which overcomes me now when addressing the people,
falling into a certain exalted tone, people cried.

I am apprehensive for my poor heart, thinking of it
only materially. Sunday before last I cut short an invitation because I feared a collapse: my heart was gal-
loping and I was frightened. And this Sunday, at another meeting, speaking after Elorrieta, I commented
on the assassination of Canalejas in the manner of this
letter, and I again fell victim to an attack of prophetism,
which left me with fever and troubled my sleep. The
truth is that sometimes I suffer pathologic exaltation—
and I remember poor Costa. I need a few days in the
country.

I am busy reading, at the same time, Herrmann's
Ethics, Cohen's *Logic of Pure Knowledge*, and Croce's
Logic. As I have told you, Cohen does not get through
to me: he is a Sadducee who leaves me cold. I understand his position well enough, but that rationalism,
or idealism, strikes me as totally repugnant. It is not
enough that it be true—if it is. I cannot, no, cannot
stand the *purity* of it all: pure concept, pure cognition,
pure will, pure reason, all that purity leaves me breath-
less: it's like putting my head in the vacuum of a bell
jar. There are some places so high that the air is so

thin that it almost asphyxiates you, giving you the urgent need to descend to an earth that can be touched, to air that can be breathed, to a place of illusions and passions and deceits and comforting superstitions (yes, superstitions) and the old lullabies of childhood. After reading some of these Germans I cross myself, say an Our Father and a Hail Mary, and dream of an impure glory and a *material* immortality *in saecula saeculorum* where I find my mother, my children, my wife, and the certainty that the human soul, this poor soul of mine and of my people, is the meaning of the universe. And reason doesn't help. No, no, no! I will not resign myself to reason.

I have had a painful report about Morente, whom I met and dealt with in Málaga. You should tell him to stop jamming his hat down on his head whenever he sees the flag of his country, and cease from flying into rages against Catholicism: the main enemy is elsewhere. Let him not fall, for God's sake, into Ferrerian fanaticism. Forget the scarecrow: the people flee, they are thrown out, they die of hunger. And more: the great anarchist-millionaires ruin everything. And the conservative pettifoggers will move against us with ridiculous repressive measures based on their wealth, not on their religion. The union of all that is sound must go forward in another camp, and in this camp there are many Catholics who can help us. There is a form of radicalism which obstructs the work of socialist justice and even of culture. And there is no reason to lose hope in Spain, and no reason to slander her. Oblivious of her history, some have invented glories for her, and now, without knowing her much better, we deny them all. All because some European gentlemen do not know us. In this sense, de Onís' harangue was unpardonable. We must avoid all categorical judgments. . . . The first thing to do is to get acquainted with the facts. And there are all those others with whom we have scarcely gotten acquainted, among them Vitoria, Soto, Melchor Cano. We scarcely even know the mystics: but perhaps we reject mysticism a priori because it is not . . . pure. Neither is reality, which is impure, sweetly and consolingly impure.

Enough for today.

An embrace from MIGUEL DE UNAMUNO

To Pedro de Mugica   Salamanca,
                                        21 January 1914

I would never have believed of you, my dear friend, even though I claim to know you, that you would have lent your ears to the idle gossip of troublemakers. The person who came to you with that story must be one of these scholars—or better, a philologist, since these people are generally fond of this sort of gossip. It's not true that I spoke ill of you, and even less true that I treat you like an old shoe. What I generally say about you, which might seem bad to some simpleton, is exactly the same as I've said to you a hundred times over in my letters. I've never hidden our differences nor my judgment in things that concern you. No one can ever say that I've ever said anything about you which I haven't said to you directly. It's true that I haven't yet answered your two last letters, but that's because my private correspondence grows more than the time I have and I see myself obliged to cut back on it. Furthermore, you are awesome in your epistolomania. You answer my letters almost by return mail and at great length, and I have more things to do—and increasingly so—than to write to friends. On the other hand, don't think that I'm flattered by someone who collects my letters and has them bound as if they were to be handed down to posterity. And I'm even less pleased that these letters are then quoted in public writings so that opinions which I perhaps want to keep private are aired in the open. I won't ever forget that kind of criticism (??) which you wrote about my *Memoirs of Childhood*, in which you asked if these memoirs didn't correspond more or less with some articles I published many years earlier in *El Nervión* in Bilbao. Do you believe that these bibliographical disquisitions are criticism or anything like it? For God's sake, friend Mugica, don't turn into a Dr. Hölle—that boring dolt to whom I sent my *Life of Don Quixote* and who came after me with a certified list of the mistakes—and he missed some— in my book, which he hadn't understood. That atmosphere of *learned* (!!!) Germany, with its pedants, its technicians, and its professionals, is horrible.

I've told you a hundred times over that by living far from your own country, in that German atmosphere, and communicating only with the erudite, philologists, academicians, and *ratés*, you have a very twisted view of all this. You claim to be better informed than we, but if so it's about some men and some things—I mean books—which don't matter here and which no one takes notice of. Your set of values is completely different from the one here. [. . .]

I repeat, what I say about you when your name comes up is exactly what I have said to you a hundred times. And I always speak of you with affection. Now, if you claim something else—*Intelligenti pauca*. And I generally don't have much occasion to speak of you, because the circles of people in which I go—and go little, since I don't often leave here (I've now spent twelve days in Madrid)—circles of young writers (younger than I), poets, novelists, and so on, I don't know if they know you. And I flee from scholars, from bibliographers, from old literati, etc., etc., etc. My world, the world I live in, is different from the world in which you seem to live. I won't say if it is better or worse, but it is other. [. . .]

[. . .]

In any case—and take it as you take what I say to you—I always will regard myself as a good friend of yours, and I calmly expect to appear as such, after my death, when they publish my correspondence.

So it is with MIGUEL DE UNAMUNO

To José Ortega y Gasset   Salamanca,
                                              3 September 1914
Ortega,

Yes, my dear friend, I need you, I need your pen, I need what you call your bad temper. And thank you. I haven't been dismissed, I've been thrown out like a rabid dog, without any prior warning or admonition, without any complaint as to my conduct. I have been given no notification nor explanation. The cause of my dismissal? In all truth I do not know. But I'll tell you a story (it's my method): A friend of mine, a Galician, very shabby in his attire, sloppy and not altogether clean (but a most intelligent man and a very good person), was introduced to another Galician, a handsome model of a man dressed in the latest fashion. When I asked my shabby friend what he thought of the well-dressed one, he told me: we were introduced, we looked at each other's clothes, and we despised each other mutually. I think the same happened as a result of my two interviews—altogether cordial on other

levels—with Bergamín, when he offered me, without
my having asked him for it, a place in the Senate *to
collaborate with him on his plans.* [. . .]

And yes, why not tell you?: there is disdain in all
this, "odium for *Kultur.*" It is indeed a blow against
the intellectuals.

I have been accused, I think, of being undisciplined,
when in fact I have succeeded in introducing some
discipline here, even if only in appearances. To say
that I do not attend to administrative duties because
I am lost in "sublimities" (?) is to lie. I am able to say
forthrightly that as a bureaucratic functionary I am as
good as anyone. I know, of course, that my exacting
standards for the faculty were resented, as was my
requesting an inspection, which implied that some professor might have been inept. [. . .]

And I repeat, friend Ortega, yes, I need you. My
cause, which is a common cause, needs you.

I arrived here on the 29th, after having spent forty
days in Figueira da Foz, Portugal, with my family.
Among the books I found on my return was your
Meditations on Quixote. Until this battle is concluded
I will not have the peace of mind to read it as I would
like.

Adiós,

an embrace from MIGUEL DE UNAMUNO

To Giovanni Papini   Salamanca,
                                        15 July 1915

Thank you, dear Papini, for your article "What Is
Spain Doing?" Thank you in the name of my country
which, because of the European war, is torn these days
by a strong, deep, civil struggle. The battle of our two

Spains seemed to be dormant or going through a truce; now, thank God, it is on fire again. Long ago, I warned against *Kultur*, I made mock of the capital "K" with its four points, like a frieze horse, and I defended our own culture. A sort of Germanization, imported by our students enjoying grants to study in German universities, was beginning to infect Spain. Everything was reduced to method, technique, specialization, and, finally, pedantry. I abhor a nation of soldiers, but I abhor even more a nation of professors. And if such professors belong to the military, oh horror of horrors! The question is whether we Latins, masters in the art of war, can best those professors of military science. And the fact is that most of our young intellectuals, trained technically in Germany, and, therefore, of the best, are on the side of the Allies. Not only in the reviews that you point out, but also in other reviews, like the *Nuevo Mundo* of Madrid, *Hispania* of London, and *La Nación* of Buenos Aires, I am upholding the cause of the Allies. And also in Italy, of course.

When your noble nation, fed up with being the victim of the Triple Alliance, heeded the call of honor and glory, our traditional cave dwellers repeated all the Austro-German insults against Italy. Because our Germanophiles do nothing but repeat. They are an army of pens directed, like the Turkish army of weapons, by German officialdom. And then came the kiss of Judas and the betrayal. They refused to inform themselves of what Salandra said about your arguments. Our cave dwellers do not wish to be informed. They have accepted as divine revelation the axiom of the invincibility of the German army and that is enough for them. They do not ask themselves who is right but rather who is stronger. Or who they think is stronger. And when that very noble Italy went to war, there

were those here—here in the land of Don Quixote!—
who said it was worse than a crime; it was a folly. The
fact is that, on the one hand, our cave dwellers, enlightened by God-given, prophetic knowledge, know
what you poor Italians do not know—Vázquez de Mella
is privy to the secrets of German High Command,
which to him is divine Providence—and, on the other
hand, the repulsive meanness of their materialistic spirit
prevents them from understanding that nobody goes
to war unless he is sure of victory. And for me, the
greatest thing about France is how she went to war
during those terrible, agonizing days of August last
year. Would Germany have gone to war if, in her blind
pedantic pride, she were not certain of victory? And
for me, that is the greatest sin of that predatory nation.
She was mistaken in her expectations—that is what
happens with the *Gott mit uns*, instead of *Wir mit
Gott*—but, if they had not had confidence (as they did,
pendantically and proudly) in victory, they would have
borne the greatest humiliations. They went out to conquer their honor and not to save it, contrary to the
spirit of our Don Quixote, the conquered hero, who
conquered by being conquered.

Everything you say in your article about Spain is
very true. My poor nation is tired, disillusioned, without faith in itself. The Cuban war, that other war into
which the United States led us with its "Remember
the Maine!"—now, on the other hand, they only exchange notes with Germany, not Spain, over the *Lusitania*—and the war with Morocco, have us dispirited.
And the Germans, counting on our Catholic cave
dwellers and a few worshipers of science—those who
still read Jules Verne in their adulthood—are taking
advantage of our depression and are trying to exac-
erbate old prejudices.

Yes, people here who think and are worth something know Italy and do her justice. And we know more: we know that in Italy they know and appreciate us better than they do in Germany, and they like us better. I have repeated again and again that perhaps the best Hispanists exist in Italy. And in France, of course. I cannot abide the German *Herr Professor*, the specialist in Calderón or Gracián, or in the period from 1561 to 1658, who comes to us with the claim of teaching us how we are supposed to learn about ourselves. I cannot abide those so-called organizers of Europe who reserve for us the role of providing for them the findings of our archives and providing them with file cards so that they can write monographs that prove that Cervantes, Calderón, Velázquez, Goya, etc., descend from the Goths. To the devil with those who propose to catalogue the universe so that they then can, carried away by their *Schadenfreude*, destroy it. And such pedantic destruction! If Werther had not committed suicide, he would have been among those who destroyed the cathedral of Reims. And not out of barbarism, but out of the pedantry of barbarism. In love with Charlotte, he imagined himself the most wretched of men; in war he would have become the most inhuman of men. We must be on our guard against the hypocritical sentimentality of those who shed tears of beer while they listen to Schumann.

It would be horrible if the *Weltanschauung* of that gross nation—gross even in its despair—were to triumph in Europe. We have only to compare the ridiculous pessimism of Schopenhauer—a methodical, professional pessimism—with the noble despair of Leopardi. The latter got to the very bottom, to the tedium, the infinite vanity of all, while the Prussian pedant stopped

214*

with the conviction that the sum of all pain exceeds the sum of pleasures. Fool! He saw only pain and pleasure and believed that it was enough to count them up, as if they were soldiers, or weigh them like cannonballs. Not even the nobility of despair! And the same applies to criticism. They will doubt or, better yet, they will pretend to doubt, professionally and methodically, they will doubt the reality of the outer world, but not the press releases of the General Staff. You have already seen those ninety-three *Gelehrte*—scholars!—dogmatically affirming—in the land of Lutheran free examination—that things they did not know were not true. Oh, research!

But now, thank God, whatever happens, that barbarous German scholasticism will not again infect the clear, noble Latin countries. I think we have saved the soul, our soul; I think we have redeemed it from *Kultur*! Humanity will not be an anthill. Because in this war we are fighting for the rights of the free Christian individual human personality; we must save man from the tyranny of the State. The born hero, *ein geborener Held*, which is, according to Treitschke, the German, will understand that you cannot dominate the world with cannons, submarines, zeppelins, microscopes, telescopes, pharmaceuticals, engineering, and all sorts of sciences and technologies and disciplines that have a cave-like, caveman-like soul and lack a sense of one's own free personality. They will see the meaning of what they call Latin anarchy. And one of those who will teach them will be that eternal Italy, that Italy of many lives, that Italy of incessant Renaissance, that cradle of free personality and of civilian life. Dante, the creator of souls, will show them!

I could say much more, for I am overflowing with

215*

thoughts inflamed by the war. But my task here at home is to awaken, encourage, and console my nation.

And so, onward, and long live Italy! And let us lock those people up in their caves.

Your very good friend, MIGUEL DE UNAMUNO

To Pedro Jiménez Ilundain   Salamanca,
                                            26 August 1915
My dear friend,

We are all of us, more or less, splashed by the dirtiness of the war. But what has stirred up the very lees of my soul is the prospect of how all this will shock human thought, shake it up.

One can and should be Anglophile or Germanophile or Francophile or a -phobe of any one of them when it is a matter of an ideal of life, thought, feeling, and action. For my part I do not conceal the fact that I pray for the defeat of technology, and even of science, of any and every ideal which has to do with getting rich, with earthly prosperity, and with territorial or mercantile aggrandizement.

If the war brings down worldly European pride and returns us to some kind of new romantic age, good luck to it! Monotony would have finally done us in, killed us off, in a Europe run by engineers, druggists, professors, scholars, travelling salesmen, soldiers, pedants, monistic philosophers, "singers of life," apaches, and such truck. And so, what if, as some fear, superstitions thought dead were to be revived?

Better superstition than that awful technological, specialist, and science-ridden Europe of the end of the 19th century.

                                I embrace you, UNAMUNO

216*

To Matilde Brandau de Ross   Salamanca,
                                  7 January 1916

My good friend,

You really don't know how pleased we were after so long a time to get a letter from you. In this house you aren't forgotten, no more than I can forget the man who was your husband and my very dear friend. Yes, I continue working in this Salamanca which, it seems to me, I shall never wish to leave. They threw me out of the rectorate and in a very gross manner, much as you kick out a nuisance of a dog, with no hint or complaint or advance warning, and I still haven't been told why—it was a political intrigue. But I still have my two teaching assignments as before, and I have even been promoted. The rectorate is only administration. Even though the post is rather lucrative here, I consider myself lucky to be out of it because the year that just ended was my most prosperous. My affairs go well. I have all the work I need. My children are growing and making progress. In two years my eldest son will be an architect, and my second son Pablo will be a doctor in another two years. The third son will have his bachelor's degree next year, and the latter two are doing well. The three girls are well. The eldest, Salomé, has worried us because of her curvature of the spine. It seems that the defect has been corrected as much as is possible. She will remain somewhat stooped, but she's in good health and cheer. It's a shame that she is not developing as she might have done without this misfortune, for she is very beautiful. My second daughter is developing a love I never had—music. The third one is growing beautifully. My dismissal permitted me to know how many good friends I have here in Salamanca, in all Spain, and especially in my native Bilbao. There was quite a to-do over it, and the min-

*217**

ister, attacked in the Senate and in Congress by those who pushed him to the wall, couldn't explain the matter. Finally, at the end of the debate, Azcárate declared that the reason it had been done was not clear. Then, in private, the minister said that he regretted what he had done. I still hope to find out what lay behind the intrigue. This summer, while in my wife's native town, Guernica, which is a small place, the King arrived. I encountered him, and when he said hello he told me to come see him, since he wanted us to talk. I have requested an audience and am awaiting my turn. And I shall go to find out the secret motivation behind their treatment of me. Of course, the affair has increased my authority and my freedom. During this year and a half, since they dismissed me, my performance as a publicist and my effectiveness in the city have increased. True, it coincided with the war, which has limited me more than anyone else here. Since it began I have resolutely taken the side of the Allies against German *Kultur*, which strikes me as the absorption of the individual into the State, the death of the free human personality, and the restoration of paganism. Besides, I am disgusted by technicism, specialization, scientism, etc., etc. Here in this country, I really don't know why, the reactionaries, the inquisitors, and the ultramontanes are the Germanophiles.

I am hoping to take a trip to Argentina and I really think it will happen. A Spanish institute named after Menéndez Pelayo, which invites lecturers, asked, as their rules require, the Council for the Development of Studies in Madrid who should come this year, and I was named. I still don't know the terms under which I would go, nor when, but I really want to see that Chile which I always so much wanted to know, even before I met Luis. After meeting him, my late good friend, my desire grew much stronger. How well I would remember him in his own land, if I get there. But these travel plans are still subject to many contingencies and depend in great part on the regularization of my relations with those in power here, with the politicians—who are abnormal. Better yet, I would say that such relations don't exist. As long as I am not given an explanation—that's all I ask—I shall accept no favor nor the slightest concession.

I also imagine that once the war is over I will be invited to France or Italy, where I have recently made many new friends by my campaigns. But for now what I most want is to know your part of America.

My literary activity, aside from reports and newspaper articles, is limited to finishing a poem, "The Christ of Velázquez," which I started two years ago. It is a mystical work, in verse. I have published an ill-tempered novel, *Mist*, which I haven't dared send you, for I hardly think it appropriate to your way of life and your frame of mind. It's rather corrosive and bitter, for I vented my bad temper and unpleasant view of life in it. The first part of my *Tragic Sense of Life* has already been translated into Italian, and three days ago a German (!!!) wrote me that he completed translating it into his native language and asked permission to publish it when the war is over. And in a short while I'm going to begin publishing collections of my essays which appeared in magazines. In short, I keep working. It is my consolation. I say "consolation" because although it might seem unlikely, the fact is that even though my life has gone well, without great misfortunes, with my wife and my eight children healthy, good, and happy, without money worries, with my own good health and the respect and affection of my countrymen, I nevertheless cannot free myself from that tragic sense of life, that constant preoccupation with our final destiny. You tell me of your eternal grief and that your life is a failure. I believe that every life is a failure and that whatever sense there may be to life can be seen only after death. I, the eternally unhappy man, understand all the depth of your misfortune. Concha, who is very well, cheerful, and delighted with her children, tells me that she's going to write you. She's in very good health. You can't tell that she is fifty-one, like me. She looks ten or twelve years younger than me. My sister María, who is very close to her, lives with us, and she also asks me to tell you hello. On your part, please be sure to greet your brother Valentín, whose brief trip here I remember well. Is he publishing anything? He is perhaps too wrapped up in his teaching in that tiny corner of Iquique, but that would be a pity.

Let us hear from you. And I promise that I will answer right away.

May this new year bring you health, faith, work, and hope. And may your grief pass away. That is what your faithful friend wishes you.

MIGUEL DE UNAMUNO

To Elvira Rezzo   Salamanca,
                                              28 June 1919

Your letter, señorita, touched me to the quick because it comes from a young girl—a girl who could be my daughter—a young girl who is both Italian and Argentine, and, finally, because the letter comes from Italy. I have always been surprised in the past to receive more letters from women than from men, when one would think that my message is quite harsh, my teachings not overly consoling. But my experience has shown me that a woman, all the more if she be young, has more courage than a man has to gaze little by little into the eyes of the Sphinx, who was—at least Sophocles thought so—also female. Man is appalled before the unfathomable mystery and, if he should chance to have more physical daring—which is not always the case—he has less moral daring. It was the faith of a woman which created Christianity when the Apostles abandoned Christ. And it may be that the feminine *I* is more universal than the masculine *I*, because woman tends to see above history—or beneath it.

I have also been impressed that in Argentina, a country we think of as superficial, given over to ephemeral life, to diversion, to making money, to pleasure, or, what is worse, to pretended pleasure, that in this same Argentina, my sermons—those of a lay monk, a secular and agnostic hermit, perhaps a desperate one, harshly preaching in age-old faraway Spain—have found a sympathetic echo. And then, your letter comes to me from Italy, where I went when I was twenty-five years old and where I returned only a year and a half ago, in September of 1917, in the throes of war's tragedy, a country to whose masters my spirit owes so much. It was in Italy that the first translation of any of my work was made: my *Life of Don Quixote and Sancho* circulates under the title of *Commento al Don Chisciotte*, as well as the first part of my capital work, *The Tragic Sense of Life*, into which I put my innermost self, the most sensitive and sorrowing side.

You write that you arrived in the Italy of your forefathers five years ago, when you were seventeen, that is, still a girl. These past five years have been, for Italy as for the world, a time of tragedy and trembling in the heart of nations. If you return to Argentina, you will be taking back the fruit of those tragic years. I trust this spiritual earthquake will have shaken the religious foundations of Humanity and that the generation raised under the sign of this apocalypse of war and of the ensuing Revolution will once again feel the anguish implicit in the Unique Problem: the final destiny of the soul of each one of us and the eternal meaning of history.

A new religious faith will arise from all this. What form it will take I don't know. But I am sure that life for life's sake will become a thing of the past, and that, just as the great Mazzini understood, life will be seen as a mission. What kind of mission? The conquest of God! Gather then from the sacred land of Dante, of Bruno, of Savonarola, of Leopardi, of Rosmini, of Mazzini, of all the great religious apostles—even when they were apostles of despair, like Leopardi—gather strength to take back to Argentina more light and strength so as not to be smothered by the materialist ideal of a self-indulgent country, one still too young. Youth is a greater danger for a country than it is for an individual man or woman. Whatever the case, when you return from luminous Italy to that juvenile, self-confident, somewhat smug Argentina, do not forget, either, that in this ancient, hermetical Spain which has bequeathed you your language, in this Spain prone now to the delirium of dissolution, there is a man, no longer young, who is driven by the sorrow of his country and the universe to the task of awakening God in the consciousness of his brothers and sisters of a common human destiny. For we do not sleep in God; rather God sleeps in us: we do not need to awake in Him, but must awaken Him in ourselves. And if you rouse others to this consciousness, you will yourself be able to sleep in peace when you lie down for the last time,

Letters

forever, and you will know that you have dreamt the
true life and will live in that dream.

Greetings to the lively Argentine Italian girl from
this ancient Spanish fighter

MIGUEL DE UNAMUNO

To Pedro Jiménez Ilundain   Salamanca,
                                      6 June 1920

Ah, what would I like better, my dear friend, than
to accept your invitation! It would suit me perfectly!
A few days of rest, and of rest only. And how good it
would be to make personal relations out of what today
is a mere epistolary relationship! What new paths would
open before me! And what I would learn! And it's not
that Paris doesn't attract me as it does others, no! I
would go there to firm up quite a few prejudices. And
even more than learning from those people, I would
want them to know me better, for them to say: "Here
we have the Spaniard!" It would even serve my projects for publishing. My going there would speed the
stated intention of *La Nouvelle Revue Française* to continue translating my works, as they began, with my
Tragic Sense.

But I can't leave here. For the past year and a half
I have been subjected to three legal prosecutions. The
three have as venue Valencia, and all three are over
alleged offenses to H.M. in writing. And I am under
provisional liberty, obliged to appear in Court on the
1st and 15th while a seventh part of my pay is withheld. Pardon has been granted; but, in order to obtain
it, I must submit to trial, and I do not want to do so.
I will not go through the farce wherein the prosecuting
attorney refuses to withdraw the accusations, or where
he withdraws two of them and then perhaps has me

*223**

found guilty on the third one, so they can then grant me a pardon.

It's a long story. I am outraged that they chose to attack me most viciously in Madrid and then enmeshed me in Valencia because of [. . .] the lady mother of H.M., the Hapsburg woman, the pernicious Austrian! Romanones wanted to fix up the matter, and even yet members of the government lend themselves to an arrangement, but now it's a lawsuit—with a Basque!— of a most personal nature, between the King—and his mother—and myself. Never before, as now, was pardon granted on the condition that one first be found guilty. Always before this the judgment on pending trials was stayed. But they know I would protest and would publicly state that that petty scoundrel Alfonso has nothing to pardon me for, while I do have something to pardon him for.

And thus, I am confined to Salamanca. Of course if I were to go to Paris, and stayed as long as I liked, they would not say a word, and would even be delighted, since my presence is no longer required at court. But I can't be out of Salamanca on any 1st or 15th of the month. My strength lies in that, and in refusing to ask for clemency, which is what they would like me to do. For similar reasons I have been unable to go to Argentina or New York: I require a restoration of justice and I will get it. When? I don't know. Within a month, a year, or in ten or twenty or fifty years. I'll live for them as long as is necessary. I have made up my mind that in my case they won't be able to bury the injustice. And let others do the same. On this head, Marcelino Domingo and those involved in the August 1917 strike have shown themselves weak. I am a Dreyfusard. It is more important—more important than what they call a collective suit—to refuse to tolerate the least outrage against the least citizen. You know the radical nature of my individuality. And, since we are all individuals, individuality is most universal. I abhor all mass dictatorship. Therefore, I cannot, I cannot go! You will not know with what sorrow I say so. I remain here imprisoned in my trampled dignity.

I did receive the newspapers and reviews you sent me. It's good to look at everything: but that Syndicalist, Bolshevik, Nationalist literature—what poor stuff it is! The war has been followed by a cataclysm of vulgarity, more of it in France than elsewhere. One can now see what terrible mental limitation exists there regarding positive conservative heroism. Those who fought most heroically for what is theirs—their France— speak nothing but foolishness. For example, have you read anything more vapid, more hollow than Barbusse in his *Clarté* manifesto? They are all of them spiritual bourgeois. They all of them believe in the *joie de vivre*.

I've just now finished reading Ludovic Nadeau's book, which you sent me, *In Prison under the Russian Terror*. Thank you! I read it almost through, in a couple of sittings. It's very interesting, very suggestive, and, for me, very useful. I'll explore it further. Thank you! I even learned a dozen French words I didn't know before. And I've read so much in French.

In any case, Lenin remains: like Marat and Nero and Diocletian and Cromwell and Luther and and and—

Your old friend, who will always love you,

MIGUEL DE UNAMUNO

To an Unknown Professor   December 1923

I write you taking advantage of the state of muteness to which these barbarians of the Suspensory have condemned me. The entourage of the Royal Gander, who have gone off with H.M. to Italy, now systematically blue-pencil whatever is written by certain names. Then, bearing another signature or without any at all, the piece goes through with no trouble. Next, those wretched slaves who scribble on that toilet paper called *El Sol* announce that there is freedom to make liberal propaganda and that the Left merely holds its breath. Wretches! They mock those who do not speak because they are wearing a gag.

I thought the Royal Gander who signed that outrageous manifesto of September twelfth, a pattern of ignominy for all Spain, was no more than a simple blusterer, a cricket-brain, a tragicomic movie-actor, but I have come to realize that he is a sack of vile abject passions; either that or a puppet for the dour, dark Martínez Anido, the director of this tyrannical farce. I have a long letter from Santiago Alba in which he tells me—and furnishes documents as proof—what that low gang has done to him. One is ashamed to be a Spaniard when civil men, who believe they are honorable, collaborate with this rabble infected with the rancor of pimps.

That invitation to inform secretly on others has stirred up the poisonous well of what Menéndez Pelayo called Spain's "friars' democracy," inciting the demagogic Inquisitorial sensibility, and it has brought into the open Spain's terrible cancer, which is not *caciquismo*, not political paternalism, but envy. Envy, envy: a hatred of intelligence.

Things were bad, bad, but this is worse. The Carlist leprosy of those who were defeated in 1820 and 1840 and in 1876 is breaking out again: priests and priest-lings, quartermaster-sacristans, and second-rate *ratés* (like Maeztu), line up on the side of this pigsty of a Suspensory. And they blaspheme by yelling "Justice!" They don't give a damn about justice. There is no justice in insulting people or preventing them from defending themselves in public, nor is it justice to allow what Silvela describes: part of the money from gambling going to the civil government of Barcelona and no investigation at all made as to what becomes of the funds in the hands of that unspeakable Martínez Anido, and of that hyena of the press, Arlegui, who serves him. And that disgusting rag of a newspaper printed on toilet paper applauds that riffraff.

I am smothering, drowning, choking in this cesspool. And Spain pains me through and through. And we must even endure their talk of mysticism! And of a new concept of freedom!

They are dishonoring us.

And then, the lies, lies, lies. They lie, not merely err, when they claim that public opinion almost entirely supports them, and they lie each time they take up a problem.

I've been told that Marañón was going to organize— I don't know whether with the permission of the Suspensory or of *El Sol* or not—a party of the left, monarchical I suppose. I've written him asking him to desist, for the task of liberals now is to endure, gag in mouth, storing up saliva now in order later to spit out the truth on that filthy pack. In Spain, liberalism and monarchy are no longer compatible.

Who could have told me that on approaching my sixtieth birthday I would feel weighed down by the malignant tradition, that traditional cancer which made bombs explode over my head when I was ten years old. Poor Spain! Poor Spain! Poor Spain! It makes one want to die.

Enough! I'm crying real tears!

MIGUEL DE UNAMUNO

To Elvira Rezzo   Salamanca,
                                 2 February 1924

You have no idea, my dear friend, how pleased I am to be back in touch with you, of whom I cherish such a fond memory. And if I did not write upon receipt of your article on my work (thank you for it!), I did you an injustice. But forgive me and also the hustle and bustle of my life, as well as the intensity of the political campaign I am conducting, practically single-handed. It is accompanied by a good deal of applause—that, yes!—but little enough help. . . . But we'll drop that matter, as it's a sad subject.

I received the *Rivista di Roma*—I was acquainted with the magazine before and do have many of the previous issues—with my story "L'assalto dellamore," which was perfectly translated by your brother, to whom I am indebted for the lines he wrote by way of introduction. I must tell you that lately I've risen a good bit, quite a bit really, in the estimation of my compatriots and *even* of my literary colleagues. The legend of my unsociability has been shattered. At the beginning of the year, after five years of absence, I went to my native Basque country, where I was granted a triumphant reception. Never have I been so overwhelmed with attention! And at my age—next September I'll be 60—this attention takes up half my life.

228*

The other half is taken up by my struggles and my household.

I would, indeed, like to return to that Italy which I visited in 1889, at age 25, and again in 1917, when I was 53, and where I was so well treated. I talked about it with Filippo Sacchi, the editor of *Il corriere della sera*, who has spread the word. If I cannot achieve this wish soon, it will be because of the present state of my country, this Spain. As long as the dictatorship lasts, I'm not thinking of leaving.

I don't know Don Juan Chabas y Martí, who I suspect might be from Valencia. As for Professor Antonio Restori, I do know something of him. Not long ago in my class I was commenting on his interpretation of a passage from the *Poema del Cid*. For I lecture not only on the Greek language but also on Castilian. So, you see, as far as I am concerned, I would like to make contact with Señor Restori.

I'm sending you three of my recent books: *Spanish Walks and Vistas*, *La tía Tula*, and the second edition of my *Peace in War*. I shall also send you *Mist*, if you don't already know it—there has been discussion of it because of Pirandello, and it has been translated into Italian, but with such cuts and abridgments it has become unrecognizable. These abridged editions strike me as a bad thing. I imagine *La tía Tula* will prove interesting to you. *Peace in War* has been declared a standard academic book for Spanish examinations in France. *Spanish Walks and Vistas* contains some of my most heartfelt writing. This year a collection of my verse, *Teresa*, will be published and I shall send it on to you.

Do consider me a friend of Italy and a friend of yours.

MIGUEL DE UNAMUNO

229*

Letters

To Carlos Vaz Ferreira

Puerto Cabras de
Fuerteventura
(Canary Islands),
My good friend,   11 May 1924

As ignominy continues to fall upon my poor Spain with the silence of a snowfall, I am in receipt today, from that Montevideo of yours, of the issue of *El Día* which carries the manifesto of the intellectuals of Uruguay concerning this confinement of mine. Thank you, brothers. Brothers in the language of Don Quixote, that most noble brotherhood. For I acknowledge gratefully your regard. The Samson Carrascos here, the university graduates, the barbers, and the rest of the national rabble, tell me that one must adjust to reality. The so-called materialist conception of history professes to believe that things, *res*, reality, make men what they are, but my historical sense of history tells me that we, men and women, persons, are the ones who make things, *res*, reality. I left the sad reality behind me there; I brought the *person*ality of Spain here with me. Not even Sancho lives there now, in Spain, since it's up to that Maese Pedro's monkey, poor General Primo de Rivera, to act as the representative figure for the country.

I will not be going back to my unfortunate country, an unfortunate fatherland today, so long as the dark General M. Anido, the ungallant runaway *caudillo* of insurgents, is on the loose, without so much as a muzzle on him. Not even the life of an honorable citizen is safe there, unless he vilely resigns himself to silencing the truth in public.

How has all this fallen upon us? Ever since 1914, with the war of the nations, there has been an exacerbation of the collective mania for persecution en-

230*

demic in my poor countrymen, who have not yet understood the mission which God—whose thought is history—reserved for Spain, the mother of those free republics across the Atlantic. The *Black Legend* took root, and a counter-legend, even more legendary, sprang up, and the blackness is smothering us. The German-ophilia of our Spanish cave-dwellers was something truly sad to behold. Our false native traditionalism contributed the lowest and most gross, most materialistic concept of caste, as a buttress: the cult of what they call masculinity. And men began to disappear inexorably, leaving room only for *machos*, he-men— and for eunuchs.

But the saddest aspect of all this is that the directors of the Directory are the dimmest, most uncultured, most unintelligent of the Spanish militia. What must they be like! The wings of one's soul break and fall off when one hears them repeat, through Gander Beak, the most hollow and vulgar *generalities* (a generality, from a general, is vacuity cubed). They abominate intelligence; even more they abominate wit and humor. Above all, they abominate originality and personality.

Still, I have hopes. I am confident that my gesture in allowing them to send me here without the sentence of any tribunal, without so much as a formal charge (not even for the crime of "extravagance," a new penal category invented by Primo de Rivera) has not been in vain. Did I say a "new" category of crime? No: he is incapable of inventing anything at all. The crime is the ancient one of heresy persecuted by the Holy Office, today resurrected. But it is the last death rattle of orthodox demagogic envy, of that terrible cave-dwellers' envy.

I hope that from all this will emerge the Spain within, the Spain of the inner depths, the Spain which is sister to the other nations of the same spiritual blood, that is, the same language. And I hope that instead of saying that there is no part of the earth without a Spanish grave, we will be able to say that there is no part of the heavens without a Spanish idea, an idea in Castilian.

My thanks to you all, men of Uruguay. Convey to your comrades, to your nation, along with my salutation, my hearty faith, my live and lively hope in the future of freedom and in the honor of Hispanic-American thought, righteous thought.

From across the sea, which can only smile at our tragic frailty, from this fortunate, bare, skeletal island, an austere piece of Africa, I send you the greetings of

MIGUEL DE UNAMUNO

To Jorge Luis Borges   Hendaye,
                                          26 March 1927

For some time now, *compañero*, I have felt a desire to write you and comment on your contributions to *La Prensa*, all the more so whenever I read some flattering reference to myself and to the fact that I remain one of those writers whose work you still follow. And right at this moment I have your brief essay on "Quevedo Humorista" before me, and, given the sorry state of my poor country, I feel full of Quevedo's bitter humor. Yes, the secret inner Quevedo is still to be discovered.

Though for my part I have already discovered him, and feel him come alive again in my own gut.

I used to feel sympathy toward the sad smile of Cervantes, the war casualty, the one-armed man from Lepanto—as Loyola was a war casualty, limping from

Pamplona—but now I am more sympathetic toward
the bitter grimace of Quevedo, a casualty from another
war, wounded in his soul. He went to prison for telling
truth, the naked truth, all of it—"*¿no ha de haber un
espíritu valiente?*" ("Is there not to be one brave soul?");
he felt like no one else the fury of the enormous monk-
ish envy, the militant friars' envy, which mothered the
Inquisition and which is, as he says, so skinny because
it only bites and never eats. How deeply he endured
Spain under the House of Austria, which enlarged
itself in the manner of moles. It battened on the roots,
on the hunger personified by Domine Cabra, Master
Goat. Even in Quevedo's tragic and macabre scato-
logical jokes, what a depth of bitterness! How he would
have mocked the officious dispatches of that clown
Primo de Rivera. Just listen to this:

> He's my man and let him beat me
> till he breaks my baptized head
> let him do it in our bedroom
> but now, Good Christ!
> to force me in some tavern
> when he's blind with drink
> to drink from the glass
> in which he spat, the pig!
> for that goes beyond
> all the laws of tender love
> and it's not the manly thing to do. . . .
> Tell me, Spain,
> is it bearable to suffer such a fate?
> Ay, my girl, I put up
> not only with blows from the State: fines,
> outrages, prisons
> gags and murder
> but something worse, the official
> dispatches which are the glass
> in which my pimp empties

> with the greatest naturalness
> all the evil humors of
> the Tyrant's catarrh
> I might forget it all, but . . . that?
> I could not have fallen lower!

And he, Quevedo, who so gravely and ascetically discoursed on the kingdom of God and of Christ's regime, what would he have to say of the tainted and cowardly Praetorian tyranny which rules today in our Spain—ours, Quevedo's and mine. . . . It is a regime of thieving hangmen, who have taken the place of judges, a Spain where, instead of justice being administered, punishment—which they call order—is meted out. The ill-fated jack of spades in the Spanish pack, the gang-foreman, General Severiano Martínez Anido, has said that justice must be sacrificed for the sake of order. And of course he, the fire-chief of the squadron that is to put out the Bolshevik fire, sets the fires himself in order to plunder and sack the frightened bourgeois household.

Believe me, *compañero*: in today's Spain, as in Quevedo's, one must free oneself from arbitrary, casual law, one must seek out wild miracles if one wants to live like a man. Or do as I've done: go into exile, slip off the gag. And let these who go in for the politics of the rear guard pirouette among the literature of the *avant-garde*.

In short, here in this Carthusian cell of a little Hendaye hotel, while I listen to the sweetly grave sound of the bells of Fuenterrabía, resounding off the stark, naked Jaizquíbel, I indulge my solitude of solitudes with all kinds of reading, especially metaphysics. And I muse on whether God will remember me always, or if these recollections of God recall themselves or are aware of themselves, so that an eternity of eternities is no more than a moment under time and the infinite circle its own center and the entire universe no more than an atom, which is to say a zero. And from this wading into the fathomless mystery of existing and insisting, I sometimes come up with ferocious mockery and sarcasm to hurl in the faces of the hangmen of my fatherland.

And that's enough unburdening.

Receiving the salutation of your grateful reader, *compañero* and—why not?—friend.

MIGUEL DE UNAMUNO

To Matilde Brandau de Ross　　　　　Hendaye,
　　　　　　　　　　　　　　　　　　15 November 1927

I am so happy, my dear friend, to learn you are again in our agitated Europe and that we can see each other. I am here on the border, and here I shall remain until I can return to my Spain. I am much better off here than in Paris, and I do more here. Furthermore, my family comes from time to time on vacations. We spend the summers here together. Around Christmas my wife will come with one of the girls and with my eldest son, Fernando, who lost his wife last July. It was a terrible blow for us all! My poor daughter-in-law was like another daughter for me, so affectionate and self-effacing. She went with her husband, my son, to the Canary Islands to get me. They were married eight years, without children. And a few days after a miscarriage— I was dreaming of being a grandfather!—she died. She left such a void behind her for us! And I am in exile, here for most of the year in a tiny student's room in this little hotel, reflecting bitterly on my country's shame.

235*

The worst of it is not the dictatorship—or better, the tyranny—but rather that the petty tyrants (all you can say about them is that they are big, brutal soldiers) aren't honest persons. Never has there been so much stealing. How could I have imagined when our Luis Ross was traveling through Spain, so full of love and understanding toward the country, that we would end up this way! As for my situation, fortunately my son the dentist can support the entire family easily. Aside from the income which stopped when my university professorship was snatched from me, my plays are beginning to bring in something and also, to a lesser degree, the translations of my work, especially those into German. But we will have the chance to talk about all this and also about you and your Chile.

I send an affectionate greeting to your brother and your sister-in-law, who I suppose are with you. I remember them well. In memory of your Luis, receive a big hug from your friend,

MIGUEL DE UNAMUNO

To Manuel Gálvez   Hendaye,
                                          15 April 1928

What a long time with so little news of you, my friend! O the days of *El solar de la raza*, *La maestra normal*, and the like. And all the rain that has rained upon us since! I went beyond rejuvenation: I'm now in re-childishment. To the point.

I've received *Síntesis*, No. 10, which you, and no one else, sent me. I know only two numbers of that journal: Bóveda sent me No. 1, and now I have No. 10. I have not even seen the issue in which my article "Hispanidad" appeared [. . .]

236*

Of what you call my *philosophy*, what would you have me say? [. . .] When I was studying Thomist philosophy, our school text—detestable!—was by a Father F. Zeferino González, O.P., who attained the rank of archbishop, of cardinal, without ever ceasing to be a rustic boor. I was always amused by the well-known phrase of his—"the lamentable consequences of this doctrine." And I'd say to myself: the lamentable consequences of a doctrine may prove that the doctrine is lamentable, but not that it is false. It reminds me of those people who are always excusing themselves because they are taken for pessimists. And what of that? If you could only see the amusing letter written me by Maritain—I met him at a P.E.N. banquet—just when my little book *L'agonie du christianisme* was published! What damage they do, and not only to truth, but to Christianity, these French converts!

And coming to the point you make, I am not sure I am not a superrationalist. In any case I believe, as Professor (not much the professor) Warner Fite, the translator into English of my *Mist*, wrote a little while back, that I never lost contact with the earth or, if you prefer, with the boards, the stage. I know I tread the boards; I know I am acting a role and I know what my role is. On the level of thought, it is something like the role played by Don Juan on the level of sensuality; and Don Juan is a profound character, essentially theatrical, who knows he is playing a role, who develops on stage and knows that it is the ultimate reality. And Don Juan, who knows how to play his role, who is all role, and only a role, convinces the spectators—or rather, the listeners, for he is not an actor in silent films: he is a voice, more than a character, and it is not by means of reason that he convinces. Now believe me, my friend, it is not only through

237*

reason that we are able to convince. More: reason is what does *not* convince in the moral order.

Another thing: do you really believe that most pagans were without a sense of painful anguish? If you had spent nearly thirty years reading, making translations, and commenting on the Greek classics to a class—and my classes consisted mostly of making translations, although I varied (to my advantage) the texts nearly every year—you would probably not think as you do. Whenever I am asked if I have taken certain themes from Nietzsche—whom I still know very poorly and fragmentarily—I would respond that he and I (he, too, was a professor of Greek) have both imbibed from the same fount: Hellenic sophistics. And he, moreover, from the richly nutritious book *Psyche*, by his friend and teacher Erwin Rohde. But those who have read the Greeks in translation and Nietzsche also in translation know that there are things in Greek and in German, more so than in other languages, which are untranslatable. No, I do not like the literary content of philosophic systems. I do not like the equation rhetoric of oratory and politics. Spencer's cosmogony is a political cosmogony, progressivist, but there are also conservative, regressive cosmogonies.

What a lot I would like to say about the systems of thought produced by the nineteenth century, and about what has sprouted from the war, the weariness it brought in its wake! But that would return me to my present *system*, to my battle against the Praetorian, police-state tyranny which is devastating, degrading, and stupefying our Spain.

And that's enough for today. But I do not forget to thank you for your work, which must help in the diffusion of my own work—and why does one write if not to *diffuse* oneself? Besides, you have done your work with enthusiasm and love—which are the same thing—and have given me thereby the greatest and best proof of friendship possible to give. Thank you, thank you, thank you.

We will write each other again, no?

Greet my comrades, especially Borges.

Much your friend, MIGUEL DE UNAMUNO

To Warner Fite Hendaye,
19 November 1928

Mr. Warner Fite
Princeton University
5 College Road
Princeton, New Jersey

It's not yet a week, my dear friend, since I received the copy of your translation of my *Mist*, as well as the Dana book and the Dewey. Just before that I had received Lord Charnwood's *Abraham Lincoln*. Knopf had already sent me three copies of your translation. I find it very good, faithful and, as far as I can judge, very much *adapted* to the English. The second Spanish edition has also just appeared, and is going nicely. Now I can say that I am *beginning* to be read in Spain, because by now my individual language has become understood and can be translated by my readers. You are quite right in what you say about Lord Charnwood's *Lincoln*, but it is the best I have chanced to read on the subject. I have gotten a glimpse of the religious man, of his melancholy a-dogmatic religion, and I have learned of his penchant for reading novels and of the fact that he wrote . . . verse. And I have explained his Gettysburg Address to myself as being in essence a grandiose melancholic religious poem.

Lincoln had the tragic sense, there's no doubt of it. I have also begun to read *Two Years Before the Mast* and *The Philosophy of John Dewey*. The diaphanous simplicity of the narrative in the first book came through to me at once: it is a classic book in the best sense—a book with class—and, like *Robinson Crusoe*, a book for both children and adults. It possesses a moving simplicity and a spontaneous poetical philosophy of life. Going from Dana's simple pages to those of Dewey, I was all the more struck, even shocked, by the confused and confusionist style of the latter. His scant literary effectiveness, the heaviness of his style, reveal the weak point of his thought. [. . .]

I do not believe that Dewey could feel the tragic sense of life inasmuch as he does not seem to feel the tragedy of consciousness. "I know who I am," said Don Quixote. But there is another step and that is "I know that I am!" And who knows that? But I think that when I finish reading the Dewey book I'll be able to say more about him and about his behaviorism, which puzzles me.

I am delighted that you like Pérez Galdós. Since he had to live from his books, he sometimes fell into what Balseiro would call *art*, but in general he was a human being who told human stories to other human beings. His weakness was to allow himself to be carried away by the voluptuosity of constructing paragraphs. A novel like *Fortunata and Jacinta*—his best, in my opinion—would have been one of the great universal novels, if he had been able to condense it. But who knows if perhaps an artistic condensation would not have taken away the charm of a story which is enjoyed in the telling. [. . .]

Life goes on here, and I cannot foresee when I will be able to return, as a Spaniard, to my poor Spain, which is being poisoned by the Praetorian pornocracy

(*pornocrateia* is the right name for it). I read now, and write but little: verse and drama. [. . .]
 You know what a true friend you have in
MIGUEL DE UNAMUNO

To Jorge Guillén   Hendaye,
3 January 1929

Yesterday, my dear friend, my wife and two of my children who spent Christmas with me left for home, and this morning, the 3rd of January, when I awoke, it was still dark out, and in my hermit's bed in this frontier cell, I read from your *Cántico*.

Once it began to clear outside, I saw from the bed the fields all covered with snow and the snow still falling silently. I took from my night-table the Gospels—my Father Astete—and read a chapter from the Epistle of St. Paul to the Colossians. Next I consulted my other classic, the other great popular Castilian classic along with Father Astete: "The Firmament. Zaragozan Calendar for 1929 arranged for all of Spain by the celebrated astronomer and unique observer don Mariano Castillo y Ocsiero," and read the entry between the 2nd and 3rd of January: "gentle winterstorm." And of a sudden I felt all the prophetic poetry of the great "celebrated astronomer and unique observer." And at the same time of the unique popular Hispanic poet, the one and only.

The case in point occurred at Coimbra, shortly after the death of the great Portuguese lyric poet João de Deus. A professor from Coimbra and Don Antonio Sánchez Moguel (who told me the tale) were boating on the Mondego, which carries out to sea the fervent tears of Camões. The Lusitanian said that João de Deus had been a great popular poet, and the Anda-

241*

lusian replied that there are no popular poets. In proof of this last assertion, he added that the boatman was certain to know nothing about João de Deus. They asked him, and the boatman answered: "*João de Deus? João de Deus? não o conheço.*" They asked what poet he knew, and without hesitation: "*Poeta? O Zaragozano!*" Our man, the great don Mariano! You know that in the lands of Portugal, as in Castile, "poet" is the same as saying calendar-maker, one who prophesies the weather, and makes judgments on the year, in verse.

I was delighted with the prediction of the "unique observer" as he prophesized for today a "gentle winter storm". [. . .] I returned to your *Cántico*, but outside the snow continued its silent song and inside me sang the gentle purity of my winter-storm [. . .].

When you visited me here, my *canciones* numbered some three hundred and sixty; now I have five hundred and eighty. This gentle snow and the closeness of your verse will add another at once. [. . .]

Besides the *Cancionero* which you saw in part here, I'd like to publish [. . .] some *cantos* to cities and towns [. . .]: to Salamanca, Bilbao, the Nervión, and Cáceres, Zamora, Oviedo, Madrigal de las Altas Torres, Ávila, Segovia, Toledo, Burgos, Córdoba, Granada, the Duero, the Peña de Francia, Erguijuela de la Sierra, Vitoria and [. . .] my Spain! [. . .]

MIGUEL DE UNAMUNO

To the Editor of Síntesis　　　　Hendaye,
13 November 1929

I am not in the habit, my dear colleague, of commenting in my turn on commentaries made on my work, and that is why I have kept silent about the very flattering statements made in *Síntesis* by Guillermo de Torre about my *How to Make a Novel*. But I have just read in the last issue of the review, dated October, the article "The Latest Versions of Spain (Waldo Frank, Keyserling, Jean Cassou)" by de Torre and now I feel I must break my habit—a habit not broken becomes routine, and finally, narrow unawareness—and break it in honor of my good friends Frank, Keyserling, and Cassou, and our good commentator, Torre. [. . .]

First, the well-worn topic of my contradictions, which Torre calls "possibles." The theme of contradiction is as inexhaustible as the theme of paradox, and in essence it comes to the same thing. Need I remind anyone that the Gospels of Jesus are woven out of contradictions and paradoxes which, along with the parables, constitute its framework? And I say nothing of Saint Paul, as full of contradictory and paradoxical feelings as of excellent dialectic. And his pharisaical dialectics were polemical dialectics.

[. . .]

In accordance with the dialectic of contradictions, of thesis, antithesis, and synthesis, my dear editor of *Síntesis*, I have come to the belief that to Europeanize Spain is the same as to Hispanicize Europe, that all co-penetration, even that of the part with its whole, is mutual; I have come to understand that the Spaniard who wishes to Europeanize the minds of his fellow-countrymen must work to make Europeans into spiritual Spaniards, and in order to make Europe known in Spain I have devoted myself to making Spain known—and therefore loved—in Europe and all over the world. Have I succeeded? Keyserling has said, and de Torre recalls it, that "for the Spaniard of today the eternal Spaniard Unamuno may perhaps be an obstacle, while, on the other hand, the European Ortega y Gasset may be the immediate road to salvation." Eternal Spaniard! I have never been paid greater honor. Because any eternal Spaniard is more than European, he is universal. And of course, much more so than the current European. Spanish eternity, like French, English, German, Portuguese, or Andorran, is more universal than is our poor sad European contemporaneity.

My motto that "we must Hispanicize Europe" has struck many as arrogant, but I should have said that we must Hispanicize the Universe, which amounts to universalizing Spain. And if I am to be truly sincere, since the Universe is spiritually God, I should say that I, the eternal Spaniard, attempt to Hispanicize God in order to divinize Spain. Or is it not possible that Unamuno, the eternal Spaniard, is trying to Unamunize God in order to divinize himself? And, in himself and through himself, to do the same for others?

And do not be shocked by my bringing God, my God, into this. All our minds, even the minds of atheists, are so involved with the idea of God that we cannot think without it. The Universe in our minds, become awareness, is the Word, and the Word, says the beginning of the 4th and mystical Gospel, is God (John 1:1). And without the word, one does not think. Mathematics? Algebra? Look here: in $(a + b) = a^2 + 2ab + b^2$ there are two letters, a and b, and the letters are the cells of written words, they are literature, and the numbers themselves, 2 or 3 or 5, are words. He who does not speak does not re-count. To tell a story is to tally an amount. And just notice how in this flight-of-the-pen commentary—and may it fly far!—to a commentary by Guillermo de Torre, I have gone so far as to encompass God. May God reward de Torre for that!

But recently I have been grieved to observe the meaning they wish to give my motto about Hispani-

cizing Europe, a—God protect me!—*fajisto* meaning
(I say *fajisto*, because the Italian *fascio* gave us our *fajo*
or *sheaf*). And a certain *fajisto* Italian writer has claimed
me as one of theirs. I recalled it with sadness when I
saw in the last issue of *L'Illustration française* a pho-
toengraving of the Duce reviewing the *fajisto* troops,
and when the soldiers presented arms, they brandished
[. . .] daggers. No, that *Fajismo* cannot be expressed
in our Castilian tongue, the most Roman of Romance
languages. No, no, no; we must reject knife-slinging
Hispanicism. [. . .]

A cordial farewell from MIGUEL DE UNAMUNO

To Bogdan Raditsa   Salamanca,
                                       16 April 1930

I was on the point of answering your previous letter
when events in Spain developed quickly, and I decided, once the main obstacle was overcome, to return
here. My reception in Irún, in Bilbao, in Valladolid,
and here in Salamanca exceeded all I could have hoped
for. There were popular demonstrations which proved
that my campaign of exile was not in vain. I was sought
out on all sides. I was preparing to go to Madrid, when
I took a fall in Zamora which bruised both my wrists
and fractured the radius of my left hand. I have scarcely
been able to use my hands these past twenty days, and
have been reduced to letting myself be dressed and
undressed. It has been less than a week that I have
the use of my hand for writing, though not without
pain. And, since I do not like to dictate, I have not
written you before.

When I left Hendaye, I had already read all the

poems of Kostis Palamás that he sent me and which are now covered with marginal annotations, for I proposed to make, in my own way, a study of such an extraordinary poet, especially of his poetic concept of the Gypsies and of Hesiod. Please tell him all this, and his daughter Nausicaa as well, whom I mean to write, just as soon as I bring my correspondence up to date. I have fallen woefully behind due to the circumstances of my repatriation and the unfortunate accident to my hands.

I also failed to notify the *Elefteron Vēma* of my change of address; I would be grateful if they continued to send me the daily, but here to Salamanca: no address is needed except my name.

As for going to Greece, and visiting the Balkans, of which I know only the desolation of Karst: it would be a splendid dream! But it cannot be at this time [. . .]. This summer I must go to a watering-place, to treat the rheumatism brought on by the accident, and then I must return to Hendaye to take care of some matters and to fetch the small library I left behind there.

I have gained back my chair at the University here, but I shall not be lecturing until the coming term, in October, unless the course of politics leads me in another direction.

The suppression of the Dictatorship, at least partially, has not resolved the problem. The number of republicans—more antimonarchical than they are anti-Alfonsite—grows larger day by day in Spain, and the coming Cortes is bound to be most lively. The Dictatorship—which the King brought about—has left all the old problems unresolved, and the Moroccan problem, the syndicalist problem, regionalism, and the economic problems are far worse than they were. Spain is about to enter a period of reconstitution, of liberty and justice, all of which can lead to confusion, so much so already that we have no time to notice what is happening outside. We must be wary lest Fascism fall upon us, now that there is nothing to fear from Bolshevism. The rather anarchistic temperament of the Spanish people is averse to the latter.

I have not published anything lately, nor have I concerned myself with other than theatrical matters. I will send you my drama *Dream Shadows*, only lately produced, and *The Other* as soon as it is produced. I do not even write for the press, because I do not care to have my writings go through censorship.

In one of the last numbers of *Elefteron Vēma*, which I read in Hendaye, I saw an account, together with some verses, of a poet, a woman, who is apparently dying of tuberculosis in some sanitarium; I don't recall her name now, but her verse moved me deeply.

Do tell Palamás that I have not forgotten him and that through him I learned to know and love his Romaic and Gypsy Greece. [. . .]

Very much your friend, MIGUEL DE UNAMUNO

To Jacques Chevalier   Salamanca,
                                        28 April 1934

You cannot imagine, my good friend, with what grief I write you this letter. I have been hoping that one of these days the agonizing situation which hangs over me might be resolved, but there seems to be no way out. I do not refer to the condition of my poor country, which is going through one of its gravest crises, a time during which those of us who have public responsibility do not know what we shall have to do. No, it is a question of something closer, more personal.

My poor wife—who will be seventy years old on St. James's Day, if she survives—is hovering between life and death. Some two weeks ago she suffered a brain hemorrhage, from which she seemed to be recovering, but then she was overcome by paralysis of her right side and aphasia. She has gone back to childhood, but since she still feels something, she clings to those of us who love her. You do not know what it is like, my friend, to lie at her side, holding her by the hand, lulling her to sleep, for she will abide no one else. We have been married forty-three years and have known each other some sixty-five years. And it is terrifying when she turns her eyes—they are also mine!—to gaze on me, as if seeking something beyond life! She scarcely recognizes anyone. And since she is suffering from complete aphasia—verbal amnesia—I can only conclude that she cannot think. But she feels, and perhaps imagines things. She is a saint, and has always had a childlike quality; her pure cheerfulness has always been my greatest shield. But now she is fading into a saint-like childhood. I was afraid that, like her brother, who died the same way, she would be in pain, unable to eat because of paralysis of the pharynx. But it seems *that* is not to be. I do not know how long this will last, but as long as it does, I cannot leave her side. And if she were to pass away soon, you understand that I could not undertake any sort of trip. I used to say that my wife, my Concha, was "my habit" (in the sense of *habitude*): when God tears her from me—His will be done!—the deepest fabric of my soul will be destroyed. And then there is still the problem of one of my sons and two daughters who cannot yet support themselves, although the other four—one was married day before yesterday—can already take care of themselves. And then there is my forthcoming retirement and not knowing what I shall do.

So you can imagine how I view public affairs, the affairs of my poor Spain, through my own pain, my poor Concha's.

Forgive this rather rambling letter. You, who know me, will understand that I have not expounded on the two sources of my great grief in order better to justify my inability to write to your university, but rather out of the need to unburden myself and because I consider you a friend who deserves to be confided in. And may it please God that when this stormy period has passed and when I regain the tranquillity of resignation to His holy will, I can come to you, serene and strong, to speak of what does not pass, of the eternal present.

To all your colleagues my deepest expression of gratitude and to you, my friend, a warm embrace from these arms of mine which every night feel the warmth and throb of other arms—they are also mine—being drained of life.

MIGUEL DE UNAMUNO

To Teixeira de Pascoaes   Salamanca,
                                             24 May 1934

My dear friend, I gather from your last letter that you did not receive the letter I wrote right after I finished reading your "São Paulo," in which I told you of my enthusiastic reaction and how I was going to dedicate to you the article for *Ahora*—enclosed—and another which I have now finished. I wrote you during the time when my poor wife was dying. She collapsed of a stroke, and half her body was paralyzed. She lost consciousness and after a long crisis—days—she left me for God on the fifteenth of this month. She turned seventy last July 29th, St. James's day; I turned seventy on September 29th. We had known each other since childhood and had been married forty-three years! She was more than my love, she was my habit—my everything. The mother of my eight children and of my grandchildren—and my mother, too. And now, changing a famous verse of Bécquer, I can say, "My God, how lonely we, the living, are!"

After her death I sent you a copy of my "Saint Manuel Bueno, Martyr, and Three More Stories," and along with it the article to which you refer. I sent both the letter and the book to Avenida Wilson, 111, 2nd. fl. right, which is the address of the dedication of your "Sao Paulo."

For the moment, I can say no more.

A strong, strong, fraternal, and Iberian embrace from your

MIGUEL DE UNAMUNO

To Matilda Brandau de Ross   Madrid,
22 December 1934

Thank God, my dear friend, that I have finally been able to find a moment in this life of mine—which is not full of agitation, but rather of meditation—to write you. I have been wanting to do so for some time, because you, more than most of my other friends, deserve it. But . . . if you only knew how the rhythm of my inner life has been altered by what has happened to me the last two or three years. First my sister died, then, in August of 1933, my poor eldest daughter, my Salomé, leaving me a grandson who along with his father, my son-in-law, lives with me, and I must take care of them. My widowed son-in-law is going to marry my other daughter, Felisa, who has been like a mother to her little nephew even before my Salomé died after a long illness. The poor little thing was very weak, as fragile in body as she was strong of spirit. And then my Concha died, as you already know, the Concha who was my joy and my faith and the serenity of my life. You knew her; you knew the one whom in the last years I called "my habit," because habit is the very essence of love. Now I know what it is to be a widower, as you have known what it is to be a widow. I never really believed in life, and she, my "habit," my Concha, never believed in death. I have never known a more serene and firm spirit—indeed, have I ever known any other spirit? She was my true mother. Then came the national tribute paid to me, but it came during a time of sad concern over the state of this my Spain, convulsed by the darkest passions. And yet I personally cannot complain. I am one of the few whom they respect. And I know less than before about the Hispanic America beyond the seas. The problems of this Spain here, my Spain, overwhelm me. I have spoken about Chile—and, of course, about you also—with the admirable Gabriela Mistral, one of the most open, generous souls I have ever met; she visited me a short while ago in Salamanca. I am writing you these lines from Madrid, where I have been called to preside over an examining committee for those aspiring to teaching posts. And now as I write you, I recall the days of your loss and your grief, when you sought refuge in our house—ours, hers and mine—and my Concha welcomed you like a sister. Shall we ever see each other again? In Chile, here in Spain, where?

I am over 70 years old but I am as solid and strong as a Basque oak, free of ailments, in perfect physical health and sound of mind. For I have to live. I have to live for my children and my grandchildren—three granddaughters from my eldest son, the son (he is 5) of my poor Salomé, and two grandchildren about to be born, one from my Fernando, whose wife will give birth for the fourth time in March, and another from my second son, Pablo, who was married this year—and I have to live for my Spain. Since, thank God, my voice is still heeded and respected here, I must make it into the megaphone for God. And that is how life passes. But we shall have created life for after our death. And then, who knows? We shall perhaps live in the eternal mind of God, which amounts to living in true, substantial history.

And now receive an embrace from my Concha, which comes to you through me from where she still lives. You have the deepest affection of

MIGUEL DE UNAMUNO

To Ramón Pérez de Ayala   Salamanca,
                                        17 December 1935
My forever beloved friend,

The day before yesterday I sent off telegrams to you and to Pastor, accepting the offer. Today I write you both. [. . .]

As regards this invitation to go to that England

whose history, literature, and life I have studied so long—just you imagine!—I've never been there before and though I read fluently in English—even the most difficult texts—I understand it with great difficulty when it is spoken, and I cannot speak it myself. Yet that is no obstacle. But there is something I must tell you. Three months ago I turned seventy-one and, though I have never boasted of better health and suffer none of the ills of my age, I am beginning to be bothered by voyages—I prefer a walk in the mountains to a day in a train—and, then too, my personal, private circumstances, familial and national, have me in such a state of mind that I find it hard to make decisions, especially about definite schedules.

But now comes the most annoying part, which you, who I believe know me somewhat, must understand. I have reached that time of "having manias" and of seeming somewhat extravagant and even *shocking*. And I am deeply hurt to be treated as some kind of exception. A case in point: I went to Paris for the inauguration of the Colegio Español, in company with Blas Cabrera, José Ortega, Cierva, and others, and you cannot imagine the number of times I felt ashamed— yes, ashamed—of myself. Everyone treated me not only most attentively, but even affectionately. But at certain formal meals or gala banquets I seemed a country rustic. At the homage given me here on the occasion of my retirement, it wasn't so bad, but I went away resolved not ever to wear a mask again. This year I was invited to Portugal. Many others were going: Duhamel, Maeterlinck, Mauriac, Curtius. [. . .] From here, from Spain, there would be Maeztu, Fernández Flores, and some others. And at the banquets, I continued to appear the bumpkin, the boor. I can't do these things, it's a real sickness. To strike the right note, the right tone with the others, would cause me real anguish. This is exactly one of the things—and don't laugh at me—which keeps me from resolving to make my entrance into the Spanish Academy. And there are several of us in the same situation, you among the others, standing at the door. Baroja, who is taken for a greater ogre—better, more of a boor—than myself, has had the greater force of will. And what hurts the most is the belief that my attitude comes from wanting to stand out, to be different. No, I'm not going to dress up as a Salamantine countryman, as a Basque rustic, like Tolstoy the muzhik, and [. . .] I realize that the truly human, the most normal, is to be in tune with the conventions of mutual intercourse, but [. . .] it's not a matter of reasoning. The few times I did comply— years ago now—I suffered. And now, with age, it's an incurable sickness. And when they tell me, "You can go anywhere you want, however you want, because you are you," they wound me deeply, when they mean to please me. It is one of the things which most hounds me.

"All very well," you will say, "but what are you getting at?" But then, no, you wouldn't say that. I fear England, I fear *that* society. And that's so despite the fact that I imagine that the true quality of a *gentleman* is something different than is supposed. And please do not smile at my pettiness.

I won't go on, now.

But to see that place, to meet those people, to breathe that spiritual air [. . .]. And who knows if I wouldn't come back cured of one of my oddities and of my city rusticity (or better, town rusticity, for my Bilbao is a town).?

You doubtless know my translator, Crawford Flitch.
What a man! What an authentic man! What an hi-
dalgo! [. . .]
And believe, I repeat, that you have a loyal and
faithful friend in

MIGUEL DE UNAMUNO

To Guillermo de Torre   Salamanca,
                                        7 January 1936

First, my dear friend, you must forgive me for my
slowness in answering you, but it's not that I'm aboil
with work, but what I do get done is between intervals
of rest. I spend hours stretched out on the bed, going
over and over, as ever, the same thing. In all truth, I
feel fatigued. If you knew the mental and emotional
effort—cerebral and *cor*-dial—it costs me to write those
commentaries for *Ahora*, and all of it so as not to lower
myself by taking the easy way out! And I make the
verbal effort to continue creating my language. The
theologians were right to say that the conservation of
the world is a continuous creation. And one of my
themes [. . .] is to teach those who listen to my writing
not only to think in Spanish, but to think the language.
[. . .]
I have received the two numbers of *Sur*. I already
had read a couple of others, at most. So that now I
know the magazine's tone, timbre, and accent, with
which I'll endeavor to come to grips. I'll take, from
my notebook of jottings, turns of phrase, aphorisms,
enough to compose—improvising the composition and
not the content—an essay, or whatever anyone wants

to call it, which I trust will satisfy my present and future readers.

As far as fees are concerned, though I am in need of everything—there are so many obligations!—I leave that to the good lights of the journal's management.

Through my son-in-law I learn that Norah is in Argentina. Greet her and her brother Jorge. And please tell Borges that in all the while that I think of writing him, months and even years have slipped by. That's what happens when one feels that there is so much to say. How many times have I paused over one of his phrases, and even at some allusion to me! And more than once I have thought to compose some gloss on his sayings-in-writing. In any case I would like him to know that quite often when I address the public but speak of my "reader," I am thinking concretely and individually of him. [. . .]

You know how much I am your friend.

MIGUEL DE UNAMUNO

To Enrique Díez-Canedo Salamanca,
10 April 1936

I address you, my good friend, to ask you to act for me in answering the organizers of the P.E.N. Congress. [. . .]

For some time now I venture out as little as possible from here, from my Salamanca. And I no longer deliver addresses either in Spain or outside Spain. I made an exception only when I was invited to London to lecture and to receive at the same time a doctorate *honoris causa* from Oxford. [. . .]

A few years ago, when I was on the point of going

to Buenos Aires, invited by the Cultural Department, I was held back by the fear that my eldest daughter would die while I was out there. And such would have been exactly the case, for she died here during the very days I would have been there.

And now? My health is not what it was, though I am not hindered in my ordinary life nor in my work. I have just spend a fortnight in bed with a severe attack of rheumatism, though I could read and write there, and even take care of rector's affairs. My family obligations—five of my eight children are still dependent on me—worry me a good deal. I feel myself—at last!—growing old, and work at putting everything in order before I am forced to take leave of this world. But what most keeps me home now is the public thing (*res publica*) in our Spain, for I foresee a catastrophe if Providence or Fate or whatever does not prevent it. [. . .] With all this I believe you have enough information to explain my decision to the Commission of International P.E.N. And that would be better than my telling them directly. For you will be able to *translate* for them matters which I leave in my political dialect.

And how would I have liked to go there with an easy spirit!—Among other reasons, in order to attend the opening performance of my *Raquel Encadenada*, which will be played by my good friend Lola Membribes, to whom I would have you give my loving regards.

My greetings also to the people at P.E.N. and please convey all my gratitude for their attentions. It seems to be God's wish that I be able to "ultra-marine" myself. If it must be . . . ! Unless all this changes . . .

And you, my good friend, you know how truly I am your

MIGUEL DE UNAMUNO

To Ramón Castaneyra Schaman   Salamanca,
22 April 1936

You cannot imagine, my very dear and unforgettable friend, what a surprise I got from your letter addressed to the Rector of this University—that is, me—in which you speak of a cablegram which I never did see. And I never saw it because the telegraph operator here, who knows well enough that I am in sound good health, handed the cable to one of my sons, and my son put it away somewhere and said nothing at all to me. Now, I don't know where such a piece of news could have gotten started! For not only am I not dead, as you can see—well, I mean, it seems to me I'm not dead—but I haven't even been on the verge of death. I've had an attack of rheumatism in my left leg, and it put me to bed for ten days, and today I'm back in bed again—whence I write you—but with no fever, and without any letup in my reading and writing and even in carrying out my business, for I am brought whatever needs a signature.

The news of my death brings to mind that other rumor which went the rounds, and which you echoed, announcing that I had been awarded the Nobel Prize in Literature. Last year, there was no award made for literature, and this year, when an award will be made, they tell me that there is a probability it will be given to me, though I have personally not made a single move. I am assured that it is so presaged by my having been granted the degree of doctor *honoris causa* about a month ago by the famous University of Oxford. I went to England to receive the degree, and gave two lectures and some talks at the University of London and before groups of English Hispanophiles, as well as at the universities of Oxford and Cambridge. I thoroughly enjoyed myself. I was highly regaled and was able to meet a goodly number of professors and English writers interested in my work. Both en route there and on my return trip I stayed over for a few days in Paris, in the house of my friend the Spanish Ambassador—the same as I did in London—and I agreed to go back there soon. But—who knows? [. . .]

Leaving aside my own personal state, and despite the fact that I cannot be really discontent—for, despite certain attacks against me, I am still one of the few public figures who is shown respect—I still do not care to comment on public matters here. I see it all darkly. What is developing and gaining force on the mainland is something no longer apparent in the civilized (??) part of Europe, and that is the syndicalism, essentially anarchist, of the C.N.T., and, on the other side, Fascism is on the rise. And one and the other are worse than barbarism, for they are forms of stupidity. The mental degeneration is frightening. The older generations are being dragged along by kids whose bodily age is between 17 and 23 but who mentally are barely five years old. And what passions! What dreams! What rancor! How much resentment everywhere! Luckily I have the consolation of my pessimism! "Consolation?" you will say. Yes, consolation, for as badly as things may go, they will not turn out worse than I fear.

How often I remember that blessed island! How often I think I would be better off in Puerto Cabras, or in La Oliva, or in Pájara, or in La Antigua, or in

Betancuria. . . . When will I ever be able to see it all again and embrace you there?

One thing I would like to tell you: You know that I had scarcely left there when I broke, for reasons I wish to forget, with Soriano. We did not speak to each other again. But I must tell you that he was sent, as you know, to Chile, and I know that there, as Ambassador, he has been able to gain the sympathies of the Chileans and of the Spanish colony. Having learned his lesson from life, he has been able to conduct himself with great tact and discretion. Of course I am delighted! And I would feel badly were they to relieve him of that post, so that he would be forced to return here to struggle and battle all over again. Whatever his faults may have been, he deserves some last years of peace now. For my part I want to forget everything that came between us.

Greet all the good friends I left in that island and accept a strong, strong embrace from your

MIGUEL DE UNAMUNO

Epilogue

Unamuno's Last Lecture
by Luis Portillo

THE CEREMONIAL HALL in the University of Salamanca is a spacious chamber, used only on formal occasions, solemn, austere, the walls hung with tapestries. Through the huge windows enters a shimmering flood of iridescent light which deepens the amber glow of the century-old plinth stones.

This was the setting.

The play was enacted on 12 October 1936, when Spanish Fascism was in its first triumphant stage. The morning was half spent. The patriotic festival of the Hispanic Race was being celebrated.

There they were on the presidential dais: the purple calotte, the amethyst ring and the flashing pectoral cross of the Most Illustrious Doctor Plá y Deniel, Bishop of the Diocese; the lackluster robes of the Magistrates; the profuse glitter of military gold braid side by side with the crosses and medals exhibited on presumptuously bulging chests; the morning coat, set off by black satin lapels, of His Excellency the Civil Governor of the Province; and all these surrounded—was it to honor or to overwhelm?—the man whose pride in his incorruptible Spanish conscience was steadfast and straight: Miguel de Unamuno y Jugo, the Rector.

From the front wall, the allegorical picture of the Republic had gone, and there shone from under a canopy the Caudillo's effigy in plump insolence. To the left and right, on crimson-covered divans, the silk of the doctors' gowns and their mortarboards with gay tassels in red, yellow, light blue and dark blue, symbolizing Law, Medicine, Letters, and Science.

A few ladies were scattered among the learned men; in a prominent place, Doña Carmen Polo de Franco, the distinguished spouse of the Man of Providence.

From a packed audience which faced the dais of the elect, with its protective balustrade of dark polished wood, there rose the confused murmur of expectancy. At the far end of the long hall glinted the rounded brasses of a military band, ready to play the obligatory hymns.

The ceremony began. Don Miguel opened it with the ritual formula, spoken in that unforgettable voice of his, thin and clear. Then Don Francisco Maldonado stepped on to the platform, short, fat, Professor of Literature and Salamancan landowner. With affected, baroque diction and vast erudition, he delivered a colorless and circumstantial address. At the end, he expressed his hope for a better future, with kindly and sincere emotion. He descended the steps among cheers and applause, bowed to the dais, and returned to his seat. He was followed on the speaker's platform by Don José María Ramos Loscertales, of Saragossa, tall and lean, with fluid gestures, flashing eyes, sober and precise of speech, his sensitive face in perpetual motion, expressing a subtle and enigmatic irony. He spoke of the mortal struggle raging at the time—yet another circumstantial speech. Its thesis: the energies of Spain at white heat in a crucible of passion—and like gold from the crucible, Spain would emerge in the end, purified and without stain, in her true colors . . . which rejected the taints artificially imposed on her. Clamorous ovation.

And then rose General Millán Astray. With ostentatious humility, he preferred to speak from his own place. His appearance was impressive. The General is thin, of an emaciation which pretends to slimness. He has lost one eye and one arm. His face and his body bear the indelible tattoo of horrible scars. These savage mutilations and gashes evoke a sinister personality; his angry and rancorous bearing kills any compassion his mutilations might have inspired.

He had been the organizer of the *Tercio*, the Spanish Foreign Legion for operations in Africa; he had been the creator of an iron, inexorable discipline to which the reckless fugitives from other social disciplines submitted of their own free will. He had gained those wounds which to many seemed glorious, to some over-exploited, and to all horribly impressive, in those fantastic Moroccan campaigns which had been Spain's bitter nightmare under the regretted aegis of King Alphonso XIII, called "The African" in his day. Yet the unquestionable nimbus which surrounded the figure of the General was due to the gruesome originality, to the mysterious paradox of his battlecry: *"Viva la Muerte!"* — "Long live Death!"

Barely had Millán Astray risen to his feet when his strident voice rang out, as though bursting from that heroic chest bedizened with a galaxy of crosses, the testimonials and rewards of gallantry.

First of all he said that more than one-half of all Spaniards were criminals, guilty of armed rebellion and high treason. To remove any ambiguity, he went on to explain that by these rebels and traitors he meant the citizens who were loyal to the Government.

In a sudden flash of intuition, a member of the audience was inspired so as to grasp the faultless logic

*265**

of a slogan which common minds had thought the product of an epileptic brain. With fervor, he shouted: *"Viva, viva la Muerte!"* — "Long live Death!"

Impervious, the General continued his fiery speech!

"Catalonia and the Basque country—the Basque country and Catalonia—are two cancers in the body of the nation. Fascism, which is Spain's health-bringer, will know how to exterminate them both, cutting into the live, healthy flesh like a resolute surgeon free from false sentimentality. And since the healthy flesh is the soil, the diseased flesh the people who dwell on it, Fascism and the Army will eradicate the people and restore the soil to the sacred national realm. . . ."

He made a pause and cast a despotic glance over the audience. And he saw that he held them in thrall, hypnotized to a man. Never had any of his harangues so subjugated the will of his listeners. Obviously, he was in his element. . . . He had conquered the University! And, carried away himself, he continued, blind to the subtle and withering smile of disdain on the lips of the Rector.

"Every Socialist, every Republican, every one of them without exception—and needless to say every Communist—is a rebel against the National Government, which will very soon be recognized by the totalitarian States who are aiding us, in spite of France—democratic France—and perfidious England.

"And then, or even sooner, when Franco wants it, and with the help of the gallant Moors who, though they wrecked my body only yesterday, today deserve the gratitude of my soul, for they are fighting for Spain against the Spaniards . . . I mean, the bad Spaniards . . . because they are giving their lives in defence of Spain's sacred religion, as is proved by their attending field mass, escorting the Caudillo, and pinning holy medallions and Sacred Hearts to their burnooses. . . ."

The General lost himself in the maze of his own vehement outburst. He hesitated, irritated and defiant at the same time. In these straits, an enthusiastic Fascist came to his rescue and shouted:

"*Arriba España!*"

The crowd bowed their heads in resignation. The man went on, undaunted:

"Spain!"

Mechanically, the crowd responded: "One!"

"Spain!" he reported.

"Great!" chorused the obedient public.

"Spain!" the Blue Shirt insisted, implacably.

"Free!" they all replied, cowed.

There was an obvious lack of warmth and listlessness in these artificially produced responses. Several Blue Shirts rose to their feet as though pushed by invisible springs, and raised their right arms stiffly in the Roman salute. And they hailed the sepia-colored photograph on the front wall:

"Franco!"

The public rose reluctantly and chanted parrot-like:

"Franco! Franco! Franco!"

But Franco's image did not stir. Neither did the Rector.

Don Miguel did not rise to his feet. And the public fell silent and sat down again.

All eyes were fastened in tense anxiety on the noble head, on the pale, serene brow framed by snow-white hair. The uncertain expression of his eyes was hidden by the glitter of his spectacles.

Between the fine curve of his nose and the silver of his Quixote-like beard, his mouth was twisted in a bitter grimace of undisguised contempt. People began

*267**

to grow uneasy. A few suddenly felt a recrudescence of their old rancorous abhorrence. Some admired the serene fearlessness of the Master and feared for his safety. The majority were gripped by the voluptuous thrill of imminent tragedy.

At last, Don Miguel rose slowly. The silence was an enormous void. Into this void, Don Miguel began to pour the stream of his speech, as though savoring each measured word. This is the essence of what he said:

"All of you are hanging on my words. You all know me, and are aware that I am unable to remain silent. I have not learnt to do so in seventy-three years of my life. And now I do not wish to learn it any more. At times, to be silent is to lie. For silence can be interpreted as acquiescence. I could not survive a divorce between my conscience and my word, always well-mated partners.

"I will be brief. Truth is most true when naked, free of embellishment and verbiage.

"I want to comment on the speech—to give it that name—of General Millán Astray, who is here among us."

The General stiffened provocatively.

"Let us waive the personal affront implied by the sudden outburst of vituperation against Basques and Catalans in general. I was born in Bilbao, in the midst of the bombardments of the Second Carlist War. Later, I wedded myself to this city of Salamanca, which I love deeply, yet never forgetting my native town. The Bishop, whether he likes it or not, is a Catalan from Barcelona."

He made a pause. Faces had grown pale. The short silence was tense and dramatic. Expectation neared its peak.

"Just now, I heard a necrophilous and senseless cry: 'Long live Death!' To me it sounds the equivalent of *'Muera la Vida!'* — 'To Death with Life!' And I, who have spent my life shaping paradoxes which aroused the uncomprehending anger of the others, I must tell you, as an expert authority, that this outlandish paradox is repellent to me. Since it was proclaimed in homage to the last speaker, I can only explain it to myself by supposing that it was addressed to him, though in an excessively strange and tortuous form, as a testimonial to his being himself a symbol of death.

"And now, another matter. General Millán Astray is a cripple. Let it be said without any slighting undertone. He is a war invalid. So was Cervantes. But extremes do not make the rule: they escape it. Unfortunately, there are all too many cripples in Spain now. And soon, there will be even more of them if God does not come to our aid. It pains me to think that General Millán Astray should dictate the pattern of mass-psychology.

"That would be appalling. A cripple who lacks the spiritual greatness of Cervantes—a man, not a superman, virile and complete, in spite of his mutilations—a cripple, I said, who lacks that loftiness of mind, is wont to seek ominous relief in seeing mutilation around him."

His words rang out crystal clear. The heavy silence gave them resonance.

"General Millán Astray is not one of the select minds, even though he is unpopular, or rather, for that very reason. Because he is unpopular. General Millán Astray would like to create Spain anew—a negative creation—in his own image and likeness. And for that reason he wishes to see Spain crippled, as he unwittingly made clear."

Epilogue

At this point General Millán Astray could stand it
no longer and shouted wildly:

"Muera la Inteligencia!" — "To death with Intelligence!"

"No, long live intelligence! To death with bad intellectuals!" corrected Don José María Pemán, a journalist from Cádiz. A few voices seconded him, many
hands were clenched to check an imprudent impulse
to applaud the aged Rector. The Blue Shirts felt tempted
to become violent, true to totalitarian procedure. But
a most unusual realization of their numerical inferiority
strangled this impulse at birth. Arguments flared up
round the names of academicians who had disappeared
or been shot. Irritated "sh's" came from various sides.
Some gowned figures had gathered round Don Miguel, some Blue Shirts round their vilified hero.

At last the clamor died down like the sound of surf
on the beach, and the groups dispersed. Don Miguel
again became visible to the assembly, very erect, his
arms folded and his gaze fixed straight ahead, like the
statue of a stoic. Once more his word dominated the
hall.

"This is the temple of intellect. And I am its high
priest. It is you who are profaning its sacred precincts.

"I have always, whatever the proverb may say, been
a prophet in my own land. You will win, but you will
not convince. You will win, because you possess more
than enough brute force, but you will not convince,
because to convince means to persuade. And in order
to persuade, you would need what you lack—reason
and right in the struggle. I consider it futile to exhort
you to think of Spain. I have finished."

The controversies flamed up again, interrupted by
sudden waves of unanimous silence.

Then Don Esteban Madruga, Professor of Common

Law, a straightforward and truly good man, took Don Miguel by the arm, offered his other arm to Doña Carmen Polo de Franco, and led them out of the room. Unamuno walked with perfect dignity, pale and calm. Franco's wife was so stunned that she walked like an automaton.

The Junta in Burgos was consulted. Franco's orders came: they were inexorable. If the offence was considered grave enough, the Rector of Salamanca was to be executed without delay. The offence was indeed considered to be so, but somebody who was better advised realized that such an act would fatally injure the prestige of the nascent "Movement of Salvation." It was therefore never carried out.

Don Miguel retired to his home. His house was kept surrounded by the police.

And shortly afterwards, thus guarded, Miguel de Unamuno died suddenly on the last day of 1936, a victim of a stroke of the brain, achieving lasting peace.

Abbreviations

The most frequently cited sources of the letters are abbreviated as follows:

Alas	Adolfo Alas, ed., *Menéndez Pelayo, Unamuno, Palacio Valdés, Epistolario a Clarín*. Madrid, 1941.
Benítez	Hernán Benítez, *El drama religiosa de Unamuno*. Buenos Aires, 1949.
Fernández Larraín	Sergio Fernández Larraín, ed., *Cartas inéditas de Miguel de Unamuno*. Santago de Chile, 1965.
OC	*Obras Completas de Miguel de Unamuno*. Madrid: Afrodisio Aguado.
Ortega	"Epistolario entre Unamuno y Ortega," *Revista de Occidente* (Madrid), Oct. 1964.
Sur	"Cartas de Miguel de Unamuno," *Sur* (Buenos Aires) 117 (July 1944), 119 (Sept. 1944), and 120 (Oct. 1944).

Notes

The text used for the *Diario íntimo* is the 1970 pa-
perback edition published by Alianza Editorial in Madrid, under the editorship of Elaine Kerrigan, Eduardo
Naval, and Aníbal Froufe. There are two more editions
extant: one is contained in Volume VIII of the Escelicer edition of Unamuno's *Obras Completas*, entitled
Autobiografía y recuerdos (1966), pp. 773-780; the
other is *Miguel de Unamuno: Diario íntimo*, with a
prologue and study by P. Félix García (Escelicer, 1970),
which contains a complete facsimile of the holograph.

In preparing the *Diary* for this volume, the editors
have abridged the original text to reduce its extreme
repetitiousness—keeping, however, enough repetition
to give the reader a notion of the obsessive character
of the author's preoccupations during the intense period of his life when he wrote the *Diary*. Omissions
within paragraphs are indicated by ellipses contained
in brackets, but omissions of entire paragraphs are not
indicated. Unamuno used a long dash to show breaks
between sections (which may correspond to entries),
and these dashes are preserved, as well as his characteristic slanted cross at the opening of a notebook
and elsewhere. It should be observed that Unamuno
rarely dated an entry.

For the most part, Unamuno quoted Biblical passages in the Vulgate, and Latin devotional texts in
their original language. The editors have put these

275

passages into English, consulting the King James Version in the case of the quotations from scripture.

This is the first translation of the *Diary* into English. At this writing, there are no translations into any other languages.

The letters in this volume, with the single exception of a letter to Jorge Luis Borges which was transcribed from the archives of the Casa-Museo Unamuno in Salamanca, have been selected and translated from various printed sources identified in the notes. Unamuno's correspondence was vast: over 40,000 letters to him and from him are contained in the archives in Salamanca. Most of his correspondence, including all of his letters to members of his family, remains unpublished. Of the letters available, the editors have chosen those that reflect, in a representative way, the course of his intellectual development; his religious concerns and preoccupations; his opinions on the political concerns of the day; his relations with friends and family; his reflections on matters of autobiography; and his hopes and fears for the Spanish nation. Several letters are included which bear directly on his religious crisis of 1897, which is recorded in the *Diary*. Some of the letters have been abridged by the editors, where they either repeat material adequately covered in other letters or deal with matters of the moment which are of little interest to readers of a later time. All deletions are indicated by ellipses contained in brackets.

In the notes, all citations of various works of Unamuno refer to the sixteen-volume edition of his *Obras Completas* (*OC*) published by Afrodisio Aguado. On occasion, the nine-volume Escelicer edition of *OC*—later than the Afrodisio Aguado, but no longer in print—has been consulted.

Notes

ix. The quotations from *Tragic Sense of Life* are from vol. 4 of the present edn., pp. 3 and 4. Some of the material in this introduction is drawn from Allen Lacy, *Miguel de Unamuno: The Rhetoric of Existence* (The Hague, 1967), no longer in print, but containing a much fuller account of Unamuno's crisis of 1897 and of the various scholarly interpretations of his religious position.

xi. *Unamuno writes in Recuerdos*: *OC*, I, 316.

Balmes: Jaime Luciano Balmes (1810-1848), Catholic philosopher, priest, and mathematician.

the first cause . . . : Recuerdos de niñez y de mocedad, *OC*, I, 310.

I bought a cheap notebook . . . : Recuerdos, *OC*, I, 312.

xii. *Ortí y Lara . . . "the little blasphemy shop on Montera Street"*: "La afanosa grandosidad española," *OC*, VIII, 719. Juan Ortí y Lara (1826-1906) was Unamuno's instructor in metaphysics.

xiii. *"Seek the kingdom of science . . ."*: quoted in Armando Zubizarreta, *Tras las huellas de Unamuno* (Madrid, 1960), p. 17.

a disturbing and strangely prescient dream: quoted in Zubizarreta, p. 123.

xiv. *own true mother as well . . . :* from *How a Novel Is Made*, in vol. 6 of the present edn., p. 442.

a letter to Pedro Corominas: quoted in Zubizarreta, p. 132. The other letters mentioned are contained in the present volume.

xvii. *Ernest Becker*: in *The Denial of Death* (New York, 1973), p. 284.

xix. *he denounced General J. Millán Astray*: The account by Luis Portillo of this last public act of Unamuno is given as the epilogue of this volume.

xx. *Ilundain's reply* . . . : Ilundain's letter is in Hernán Benítez, *El drama religiosa de Unamuno* (Buenos Aires, 1949), pp. 269-274.

xxi. *Tragic Sense*: the quotation is from vol. 4 of this edn., p. 349.

xxii. *Bonhoeffer*; Dietrich Bonhoeffer (1906-1945), *Letters and Papers from Prison* (tr., London, 1959), p. 160.

xxvi. *Emilio Salcedo*: See his *Vida de Don Miguel* (Salamanca, 1964), pp. 421-422.

DIARY

According to an editorial note in the Alianza edition, the notebooks ("cuadernillos," as Unamuno called them) were of the small kind, on lined paper, used by students. The first four are 21 by 16 cms., the fifth is 15 by 10.5 cms. Unamuno prefaced each notebook with a sort of cross, reproduced in the present edition. He separated paragraphs with a long dash; a somewhat shorter dash is used in this edition.

3. *Leopardi, Amiel, Obermann: Obermann*, a much-admired novel by Etienne Pivert de Sénancour (1770-1846), French romantic, written in the Jura region as a series of letters. Giacomo Leopardi (1798-1837), Italian poet frequently quoted by Unamuno throughout his work and whose "La ginestra" he translated in 1899. Henri Frédéric Amiel (1821-1881), Swiss writer, author of a *Journal intime*, one of Unamuno's favorite books. Leopardi, Amiel, and Sénancour were all greatly admired by Unamuno: he called them "cardiac" writers since they wrote as much with their hearts as with their pens.

4. *Augustine*: The translation is from *The Confes-*

Notes

sions of St. Augustine, tr. John K. Ryan (New York, 1960), p. 230.

Spinoza's proposition: "A free man thinks of death least of all things, and his wisdom is a meditation not of death but of life." *The Ethics*, from *The Chief Works of Benedict de Spinoza*, tr. R.H.M. Elwes, Vol. II (New York, 1952), p. 232.

those verses from the Odyssey: tr. Robert Fitzgerald (New York and London, 1961), Book VIII, lines 579-580:

> That was all gods' work weaving ruin there
> So it should make a song for men to come.

Spencer: Herbert Spencer (1820-1903), English philosopher. Unamuno was a great admirer of Spencer in the 1880s and translated a good many of his essays into Spanish even after he violently rejected his materialism.

6. *St. Augustine*: tr. Ryan, p. 270.

beneath history: the unspectacular continuity of humankind underlying "recorded" history was dubbed *intrahistoria* ("infrahistory") by Unamuno in his five essays *En torno al casticismo* (1895; in book form 1902); the contrast between *historia* and *intrahistoria* provides one of the major themes of his 1897 novel *Peace in War* (vol. 1 of the present edn.).

7. *"Suffer little children . . ."*: "But Jesus said, Suffer little children, and forbid them not, to come unto me: for of such is the Kingdom of heaven" (Matt. 19:14). "But Jesus called unto him, and said, Suffer little children to come unto me, and forbid them not: for of such is the kingdom of God" (Luke 18:16)

D.J.J.: Don Juan José (de Lecanda). Father Lecanda had been a friend of Unamuno since the latter's adolescent years in Bilbao. In his lovely and gentle memoir of his childhood, *Recuerdos de niñez y de mo-cedad*, 1908 (*OC*, I, p. 314), Unamuno recounts his experiences as a member of a religious congregation of which Lecanda was director. Unamuno's article "En Alcalá de Henares, Castilla y Vizcaya" (1889, *De mi país, OC*, 146-163) is dedicated to "mi muy querido amigo don Juan José de Lecanda."

Immediately after the crisis of March 1897, the priest invited Unamuno to spend Holy Week with him in Alcalá. Unamuno probably began to write the *Diario* in Alcalá a few days before 14 April 1897 and must have returned to his teaching duties shortly thereafter.

Imitation of Christ: the translation is from *The Imitation of Christ, by Thomas à Kempis*, in *The Consolation of Philosophy*, ed. Irwin Edman (New York, 1943), p. 264.

8. *when the crisis broke upon me*: See introduction, above, pp. xiv-xv. The crisis is generally considered the turning point of Unamuno's career: from then on the problem of personal immortality and the existence of God becomes the axis of his thought and writings.

in the calm of Alcalá: following upon his spiritual crisis and his three-day seclusion in the monastery of San Esteban in Salamanca, Unamuno spent Holy Week in Alcalá de Henares with Father Juan José de Lecanda.

Fr. Faber: Frederick William Faber (1814-1863), English Oratorian and spiritual writer.

Early in life, Faber was involved in the Oxford Movement with Newman. He became an Anglican priest in 1839, but in 1845, after Newman's conversion to Roman Catholicism, Faber followed him, being ordained a Roman priest in 1847. Cardinal Manning compared his preaching to that of St. Bernard. Faber's principal works, in addition to many hymns, are *All for Jesus* (1853), *Growth in Holiness* (1854), *The Blessed Sacrament* (1855), *The Creator and the Creature* (1856), *The Foot of the Cross* (1858), *Spiritual Conferences* (1859), *Bethlehem* (1860), and *The Precious Blood* (1860), all translated into several European languages.

It was probably Father Juan José de Lecanda (see earlier note) of the Oratorians of Alcalá de Henares who introduced Unamuno to Faber's works Although the Unamuno Museum-Library in Salamanca has only an ·1886 edition of *Bethlehem*, the library at the Pontifical University of Salamanca contains several of Faber's books in Spanish translation, which show signs that Unamuno read them with some care.

In this case, Unamuno is quoting from *La preciosa sangre*, chapter 1, and the English given is a retranslation. It is therefore of interest to quote the original text as it appears in *The Precious Blood* (10th Amer. edn., Baltimore, n.d., p. 27): ". . . the real dates in a man's life are the days and hours in which it came to him to have some new idea of God. To all men perhaps, but certainly to the thoughtful and the good, all life is a continual growing revelation of God. We may know no more theology this year than we did last year, but we undoubtedly know many fresh things about God. Time itself discloses him. The operations of grace illuminate him. Old truths grow: obscure truths brighten. New truths are incessantly dawning. But a new idea of God is like a new birth."

The best study to date on Unamuno and Faber's works is Armando Zubizarreta, "Don Miguel de Unamuno, lector del P. Faber," *Salmanticensis* (Salamanca), VII (1960), fasc. 3, 667-701.

12. *"Amends can be made . . .":* The original English reads, "All the actions of life are reparable, except the last, and that is absolutely irreparable, even by any

supernatural process. Moreover, that last act—which
is death—fixes all the other actions of life, and gives
them their final meaning." Faber, *Spiritual Conferences*
(new edn., Philadelphia, 1957, p. 56).

13. *mecum eris in paradiso*: ". . . today shalt thou
be with me in paradise" (Luke 23:43).

Dimas: St. Dimas, traditional name given to the
Good Thief crucified to Christ's right. An apocryphal
gospel tells of how Dimas, the leader of a band of
robbers, helped the Holy Family go peacefully during
their flight to Egypt.

15. *lilies of the field* . . . : Matt. 8:26, 28; Luke 12:
24, 27.

16. *"What is truth?"*: See Unamuno's essay by this
title in *The Agony of Christianity and Essays on Faith*,
vol. 5 of this edn., pp. 165-184.

My rebellion . . . : See *Peace in War*, vol. 1 of this
edn., pp. 68-72, where Unamuno's youthful struggle
with the doctrine of Hell is reflected in his portrayal
of Pachico Zabalbide's effort to "rationalize his faith."

19. *infinite vanity of all that is*: "infinita vanità del
tutto," the last line of Leopardi's "A se stesso."

20. *Stupefy yourself with work*: here, an echo of Pascal's notion of the perils of *divertissement*.

21. *ye shall be as gods* . . . : Genesis 3:5.

O felix culpa: "happy fault," from St. Augustine,
who called the original sin a *felix culpa* because it led
to the redemption by Christ.

22. *wretched death's body*: "O wretched man that I
am! Who shall deliver me from the body of this death?"
Romans 7:24.

24. *"And he said unto them* . . ."*: See below, the
letter of 25 May 1898 to Ilundan, pp. 129-132.

26. *The Superman*: For Unamuno's reading of
Nietzsche and the latter's influence on his thought, see

The Tragic Sense of Life, vol. 4 in the present edn., p. 57n.

Be ye therefore perfect . . .": Matt. 5:48.

Stirner: Max Stirner was the pseudonym used by Johan Kaspar Schmidt (1806-1856), author of *Der Einzige und sein Eigentum* (1845), translated as *The Ego and His Own*. In reaction against the systematic philosophy of Hegel, Stirner, who had an impact on Nietzsche, argued that the only thing we have certain knowledge of is the individual, who must cultivate his uniqueness against all generalities. He was roundly attacked by Marx and Engels in *The German Ideology* (1845).

27. *"Behold the handmaiden . . ."*: Luke 1:38.

28. *Imitation of Christ*: The entire passage reads, "Give to God that is his and ascribe to thyself that is thine: give God thanks for his grace and to thyself guilt and pain." Tr. from the Edman edn.

29. *I have a letter from Leopoldo*: Leopoldo Gutiérrez Abascal, a close friend of Unamuno, was one of the first to know of Unamuno's religious crisis, in a letter of 31 March 1897. In January 1898 Unamuno sent Gutiérrez the notebooks making up the diary of his crisis. The latter replied later in the year, expressing his affection and stating that he was much moved by the contents of the notebooks. "Nevertheless," he warned, "I believe that it is dangerous to make such confidence. Be careful, especially with the literati." A paragraph later, he wrote, "You have suffered much and much suffering still lies ahead for you. I did not find in them [the notebooks] a single happy note, in the midst of such sorrow." The letter is quoted from Armando Zubizarreta, *Tras las huellas de Unamuno* (Madrid, 1960), p. 121, in an essay on "La inserción

de Unamuno en el cristianismo: 1897," which contains a discussion of the relations between the two men.

In Madrid late in 1918, Unamuno attended his friend Leopoldo on his deathbed. After his death he published a moving tribute to a man who also counted José Ortega y Gasset as a friend. The eulogy is reprinted in the Escelicer edition of *OC*, VIII, pp. 558-560, under the title "Leopoldo Gutiérrez Abascal: Recuerdos íntimos." Of all Unamuno's friends Gutiérrez was the most sympathetic to his attempt to regain his faith.

Erquiza: Crescensio de Erquiza, another friend. Unamuno's cross marks his death.

30. *D.J.J.*: see above, note for p. 7.

32. *Harnack, II, p. 10*: the entire quotation runs "Die Virginität ist die specifisch christliche Tugend und der Inbegriff aller Tugenden . . ." and is from Harnack's *Lehrbuch der Dogmengeschichte*, Vol. II (Freiburg i. B., 1888).

Adolf von Harnack (1851-1930), German Protestant theologian and Church historian, best known for his monumental *Dogmengeschichte* (1886-1890), or *History of Dogma* (English tr., 1899), which Unamuno was reading avidly during the period he kept his diary. The edition of Harnack used by Unamuno is the third and definitive one.

Harnack's writings are among the most annotated in the Unamuno library. Remarkably erudite, they recount how early Christian faith hardened into dogma as it encompassed Greek philosophy and Roman law. Harnack advocated a cleansing of all "non-essential" matter in Christian teaching and a return to faith as "the beginning, middle, and end of all religious fervor." His research and thought had a great impact on Unamuno's thinking and writing well into the twentieth century.

Harnack, II, p. 9: the passage referred to runs as follows (*History of Dogma*, Vol. III, Boston, 1901, p. 127): "The Church would hardly have succeeded in following out the free path opened up to it by Constantine had it not had in its midst, beside its transcendent promises, a power to which all, Greek and barbarian, polytheist and monotheist, learned and unlearned, required ultimately, if reluctantly, to bow. And that power was the asceticism which culminated in monachism."

33. *Maestro Granada*: Luis de Granada (1505-1588), Dominican ascetic writer, translated *Imitation of Christ* and wrote a great deal in Latin, Portuguese, and Spanish. His most important works are *Guía de pecadores* (1567) and *Introducción del símbolo de la fe* (1583). The quotation comes from the *Guía de pecadores*, Ch. II, lines 18-20 (in the *Clásicos castellanos* edn., Madrid, 1953, p. 20).

36. *My little Raimundín*: Cf. above, introduction, p. xiv.

Denifle's book: Heinrich Seuse Denifle, *Das geistliche Leben. Blumenlese aus den deutschen Mystikern und Gottesfreunden des 14. Jahrhundertes* (Graz, 1873; 4th edn., 1895). Denifle (1844-1905), Austrian, was a Dominican historian of the Middle Ages.

38. *Imitation*: translation from *The Imitation of Christ*, ed. Harold C. Gardiner, S.J., p. 107.

Sirach 1 . . . Denifle: In *Das geistliche Leben*, p. 32, Denifle writes: "O was grosser Weisheit liegt an der Furcht und emsigen Bertrachtung des Todes! Diese Furcht is en Anfang aller Weisheit,[2] und ein Weg zu aller Seligkeit." ("O what great wisdom lies in the fear and steady contemplation of death! This fear is the

beginning of all wisdom and a way to all blessedness.")
Footnote 2 reads "Sirach, I, 16." Sirach is another
name for the apocryphal book of Ecclesiasticus, which
reads at 1:16: "To fear the Lord is the fullness of
Wisdom . . ."; cf. Psalm 111:10: "The fear of the Lord
is the beginning of wisdom."

The quotation cited as Sirach 7:40 is not to be found
in ch. 7.

40. *Integralists*, *Carlists*, *Mestizos*, *Neos*: political
factions in Spain.

Integralists: followers of a movement produced by a
schism within the Carlists; they sought to combat liberalism wherever it appeared.

Carlists: originally followers of Don Carlos (1788-
1855), who laid claim to the throne of his deceased
brother Ferdinand VII. Before his death, Ferdinand
repealed the Salic Law so that his daughter Isabel II
could succeed him. The so-called Carlist Wars were
civil conflicts (1833-1840; 1870-1875) between the
extremely traditional Carlists and the central government. See *Peace in War*, vol. 1 in this edn., introduction.

Mestizos: in the colonies, the children of mixed Spanish and Indian parentage.

Neos: apologists who made of Catholicism a political
program to combat liberalism and secularism. Both
Neos and Integralists published in *El Lábaro*, a periodical of the diocese of Salamanca.

43. *Homer . . . theme to sing*: cf. above, note for p.
4.

50. *"God wills," said Fénelon*: Unamuno took this
passage from Frederick William Faber's *Growth in
Holiness; or The Progress of the Spiritual Life*. We quote
the entire passage from the seventh American edition
(Baltimore, 1864), pp. 43-44: "I do not know a better

picture of recollection than Fénelon's description of grace, which he sent to a person who was just going into a convent. 'God would have you wise, not with your own wisdom, but with His. He will make you wise, not by causing you to make many reflections, but on the contrary by destroying all the unquiet reflections of your false wisdom. When you shall no longer act from natural vivacity, you will be wise without your own wisdom. The movements of grace are simple, ingenuous, infantile. Impetuous nature thinks much and speaks much. Grace thinks little and says little, because it is simple, peaceable, and inwardly collected. It accommodates itself to different characters. It makes itself all to all. It has no form nor consistence of its own; for it is wedded to nothing, but takes all shapes of the people it desires to edify. It measures itself, humbles itself, and is pliable. It does not speak to others according to its own fulness, but according to their present needs. It lets itself be rebuked and corrected. Above all things, it holds its tongue, and never says anything to its neighbour which he is not able to bear: whereas nature lets itself evaporate in the heat of inconsiderate zeal."

In a footnote, Faber specified his source as *Lettres*, V, p. 398.

Fénelon: François de Salignac de La Mothe-Fénelon (1651-1715), archbishop of Cambrai, author of *Télémaque* (1699); denounced as a heretic for his quietism, he was condemned by the Pope in 1699.

53. *Canillas . . . Calzada*: towns near Salamanca.

54. *Pompeyo Gener*: (1848-1921), Catalan critic, historian, and anti-religious philosopher, a follower of the positivists Comte and Littré, influenced by Renan.

57. *The crisis . . . on me*: Armando F. Zubizarreta, in his "Desconocida antesala de la crisis de Unamuno:

1895-1896" (*Tras las huellas de Unamuno*, Madrid, 1960), indicates that by 1895 Unamuno was already convinced of the limitations of intellectualism but was inhibited by the atheistic humanism of the period and the fear of what his friends would say if he made open confession of his change of mind.

Martínez Ruiz: José Martínez Ruiz (1873-1967), better known as Azorín, outstanding essayist, novelist, dramatist. A member of the Generation of 1898, he was most responsible for the diffusion of the idea of such a "Generation."

Navarro Ledesma: Francisco Navarro Ledesma (1869-1905), journalist and critic, author of a life of Cervantes (1905).

58. *Harnack*: cf. above, note for p. 32.

60. *Act as if you did believe and you will come to believe*: an echo of Pascal's *Pensée* 233 (Braunschvig edn.), "You would like to attain faith, and do not know the way; you would like to cure yourself of unbelief, and ask the remedy for it. Learn of those who have been bound like you, and who now stake all their possessions. . . . Follow the way by which they began, by acting as if they believed, taking holy water, having masses said etc. Even this will naturally make you believe, and deaden your acuteness." (*Pascal's Pensées*, intro. by T. S. Eliot, New York, 1958, p. 68.)

From the prologue to Arzadun's work: Cf. "Prólogo al libro *Poesías* de Juan Arzadun," *OC*, VII, 140-147. The prologue is dated "Salamanca, May 1897" and the excerpt Unamuno includes in the diary is to be found, with some changes and additions, on p. 144.

Juan Arzadun, born in Bilbao, and Unamuno's childhood friend, was a military man and the author of *Poesías* (Bilbao, 1897).

61. *"O wretched man . . ."*: Romans 7:24.

Notes

65. *in-me-myself-ism*: the Spanish is *ensimismarme*.

My anonymous contributions: The weekly *Lucha de Clases*, official organ of the Agrupación Socialista de Bilbao (Socialist Party of Bilbao) was founded in 1894, its first issue appearing on 7 October 1894. On 11 October 1894 Unamuno wrote an enthusiastic letter (included in this volume) to the director, Valentín Hernández, and in 1894 and 1895 the periodical published three more letters and an article, all signed by Unamuno. For about two years—from October 1895 to April 1897—he contributed regularly. (Between 1894 and 1897 he also wrote articles on socialism for other publications.) During March 1897, the period of the crisis, he contributed nothing and on 10 April 1897 there appeared his article "Fuera credos!" which was an attack on all political dogmas. Thereafter, his contributions were very rare, and they end in 1904. Unamuno left the Socialist Party at the end of 1896 or beginning of 1897.

70. *D[eath]*: Unamuno here used the letter *M* as an abbreviation of *Muerte*.

74. *city of Sychar*: Unamuno gave Siquem-Sychem, but the episode occurred in Sychar (John 4:5).

Except ye see signs: Unamuno is wrong here both about the person(s) addressed and the verse. Christ was not addressing "the Jews," but a certain nobleman of Cana. The words Unamuno quotes appear in John 4:48, not 4:45 as he gave it.

76. *Imit.*: in the Gardiner edition, the entire passage (p. 94) reads: "I am He who raises those who are sorrowful to help and comfort, and lifts up those who know their own unsteadiness to be grounded in the sight of my Godhead forever."

Carlyle: Unamuno's library contained several of

Thomas Carlyle's works, and he translated much of the English writer's *The French Revolution*.

77. *Dionysius the Areopagite*: the name given to the author of writings that exercised enormous influence on medieval thought, a supposed disciple of St. Paul, converted by him to Christianity.

The works of Dionysius (most commonly referred to as the Pseudo-Dionysius), which reconcile neo-Platonism and Christianity, were probably written at the end of the fourth or the beginning of the fifth century and are printed in Migne's *Patrologia Graeca*, vols. 3-4.

Didon: Le P. Henri Didon (1840-1900), French preacher and theologian. His most important work, *Jésus-Christ*, in two volumes, appeared in 1890; translated into English the next year.

The quotation is from *Jésus-Christ* (Paris, 1891), I, p. 259.

78. *"They place their idea in place of God's thought."*: From *Jésus-Christ*, I, p. 260: "Le Règne de Dieu, pour les Juifs égarés par les préjugés politiques et religieux, n'est que leur propre règne. Tous mettent leurs idées à la place de la pensée de Dieu [. . .]."

79. *St. Cyril*: (315?-386), bishop of Jerusalem, remembered for his eighteen *Cathecheses* dealing with the mysteries or sacraments of baptism, confirmation, and the Eucharist.

"Blessed are those . . . be comforted.": "Blessed are those that mourn: for they shall be comforted" (Matt. 5:4). "Blessed are ye that weep now: for ye shall laugh" (Luke 6:21).

SELECTED LETTERS

85. TO PEDRO DE MUGICA, 26 JULY 1890: From Fernández Larraín, pp. 121-125. Pedro de Mugica,

born in Bilbao, taught philology for over half a century at the University of Berlin. Over one hundred of Unamuno's letters to him survive—in Chile, where they were sent for safekeeping by their recipient, who feared keeping them in his possession because of Unamuno's frequent critical remarks about German militarism.

86. *my work on the war*: the novel *Paz en la guerra*, published in 1897; tr., *Peace in War*, vol. 1 of the present edn.

La Guerra . . . Euskaldune: newspapers, in Castilian and in Basque, from the time of the Second Carlist War.

87. TO PEDRO DE MUGICA, 1 SEPT. 1890: From Fernández Larraín, pp. 125-128. The events of the Carlist War that Unamuno mentions—the rock-throwing contests, the entrance of Don Carlos into a Spanish town, the battle of Somorrostro, the Carlist pilgrimages, the bombardment of Bilbao, the Glorious Revolution of '68, and others—figure prominently in his novel.

my fiancée: Concepción Lizárraga y Ecenarro de Unamuno (1864-1934), known familiarly as Concha or Conchita.

90. TO JUAN ARZADUN, 18 DEC. 1890: From *Sur*, 119 (Sept. 1944), pp. 33-42. Juan Arzadun, a Basque who was the same age as Unamuno, was for many years his intimate friend. In his youth he wrote poems, stories, and plays, but then took up a successful military career, retiring in 1930 as a general in the Spanish artillery.

96. *Guiris*: the Basque anti-Carlist partisans of Maria Cristina, regent for her daughter, Isabella II, during the 1830s; later, the name was given generally to partisans of the Liberals.

97. *Diderot*: "Lettre au sujet des observations du

Chevalier de Chartellux sur le traité du mélodrame,"
Œuvres complètes de Diderot (Paris, 1875), VIII, 509.

98. TO JUAN ARZADUN, 17 JUNE 1892: From *Sur*,
119 (Sept. 1944), pp. 43-50. Unamuno had been appointed to his chair at the University of Salamanca in
1891.

99. *Deusto*: Jesuit college near Bilbao.

102. *Old Times and Middle Times: Tiempos antiquos
y tiempos medios*, Unamuno's title for a series of articles
published in the literary supplement of the Bilbao
newspaper *El Nervión* in 1891 and 1892. In 1907 he
added to these articles and published them as a book,
Recuerdos de niñez y de mocedad (Memoirs of Childhood and Youth). One section of the *Recuerdos* was
translated into Italian in G. Beccari, *Piccola antologia
spagnola* (Florence, 1926), but unfortunately there have
been no English translations. This book remains both
a prime source for understanding Unamuno's early life
in Bilbao and a powerfully poetic and universal evo-
cation of the form of human existence which is childhood. See Manuel García Blanco's discussion of these
newspaper articles in *OC*, I, 16-19.

103. *Zeferino González* ...: González (1831-1894),
theologian, cardinal, and primate of Spain; both volumes of his *Filosofía elemental*, which Unamuno
detested, are in the Unamuno library in Salamanca.
Juan Ortí y Lara (1826-1906), ultra-conservative
Catholic, Unamuno's professor of philosophy at the
University of Madrid. Urbano González Serrano (1848-
1904), another Spanish philosopher. The other two,
evidently professors of philosophy, could not be identified.

105. *These words*: Unamuno wrote what follows in
red ink.

Notes

106. *Concha . . . we await what will come*: a reference to her pregnancy.

106. TO JUAN ARZADUN, 3 AUG. 1892: From *Sur*, 119 (Sept. 1944), pp. 51-53.

I am avenged: These strange words linking vengeance and fatherhood may possibly have some reference to Unamuno's older brother, Félix, with whom he was never on good terms.

La Débâcle: a novel by Emile Zola, published in 1892, a vivid portrait of the Franco-Prussian war.

107. *Enrique Areilza*: a childhood friend of Unamuno; in their youth they often took walking trips into the mountains near Ceberio. A physician who was sharply critical of Unamuno's egoism and his religious position and who espoused atheism for many years, Areilza died a Catholic.

Somorrostro: a valley region northwest of Bilbao, the site of a bloody battle during the Second Carlist War which was depicted in *Peace in War*.

108. *What his name will be*: Unamuno's eldest child was named Fernando.

109. TO PEDRO DE MUGICA, 28 MAY 1893: From Fernández Larraín, pp. 195-198.

Hölderlin: Friedrich Hölderlin (1770-1843), German poet; friend of Hegel, Schelling, and Schiller; died insane; deeply influenced the thought of Martin Heidegger.

Lange: Friedrich Albert Lange (1828-1875), German philosopher; in his *History of Materialism* (1866; tr. 1877), he argued that materialism provided a framework for science, while idealism had the same effect for poetry and religion.

110. *Münsterberg*: Hugo Münsterberg (1863-1916), German psychologist who taught at Heidelberg and after 1892 in the U.S.A. at Harvard.

Notes

Amicis: Edmondo de Amicis (1846-1908), author of a very successful novel, *Cuore* (1886); he also wrote on the hardships of Italian emigrants and the lot of Italian workers.

the prattle of Bebel: August Bebel (1846-1913), eminent German socialist, opposed to revisionism, in favor of the class struggle and solidarity of the international proletariat; Bismarck's enemy.

111. TO PEDRO DE MUGICA, 1893: From Fernández Larraín, pp. 211-213.

113. TO VALENTÍN HERNÁNDEZ, 11 OCT. 1894: From Carlos Blanco Aguinaga, "El socialismo de Unamuno, 1894-1897," *Revista de Occidente* (Madrid), Aug. 1966, pp. 167-169. The letter was published on the first page of the Bilbao weekly *La Lucha de clases* (The Class Struggle), on 21 Oct. 1896. In 1894 Unamuno joined the Agrupación Socialista de Bilbao, a party founded in July 1886, and remained a member until early 1897. *La Lucha de clases*, the official organ of the Agrupación, first appeared on 7 Oct. 1894, under the directorship of Valentín Herández. Various of Unamuno's contributions to the weekly are included in the Escelicer edition of *OC*, XI, 477ff.

117. TO LEOPOLDO ALAS, 31 MAY 1895: From Alas, pp. 49-56. *Leopoldo Alas*: (1852-1901), pen-name "Clarín," was a famous novelist, short-story writer, and widely-read critic.

these plains: the countryside around Salamanca.

discussion of adolescence: cf. letter of 28 May 1895, pp. 46-48 of same collection. Unamuno had read in one of Alas's articles that adolescence is not a period of energy but a critical age, despite its etymology. In the deleted part of this letter Unamuno, speaking as a philologist, discusses the roots of the word *adolescent*, refers to the use made of it by classical writers, and

294

then expresses the hope that Alas will not misinterpret his observations as pedantry.

On Authentic Tradition: En torno al casticismo, a series of five essays published in the review *La España Moderna* between February and June of 1895 and brought out in book form in 1902. (Not tr. into English.) The point of these essays is to refute a narrow interpretation of the essence of Spain, to show that history records only the tempestuous surfaces of things and that beneath history lies "infra-history," the slow, silent, uninterrupted, and unspectacular flow of life, at which level those characteristics separating one people from another are insignificant. Unamuno thus advocates that Spanish intellectuals choose two directions at once: a profound knowledge of the grass roots, of the national landscape and its people, and a well-developed receptivity to invigorating currents from abroad.

118. *my place in the university*: Unamuno was appointed to the chair of Greek at the University of Salamanca in 1891.

119. *my remarks on the mystics*: In *En torno al casticismo* Unamuno contrasted the introspective, "egotistical" nature of the Spanish (Castilian) mystics with the outgoing nature of St. Francis of Assisi, the main exemplar of Italian mysticism.

my teacher Menéndez Pelayo: Marcelino Menéndez y Pelayo (1856-1912), great literary historian and critic, one of Unamuno's university professors, and member of the examining board which granted him his chair at Salamanca.

Zeferino: See note to p. 103.

121. *my anticasticismo*: In *En torno al casticismo* Unamuno emphasizes that what is considered "traditionally" Spanish (*castizo*) actually separates Spaniards from the rest of humanity.

121. TO JUAN ARZADUN, 30 OCT. 1897: From *Sur*, 119 (Sept. 1944), pp. 53-59. For a direct, personal account of Unamuno's religious crisis, see also his letter of 3 Jan. 1898 to Jiménez Ilundain, as well as his Diary, both in the present volume.

122. *my own children*: The two older sons were Fernando and Pablo. The "sick one" was Raimundo, the "little girl" Salomé, named for Unamuno's mother.

124. TO PEDRO DE MUGICA, 2 JAN. 1898: From Fernández Larraín, pp. 260-262.

126. TO PEDRO JIMÉNEZ ILUNDAIN, 3 JAN. 1898: From Benítez, pp. 255-263. The published correspondence between Unamuno and Ilundain—36 letters by Unamuno and 21 by Ilundain, written between 1897 and 1922, which take up pp. 244-458 of the Benítez book—is a treasure-trove for anyone wishing to follow Unamuno's intellectual development and public career from his religious crisis (detailed in this letter of 3 Jan. 1898) until the period just before his exile in 1923. In Ilundain, Unamuno had one of his most persistent and sympathetic correspondents, although Ilundain was often critical of some of his most fundamental points of view, especially as regards religion.

Pedro Jiménez Ilundain was born in Pamplona in 1865, moved to Paris at the turn of the century, and in 1921 immigrated to Buenos Aires, where he died in 1943. A successful businessman with deep literary and philosophical interests, he was politically liberal and generally opposed to religion during the greater part of his life, professing an atheism he later abjured by returning to Catholicism. He saved almost all of the letters Unamuno wrote him and made copies of certain of his own. After his death, his heirs arranged to have all the surviving correspondence made public.

Notes

The correspondence between the two men was initiated by Ilundain in two letters written from Gallarta
in 1897. He praised Unamuno's first novel, *Peace in
War*, remarking that like young Ignacio Iturriondo,
one of the characters, he was the son of a candy-store
owner devoted to the conservative Carlist movement.
Characteristically, he tempered his praise for the novel
with strong criticism, particularly of the last several
pages, which he recommended (with sound sense, some
readers may feel) be reduced from several printed pages
to three or four lines in any subsequent edition. He
wrote Unamuno that he perceived him as something
of "an atheist-mystic, a skeptic-believer," and thus a
fascinating thinker but one difficult to follow. He pur-
sued some of the same themes in his second letter,
before Unamuno wrote him back.

St. Paul . . . "him declare I unto you": St. Paul's
speech on the Areopagus (Acts 17:22-23).

Evangelical Meditations: a series of religious essays
Unamuno planned to write during his religious crisis.
The only one to be published was "Nicodemus the
Pharisee" (see vol. 5, pp. 113-147 of this present
edition).

128. *the struggle between these two beings*: Rom. 7:24.

129. *John Stuart Mill, Claude Bernard, Littré: Claude
Bernard*: French physiologist (1813-1878), proved role
of pancreas in digestion; *Littré*: Emile Littré (1801-
1881), French lexicographer, positivist, disciple of
Comte, known for his monumental dictionary of the
French language. Unamuno's remark about John Stuart
Mill ending up in the faith of his childhood is of course
wrong on several counts. That Mill had a childhood
in the ordinary sense of the word is dubious; that during his early years he had religious faith is improbable;

and that he spent his final days as a religious believer belies the facts.

129. TO PEDRO JIMÉNEZ ILUNDAIN, 25 MAY 1898: From Benítez, pp. 264-269. The various meditations Unamuno discusses here—"The Social Kingdom of Jesus," "The Prayer of Dimas," and "St. Paul on the Areopagus"—are all prefigured in his diary entries in 1897.

131. *"be ye therefore perfect"*: Matt. 5:47.

132. TO LEOPOLDO ALAS, 9 MAY 1900: From Alas, pp. 84-99.

the article . . . which you devote to my "Three Essays": Unamuno's "Three Essays" (*Tres ensayos*), published in 1900, are "Adentro!" ("Go Within Yourself!"), "La ideocracia" (Ideocracy), and "La fe" (Faith). The first two are to be found in *OC*, III, 418-427 and 428-440. The third essay is in *OC*, XVI, 99-113; tr. in vol. 5 of the present edition, pp. 148-164. For Leopoldo Alas ("Clarín"), see above, note for p. 117. Clarín's critique or review of *Tres ensayos*, published 7 May 1900 in *Los Lunes de El Imparcial* (Madrid), is reproduced in Manuel García Blanco, *En torno a Unamuno* (Madrid, 1965), pp. 209-214.

133. *Valera*: Juan Valera y Alcalá-Galiano (1824-1905), diplomat, critic, and outstanding novelist. He published the novel *Morsamor* in 1899.

Ganivet: Ángel Ganivet (1865-1898), novelist and essayist; his best-known work is *Idearium español* (1897). Cf. "Ganivet, Philosopher" in *Our Lord Don Quixote*, vol. 3 of the present edn., pp. 368-373.

134. *Campión*: Federico Balart Campión (1831-1905), critic and poet, now mainly forgotten.

Blasco Ibáñez: Vicente Blasco Ibáñez (1867-1928), noted novelist and political writer; his 1898 novel *La*

Notes

Barraca (*The Cabin*) represented naturalism in Spanish literature.

Galdós: Benito Pérez Galdós (1843-1920), most celebrated of Spanish novelists of the nineteenth century. Unamuno's attitude toward his work was often unjustly negative.

Pereda: José María de Pereda (1833-1906), celebrated regional novelist; conservative in politics.

Teresa: Clarín's play was badly received in March 1895.

Maeztu: Ramiro de Maeztu (1874-1936), influential journalist and essayist; in his early years a Nietzschean radical, in his later years a Fascist sympathizer.

135. *Heautontimorumenos*: From Greek, "self-tormentor." A comedy by Terence (163 B.C.) adapted from a play of the same name by Menander.

As St. Paul said: Romans 7:19.

137. *"uprooted," as Barrès might say*: Maurice Barrès (1862-1923), French writer to whose novel *Les Déracinés* (1897) Unamuno is alluding.

138. *translation of Schopenhauer*: The translation is *Sobre la voluntad en la naturaleza* (*On the Will in Nature*; Madrid, 1900, 244 pp.), from *Über den Willen in der Natur* (1836), by the German philosopher of pessimism Arthur Schopenhauer (1788-1860), a decisive influence on Unamuno. Clarín commented: "This begins well, at least. A truly direct translation from the German, from the hand of a professor who truly knows German—and Spanish, Señor Unamuno. It is a pleasure to read this translation, which does not have the flavor of German—or French—but of pure, simple, normal Spanish." Quoted from Manuel García Blanco, "Unamuno, traductor y amigo de José Lázaro," *Revista de Occidente* (Madrid), 19 Oct. 1964, p. 110.

Notes

an article of his on teaching: "La enseñanza del Latín en España" (orig. 1894), *OC*, III, pp. 306-329.

140. *protagoric*: In his review, Clarín says, "Braunschweig has said about truth and its relativism something more *protagoric* than what Unamuno now says." Protagoras (c. 480-c. 421 B.C.), Greek sophist.

141. *Rodó*: Jose Enrique Rodó (1871-1917), Uruguayan writer, whose most important book, *Ariel*, was published in 1900. In this book, he urged South American youth to uphold spiritual values (Ariel) against the naturalism and utilitarianism (Caliban) he attributed to North America. The "classic leisure" Rodó explained is *otium*.

Mercure: the literary journal *Mercure de France*.

Ochoa: Eugenio de Ochoa (1815-1873), critic and scholar.

Horizontes, by the man who wrote . . . Dolores: Federico Balart Campión's *Dolores* (1889) was a collection of essays. His second volume of poems was *Horizontes* (1897).

Martínez Ruiz: José Martínez Ruiz (1873-1967), most commonly known as Azorín, essayist, critic, playwright, novelist.

Morsamor, The Cabin, Campión, Ganivet: see earlier notes to this letter.

Doña Emilia: Condesa de Pardo Bazán (1852-1921), short-story writer, critic, and novelist.

142. *a pupil of Don Marcelino*: Marcelino Menéndez y Pelayo. See above, n. to p. 119.

"Joaquín Rodríguez Janssen": Unamuno's indirect satirical attack on the followers of Menéndez y Pelayo appeared 5 May 1895 in *Revista Nueva*; not in *OC*.

Echegaray: José Echegaray (1832-1916), playwright who shared the Nobel Prize in literature in 1904 with Frédéric Mistral.

Notes

143. *Landscapes: Paisajes* (1902), a collection of lyrical travel articles.

Regenta: La Regenta (1885), Clarín's greatest novel, one of the finest produced in nineteenth-century Spain, a powerful and detailed picture of life in the cathedral city of Vetusta (actually Clarín's Oviedo).

145. *the influence of my novel on Galdós' "Luchana"*: *Luchana* (1899) belongs to the third series of Galdós' *Episodios nacionales*.

Guimerá: Ángel Guimerá (1845-1924), outstanding Catalan man of letters of the nineteenth century; his two masterpieces are *María Rosa* (1849) and *Terra baixa* (1897).

in my drama: the reference is to *La esfinge* (The Sphinx), originally called *Gloria o paz* (Glory or Peace), the story of the conflict between the need for glory, the glory of living in history, and the need for the tranquility of living in eternity. The protagonist's wife, childless, urges him to be a man of action, a revolutionary leader, but he resigns from the cause in the hope of finding spiritual meaning within himself and then is abandoned and killed.

145. TO LEOPOLDO ALAS, 10 MAY 1900: From Alas, pp. 100-105.

the clipping from El Imparcial: the review of Unamuno's *Tres ensayos*, printed in *Los Lunes de El Imparcial*, 7 May 1900.

146. *"Faith"*: ("La fe"), the third of Unamuno's "Three Essays," translated in vol. 5 of this edn., pp. 148-164.

Hermann, Harnack, Ritschl: Wilhelm Herrmann (1846-1927), German Protestant theologian who assimilated religion to ethics and was frequently quoted by Unamuno in *The Tragic Sense of Life*; Adolf von Harnack (1851-1930), German Protestant theologian and church historian who exerted a profound influence on Unamuno; Albrecht Ritschl (1822-1889), German Protestant theologian who emphasized religion as a vehicle for human values.

González Serrano: See above, note to p. 103.

Campoamor: Ramón de Campoamor (1817-1901), popular Spanish poet.

147. *the thesis of "Ideocracy"* . . . *erroneous*: Clarín's review found this essay dangerous in its tendency toward ideophobia.

my description of the little church of Alzola: See the essay "Faith," pp. 161-163, where Unamuno contrasts Notre Dame in Paris ("a cemetery of fetishism") with a simple country church in Alzola, a Basque village.

149. TO MIGUEL GAYARRE, 27 SEPT. 1900: From Fernández Larraín, pp. 301-304. The identity of Miguel Gayarre is obscure, but clearly he was not at all sympathetic towards Unamuno. At the end of the letter as printed, there is appended a short note written to Pedro de Mugica in Berlin (see p. 85n. in this volume), from Pamplona, dated 28 Oct. 1900, the first paragraph of which reads: "Friend Mugica: Here is his letter. It is a good example. I haven't answered it and don't think I will. If I see *Unamuno* in Madrid we'll speak about it. *I don't know what pleasure he derives from thinking that everyone else is stupid.* If you see Chaba tell him that I received his letter and *show him this epistolary sermon so he'll see what a Spanish philosopher has in his head.*" (Italics in original.)

Harnack: see above, n. for p. 32.

Sabatier: Auguste Sabatier (1839-1901), professor in the Protestant faculty of Strasbourg and later director of the department of religion at the École des Hautes Etudes in Paris. Unamuno's library contains his *Esquisse d'une philosophie de la religion d'après la psychologie et l'histoire* (Paris, 2d edn., 1896). In his letter to Gayarre, Unamuno is incorrect about the exact title.

151. *primus in orbe terror fecit deus*: "it was fear that first created gods in the world." Statius (Loeb edn., 1928), vol. I, p. 500.

"*Lautphysiologie*": German for physiology of speech sounds.

152. *Spallanzani*: Lazzaro Spallanzani (1729-1799), Italian biologist who studied the circulation of the blood, digestion, and reproduction.

"*Life . . . Linguistic Biology*": "Vida del romance castellano, ensayo de biología lingüística," not published until 1958, when it appeared as "Historia de la lengua española," in *OC*, VI, 924-978.

that ape Caligula: Kaiser Wilhelm II.

152. TO PEDRO JIMÉNEZ ILUNDAIN, 19 OCT. 1900: From Benítez, pp. 319-324.

153. *Barco*: Juan Barco, was a childhood friend of Unamuno. After 1897, Barco was sharply critical of Unamuno's preoccupation with religion. The relationship between the two men suffered an open break in 1902 when Barco told Unamuno falsely that Ilundain had ridiculed him behind his back.

154. *Completely a Man: Todo un hombre*, not the novela *Nada menos que todo un hombre*, but the novel that came out in 1902 under the title *Amor y pedagogía* (Love and Pedagogy), Unamuno's comic masterpiece. The names of the characters as given in this letter do not correspond to those he finally used.

155. *Platonic doctrine of recollection*: see *Phaedo* 73-76.

From Kant to Nietzsche: Unamuno read this work by Jules de Gaultier in the *Mercure de France* of 1899-1900, and he never mentioned it except with strong distaste. In a letter of 7 Dec. 1902 to Ilundain (Benítez, p. 376), he wrote: "I hate rationalism, and I have to proclaim what Kierkegaard called irrationalism. One must fortify the instinct for life against what has been called the instinct for knowledge by that repungnant Gaultier, the author of that indecent, repulsive, and inhuman study, *From Kant to Nietzsche*."

156. *Petronius Sienkiewicz*: Henryk Sienkiewicz (1846-1916), Polish novelist, best known for *Quo Vadis?*, a novel set in the Rome of Nero; won the Nobel Prize for literature in 1905.

Fabiola: Fabiola, or The Church of the Catacombs, an immensely popular, much-translated novel (1854) by Nicholas Patrick Stephen Wiseman (1802-1865), Roman Catholic archbishop of Westminster, and founder of the *Dublin Review* (later the *Wiseman Review*). The son of an Irish merchant, Wiseman was born in Seville and consecrated by his mother as an infant at the altar of the cathedral there to a life of service to the Church. At his death a street in Seville was re-named "Calle del Cardenal Wiseman."

Pérez Escrich: Enrique Pérez Escrich (1829-1897), popular author of such works as *El cura de aldea* (*The Village Priest*) and *La mosquita muerta* (The Hypocrite); despite his fame and success, he died very poor.

157. *translate this formula as you wish*: the word *salud* can mean either health or salvation, depending on context.

157. TO JUAN ARZADUN, 12 DEC. 1900: From *Sur*, 120 (Oct. 1944), pp. 55-61. For Arzadun, see note for p. 90.

Maese Pedro: Maese Pedro or Master Peter is the puppeteer in *Don Quixote*, Part II, Chap. 26. Cf. "Maese Pedro, notas sobre Carlyle," *OC*, III, 522-532, first published in May 1902 in *La España Moderna* (Madrid).

Taine: Hippolyte Taine (1828-1893), French historian. Because Taine was a determinist, Unamuno disliked him as "a great falsifier." In his essay "Maese Pedro," he disparages him for his treatment of Carlyle in his *Histoire de la littérature anglaise*.

158. *Petion . . . Seagreen Incorruptible*: See *Tragic Sense*, vol. 4 of this edition, pp. 387-388.

Vigo: port city in Galicia, northwestern Spain.

Doña Emilia: Condesa de Pardo Bazán (1852-1921), novelist.

Echegaray: José Echegaray (1832-1916), outstanding Spanish dramatist; won the Nobel Prize in Literature, 1904.

Cajal: Santiago Ramón y Cajal (1852-1934), essayist, physician, and histologist; won the Nobel Prize in medicine, 1906.

Maeztu: Ramiro de Maeztu (1874-1936), important critic and essayist.

159. *Natorp*: Paul Natorp (1854-1924), one of the most influential representatives of the Neo-Kantian school at Marburg, headed by Hermann Cohen.

Joaquín Costa: (1846-1911), Spanish literary and juristic scholar and reformer.

160. *the Basque sentiment*: Basque separatism, which Unamuno always opposed, despite his love for his native region.

161. *Guernicaco*: song supporting Basque separatism.

fueros: special legal privileges which traditionally afforded the Basque provinces a measure of autonomy.

Doña Emilia: see above note to p. 158.

St. Ignatius: Loyola (1491-1556), also a Basque, of

whom Unamuno wrote at great length in *Life of Don Quixote and Sancho*, vol. 3 of the present edn.

Catalanism: separatist movement of Catalonia, centered in Barcelona.

162. TO FEDERICO URALES, 1901: From Urales, *La evolución de la filosofía en España* (2nd edn., Barcelona, 1968), pp. 160-165; originally published in Barcelona in two volumes in 1934. The most probable date for this letter is 1901, or not later than 1902. Urales, born Juan Carret (1864-1942), was an often-arrested Spanish anarchist who in 1898 founded *La Revista Blanca*, an important publication of the Spanish labor movement. The journal continued until 1905, after which date Urales devoted himself mainly to writing. His book on the evolution of Spanish philosophy was published in installments in *La Revista Blanca* between 1900 and 1902, and tended to show the radical and anarchistic tendencies of various Spanish thinkers.

164. *Wundt*: Wilhelm Wundt (1832-1920), German philosopher and psychologist; his *Grundzüge der physiologische Psychologie* (Leipzig, 1893), is in Unamuno's library. *James*: William James (1842-1910), the American philosopher. *Bain*: Alexander Bain (1818-1903), Scottish philosopher. *Ribot*: Théodule Armand Ribot (1839-1916), French philosopher and experimental psychologist; several of his books are in Unamuno's library.

"*Nicodemus*": see *The Agony of Christianity and Essays on Faith*, vol. 3 of this edn., pp. 113-147.

165. *Baur*: Christian Baur (1792-1860), German theologian who studied the origins of Christianity. *Harnack*: see above, note to p. 32. *Ritschl*: see above, note to p. 146.

Renan: Ernest Renan (1823-1892), best known for

his *Vie de Jésus*. *Réville*: Jean Réville (1854-1908), Protestant pastor, teacher, and writer. *the two Sabatiers*: Auguste Sabatier (1839-1901), Protestant theologian; his son, Paul Sabatier (1858-1928), is best-known for his *Vie de St. François d'Assise* (1893). *Stapfer*: Philipp Albert Stapfer (1766-1840), Swiss politician who moved to France to help develop the Protestant church there. *Menegoz*: Eugène Menegoz (1838-1921), French theologian and pastor of the Lutheran church in Paris.

Schleiermacher: Friedrich Schleiermacher (1768-1834), German theologian whose major work, *Der christliche Glaube* (2 vols., 1821-1822), made a deep impression on Unamuno. Highly romantic in his theology, Schleiermacher presented religion as lying closer to poetry than to science and linked it to feelings rather than facts and propositions.

Bakunin: Mikhail Bakunin (1814-1876), Russian revolutionary and anarchistic theoretician.

Kierkegaard . . . and Tolstoy: Unamuno was one of the earliest Europeon thinkers ouside Denmark to recognize the importance of Søren Kierkegaard (1813-1855), whose works he began reading in Danish in 1900. He owned fourteen volumes of K.'s works, which are still in his library in Salamanca. While he is correct about Kierkegaard's influence on Ibsen, his similar assertion about Tolstoy is a mistaken conjecture.

166. *the Portuguese poet*: Abilio Guerra Junqueiro (1850-1923), poet, satirist, enemy of religious dogma, and one of Unamuno's favorite writers.

my work as a socialist propagandist: La Ciencia Social of Barcelona put out only eight issues before it was shut down by the government. Unamuno published in this journal four articles: "La dignidad humana" (Jan., 1896); "La crisis del patriotismo" (March, 1896);

Notes

"La juventud 'intelectual' española" (April, 1896); and "Civilización y cultura" (May, 1896). The texts of these articles can be found in *OC*, III, 441-480.

Maeterlinck: Maurice Maeterlinck (1863-1949), Belgian-French writer and dramatist, won the Nobel Prize in 1911; *Le Trésor des humbles*, 1896.

167. TO PEDRO DE MUGICA, 11 FEB. 1903: From Fernández Larraín, p. 318.

168. TO ANTONIO MACHADO, AUG. 1903: An open letter from Unamuno to Machado, entitled "Vida y arte" ("Life and Art"), published in *Helios* (Madrid), Aug. 1903, pp. 46-50, and reprinted in Manuel García Blanco, *En torno a Unamuno* (Madrid, 1965) and in the Escelicer edn. of *OC*, IV, 877-880. Antonio Machado (1875-1939), the most eminent poet of the Generation of '98 in Spain and kindred soul to Unamuno.

your brother Manuel: Manuel Machado y Ruiz (1874-1947), also a well-known poet.

your little book of verse: *Soledades* (Solitudes), published at the end of 1902 and dated 1903. Machado sent Unamuno a copy, inscribed "To Don Miguel de Unamuno, Sage and Poet. Devotedly, Antonio Machado."

your two-year stay in Paris: Machado spent June to Oct. 1899 in Paris with his brother, and returned for several months in 1902.

Léon Bazagette: (1865?-1929), translator and critic of art and literature.

169. *Rubén Darío*: (1867-1916), born Félix Rubén García y Sarmiento in Nicaragua, the most important figure of Hispanic Modernism and a great admirer of the French Symbolists. See Unamuno's letters to him in this volume, pp. 188 and 189.

Gómez Carrillo: Enrique Gómez Carrillo (1873-

1927); born in Guatemala, he left for Europe in 1891 and was passionately fond of the city of Paris.

170. *Tamayo*: Manuel Tamayo y Baus (1829-1898), renowned Spanish playwright, whose best work is *Un drama nuevo* (1867), a tragedy of infidelity set in Elizabethan England.

Hérédia: José María de Hérédia (1842-1905), French Parnassian poet, born in Cuba of a Spanish father and a French mother. His fame rests on his *Les Trophées* (1893), which contains 118 sonnets as well as other poems.

172. *Plato*: the reference here is to his well-known conviction that poetry is subversive of right order, expressed in Book X of *Republic*.

172. TO PEDRO DE MUGICA, 2 DEC. 1903: From Fernández Larraín, pp. 321-324.

176. TO PEDRO DE MUGICA, 19 OCT. 1904: From Fernández Larraín, pp. 333-335.

The King: Alfonso XIII of Bourbon and Hapsburg-Lorraine (1886-1941); abdicated 1931.

177. *Luque*: Augustín Luque (1850-1937), Spanish general.

178. TO PEDRO JIMÉNEZ ILUNDAIN, 9 MAY 1905: From Benítez, pp. 399-401.

your question . . . God: This letter directly answers a question Ilundain asked in a letter written from Paris on 25 Apr. 1905 about what Unamuno meant by the word "God," used so frequently in his writings. Ilundain remarked that for him the word had no more content than the letters that spelled it.

Treatise on the Love of God: Tratado del amor de Dios, at this time Unamuno's working title for the work that was published as *The Tragic Sense of Life*.

Büchner: Friedrich K.C.L. Büchner (1824-1919),

German physician, whose *Kraft und Stoff* (*Energy and Matter*), 1855, was a materialistic view of the cosmos.

Haeckel: Ernst Heinrich Haeckel (1834-1919), German evolutionist and materialistic monist.

179. TO PEDRO DE MUGICA, 10 NOV. 1905: From Fernández Larraín, p. 346.

180. TO JOSÉ ORTEGA Y GASSET, 17 MAY 1906: From Ortega, pp. 3-4. José Ortega y Gasset (1883-1955), essayist, critic, philosopher, was the author of *The Revolt of the Masses*, *Man and Crisis*, *On Love*, and *The Origins of Philosophy*, to name only a few of his influential works. The story of the relations between Spain's two leading thinkers of the twentieth century is complicated. Ortega was a champion of clarity and rigorous thinking, an outspoken admirer of German culture (which Unamuno contemptuously called *Kultura*), a Europeanizer as against Unamuno's confessed anti-scientific "Africanism." Ortega had scant patience with Unamuno's contradictions and about-faces, his personalism, and his obsession with the question of immortality. If one of Unamuno's favorite writers was Kierkegaard, Ortega avowed he could not abide the Dane. Indicative of the wide gulf between the men is the fact that Unamuno never contributed to the *Revista de Occidente*, the journal Ortega founded in 1924. For a summary of their relationship, see Martin Nozick, *Miguel de Unamuno: The Agony of Belief* (new edn., Princeton, 1982), pp. 194-196. See also Unamuno's letter about Ortega to Mugica in this vol., p. 179.

you write: Ortega's letter, which Unamuno is answering, has not been found.

For nothing worth proving: Alfred Lord Tennyson, "The Ancient Sage."

181. *Treatise . . . God*: see note to p. 178.

I am writing verse: Unamuno's first volume of collected verse is *Poesías* (1907). In time he became a extremely prolific writer of poetry.

181. TO JOSÉ ORTEGA Y GASSET, 30 MAY 1906: From Ortega, p. 5. Ortega's letter to Unamuno has not been found.

182. *the talk I gave at the Zarzuela*: "Conferencia en el Teatro de la Zarzuela de Madrid, el 25 de febrero de 1906," *OC*, VII, 658-680; originally published in *El Imparcial* (Madrid), 26 Feb. 1906. After discussing the army, Unamuno referred to Parliament as made up of representatives of rich landowners and accused the press of being controlled by wealthy advertisers. He continued by stressing his opposition to Basque and Catalan separatism and by deploring the low level of national culture. He attacked Roman Catholicism as "the most active element in the de-Christianization of the people," adding "I am a man who doesn't need some wholesale-peddler of divine grace in order to come to terms with God." Finally, he stated that he believed only in "inner, personal revolution," not "revolution from above, below, or in the middle." "Revolution from above" was one of the political slogans of the conservative politician Antonio Maura, prime minister from December 1903 to December 1904 and again from January 1907 to October 1909; the Liberals who opposed him, and who were in power at the time of Unamuno's talk at the Zarzuela in Madrid, spoke of "revolution from below." See Raymond Carr, *Spain: 1808-1939* (Oxford, 1966), pp. 477-489.

learned Germania: Ortega studied (1905-1907) at Leipzig, Berlin, and Marburg.

182. TO JUAN MARAGALL, 4 JAN. 1907: From *Unamuno y Maragall: epistolario y escritos complementarios* (Barcelona, 1951), pp. 45-47. Juan Maragall (1860-

1911) was a Catalan poet and essayist who also wrote in Castilian; he was much admired by Unamuno.

183. *L'infinita vanitá del tutto*: "the infinite futility of everything," from "A se stesso" by the Italian poet Giacomo Leopardi (1798-1837), often quoted by Unamuno.

a piece I published in El Imparcial: "La cultura española en 1906," published in *Los Lunes de El Imparcial* (Madrid), December 1906, where he called Maragall a "noble, serene poet." *OC*, V, 319-325.

184. *Maura*: See note for p. 182.

184. TO JUAN MARAGALL, 15 FEB. 1907: From same source as foregoing letter, p. 56.

186. TO NIN FRÍAS, 19 JULY 1907: From *Trece cartas inéditas de Miguel de Unamuno a Alberto Nin Frías* (Buenos Aires, 1962), pp. 83-88. Alberto Nin Frías (1882-1937), was a Uruguayan writer. In 1902, Unamuno reviewed his "Ensayos de crítica e historia y otros escritos," *OC*, VIII, 180-186.

Taine: Hippolyte Taine (1828-1893); despite Unamuno's claim here that he admired Taine, he generally spoke disparagingly of him.

the Sabatiers: see above, note to p. 165.

Réville: see note to p. 165.

Amiel: Henri Frédéric Amiel (1821-1887), like Rousseau a Swiss; his *Journal intime* was much quoted by Unamuno.

in your own book: Ensayos sobre la filosofía de la historia de España.

187. *infrahistory*: one of Unamuno's favorite themes, elaborated in *En torno al casticismo* (On Authentic Tradition), 1895, 1902, and given flesh in *Peace in War*; the silent, ongoing, unspectacular events that underlie those recorded in books of history.

St. Teresa: Santa Teresa de Jesús (1515-1582), great Spanish mystic.

St. John of the Cross: San Juan de la Cruz (1542-1591).

Bossuet: Jacques Benígne Bossuet (1627-1704), French prelate, writer, and orator; condemned Fénelon's quietism.

Hildebrand: Gregory VII (1020-1085), pope from 1073 to 1085, famous for his conflict with Henry IV.

Ganivet: Ángel Ganivet (1865-1898), Spanish essayist and novelist, known especially for his *Idearium español* (1897), an attempt to analyze the Spanish temper. He and Unamuno met in the spring of 1891 when they were both taking competitive examinations for teaching posts. After two months of close friendship, they never saw each other again. Five years later Unamuno saw Ganivet's articles in *El Defensor de Granada* and they began a correspondence which lasted from 1896 to 1898. Their exchange of public letters in *El Defensor* was republished by Unamuno in 1912 as *El porvenir de Espāna* (Spain's Future), *OC*, III, 953-1015. Ganivet wrote two novels, *La conquista del reino de Maya por el último conquistador español*, *Pío Cid* (1897) and *Los trabajos del infatigable Pío Cid* (The Conquest of the Mayan Kingdom by the Last Spanish Conqueror, Pío Cid; The Works of the Tireless Pío Cid). Unamuno refers here to the second novel (1898).

188. TO RUBÉN DARÍO, 26 SEPT. 1907: From Manuel García Blanco, *America y Unamuno*, pp. 62-63. Rubén Darío (1867-1916), born Félix Rubén García y Sarmiento in Nicaragua, was the outstanding exponent of Hispanic Modernism.

everything disagreeable I may have said about you: As Unamuno confesses in an essay "¡Hay que ser justo y bueno, Rubén!" ("One Must Be Just and Good,

Rubén!"), published in *Summa* (Madrid), 15 March
1916, and found in *OC*, VIII, 518-523, he once said
of the Nicaraguan poet, whose features were unmis-
takably Indian, that "Rubén's Indian feathers are dis-
cernible under his hat." The remark reached Darío's
attention and on 5 Sept. 1907 he wrote Unamuno a
letter from Paris, expressing not anger but great admiration for Don Miguel. The letter begins, "It is with
a feather under my hat I write you," and it ends,
"Therefore, be just and good"—words which Unamuno picked up in his essay.

189. *Poesías*: Unamuno's first volume of poetry,
published in 1907.

your piece on the legend of Verlaine: see Rubén Darío,
Obras completas (Madrid, 1950), II, 292-299. Darío—
but not Unamuno—was a passionate admirer of the
French poet Paul Verlaine.

189. TO RUBÉN DARÍO, 10 NOV. 1907: From same
source as foregoing letter, pp. 64-66.

191. TO LUIS ROSS, 16 DEC. 1907: From Fernández
Larraín, p. 383. On Luis Ross (1883?-1908), see
Unamuno's essays "La tragedia de Luis Ross" (*OC*,
VIII, 429-438) and "Prólogo a *Más allá del Atlántico
de Luis Ross Mugica*" (*OC*, VII, 223-237).

These tributes to the young Chilean Luis Ross are
among the most moving essays by Unamuno. The
relationship between the two men began when Unamuno was attracted by Ross's letters to him from Chile.
Then the young man, not long married and accompanied by his pregnant wife Matilde Brandau de Ross,
came to Spain. First they went to Galicia, then to
Salamanca for a visit which lengthened into a month
and a half, and which Unamuno described as a "spiritual holiday" for himself. The bond between the two
men, separated by two decades in age, grew stronger.

Unamuno said that it was as if they had known each other from infancy, and he was totally captivated by Ross's "moral integrity."

Ross and his wife went on to Madrid, where their child was stillborn, and not long afterward, Ross too died, of appendicitis, at the age of twenty-five. Unamuno called his death "a misfortune for Chile and for Spain," and soon wrote that "Luis Ross's death revealed to me further secrets of Providence and makes me reflect on the noblest and purest form of intelligence, which is the splendor of virtue."

191. TO PEDRO JIMÉNEZ ILUNDAIN, 16 JAN. 1908: From Benítez, pp. 419-421.

my Memoirs of Childhood and Youth: Recuerdos de niñez y de mocedad (Madrid, 1908), *OC*, I, 235-348, originally published in the Bilbao newspaper *El Nervión* in 1891 and 1892, under title *Tiempos antiquos y tiempos medios* (Old Times and Middle Times).

192. *my Quixote: Vida de Don Quixote y Sancho, según Miguel de Cervantes, explicada y comentada por Miguel de Unamuno* was first published in Madrid in 1905. It has seen many subsequent editions and has been translated into German, French, and Italian. It was published in 1927 (New York) in a translation by Homer P. Earle, and it appears in Anthony Kerrigan's translation as a part of *Our Lord Don Quixote*, vol. 3 of the present edn.

Treatise on the Love of God: see above, note to p. 178. [*of the Jesuits*]: In the text of this letter as reprinted by H. Benítez (S.J.), these words do not appear. Instead there is an ellipsis, apparently editorial in origin, and a note (p. 421) in which Benítez indicates that Unamuno referred here to "the members of a religious order of Spanish origin," for whom he felt "aversion, despite his high regard for the order's founder" (St. Ignatius of Loyola).

193. *a trip to Spanish America*: Unamuno never made this journey.

193. TO LUIS ROSS, 1 OCT. 1908: From Fernández Larraín, pp. 387-388.

194. TO MATILDE BRANDAU DE ROSS, 23 OCT. 1908: From Fernández Larraín, p. 389. See note to letter of 16 Dec. 1907. After the death of her husband, Unamuno accompanied his young widow, Matilde Brandau Galindo de Ross, a Chilean jurist and educator, to Lisbon, where her ship departed for Chile. For the next three decades the epistolary friendship continued between Matilde Ross and Unamuno, whose wife also wrote occasionally. For additional letters to Sra. Ross in this volume, see pp. 217, 235, and 250.

195. TO PEDRO DE MUGICA, 13 APR. 1909: From Fernández Larraín, pp. 349-350.

Julius Kaftan: (1848-1926), professor of religion at Berlin and representative of the Ritschlian "liberal" theology. His books *Dogmatik* (Tübingen, 1909) and *Die Wahrheit der christlichen Religion* (Basel, 1888) are both in Unamuno's library at Salamanca.

197. TO TEIXEIRA DE PASCOAES, 4 MAR. 1909: From *Epistolario Ibérico, Cartas de Pascoaes e Unamuno* (Nova Lisboa [Angola], 1957), pp. 38-39. Teixeira de Pascoaes (1877-1952), pseud. of Joaquim Pereira de Vosconceios, an eminent Portuguese poet, was one of Unamuno's favorites. A constant in Unamuno's life and thought was his fondness for Portugal, its landscape, its people, and its literature. The correspondence between the two men lasted from 1905 to 1934.

198. *Amarante*: Teixeira's family estate, where Unamuno stopped during one of his many visits to Portugal.

Notes

Senhora da Noite: Lady of the Night (1909), a long poem.

Souls and Things of Portugal: became *Por tierras de Portugal y de España* (Through Regions of Portugal and Spain), 1911, which included the essays on the various places mentioned in the letter.

Corrêa de Oliviera; Antonio Corrêa de Oliviera (1879-1960), Portuguese writer; *Elogio de los sentidos* (In Praise of the Senses).

199. TO CASIMIRO GONZÁLEZ TRILLA, 2 OCT. 1909: From "Doce cartas inéditas a González Trilla," *Revista de la Universidad de Buenos Aires*, No. 16 (Oct.-Dec. 1950), pp. 547-548. Casimiro González Trilla (1880-19??), taught Spanish literature at the University of Zaragoza and then that of Madrid.

in my native region: Bilbao.

200. *La Vida es sueño*: drama by Pedro Calderón de la Barca (1600-1681).

200. TO CASIMIRO GONZÁLEZ TRILLA, 12 NOV. 1909: From same source as foregoing letter, pp. 548-549.

The year 1909 was filled with political unrest in Spain. Melilla, a garrison town in North Africa belonging to Spain, was reorganized at the orders of Antonio Maura, the conservative governmental minister who feared war with the Moors. Incidents precipitated a Spanish attack on the Moors, and the active reserve was mobilized. Losses in North Africa were heavy, and the war was very unpopular, especially in Madrid and Barcelona. In late July a general strike was called in Barcelona to protest mobilization, and violence broke out during "the tragic week" ("la semana trágica"). Order was not restored until August 1, when military courts began to function and executed the leaders of the outbreak, including the anarchist Francisco Ferrer (1849-1909), who was shot.

Ferrer's execution aroused a furor in Spain, much of the same sort the Sacco-Vanzetti affair later did in the U.S. In 1909 Unamuno was anti-Ferrer, but later, in 1917, he confessed that his approval of Ferrer's execution had been a mistake.

When Trilla received this letter from Unamuno, he allowed it to be published in newspapers. When Unamuno found out he sent him a postal card (10 June 1910): "You were wrong in making my letter to you on the Ferrer case public. It is not that I'm afraid of making my ideas known, but the letter was a very private one, and it has a tone, an emphasis, that should never be used in anything meant for the public. A thing said confidentially loses its truth—yes, its truth— when made public. But what's done is done, and I just hope it will not happen again. Everything is all right here. I wish you a good year of good health, faith, liberty, and work. MIGUEL DE UNAMUNO."

Ferrer . . . his schools: In 1901 Ferrer founded the coeducational and anarchist Escuela Moderna de Barcelona.

201. *Jews, scientists, and dolts*: It is important to recognize that Unamuno was not an anti-Semite. Throughout his letters to Pedro de Mugica (Fernández Larraín, *Cartas ineditas de Miguel de Unamuno*, Santiago de Chile, 1965), he speaks admiringly of the Jews. For example, in 1895 (p. 230), "The more the anti-Semites speak about the Jews, the more attractive I find the Jews." And in 1898 (p. 261), "But why this prejudice against the Jews which comes out in your letters from time to time? I admire those people, and let me be frank about it. I admire them for many reasons, including their anti-military and cosmopolitan spirit and their opposition to anything symbolized by that intolerable Emperor [Kaiser Wilhelm]." And in

1933 ("De nuevo la raza," *OC*, VI, 908) he asked, with regard to German anti-Semitism, "What is this persecution of the Jews if not savagery?"

202. TO PEDRO DE MUGICA, 7 JUNE 1911: From Fernández Larraín, p. 351.

203. TO JOSÉ ORTEGA Y GASSET, 21 NOV. 1912: From Ortega, pp. 19-22. Unamuno is answering a letter of 1 Oct. 1912 from Ortega, which has not been found. For Ortega's relation with Unamuno, see above, note to p. 180.

de Onís, the neophyte: Federico de Onís (1885-1966), born in Salamanca, son of the university librarian, and Unamuno's disciple. In 1916 he came to Columbia University, where he was head of the Spanish department for several decades. With Anthony Kerrigan, Martin Nozick, and Herbert Read, he was one of the original editors of the present Selected Works of Miguel de Unamuno in English translation.

204. *last Sunday . . . this sleepy city awake*: see "Discurso en el Círculo Mercantil de Salamanca, el 11 de noviembre 1912," *OC*, VII, 831-852.

Canalejas: José Canalejas (1854-1912), several times a cabinet minister, prime minister from 1910 to 12 Nov. 1912, when he was assassinated. Although a devout Roman Catholic, he wished to check the growth of religious orders and to subject the clergy to the laws of the land.

205. *Ferrerian anarchism*: see letter of 12 Nov. 1909 to González Trilla and accompanying note to p. 200.

Nakens: José Nakens (1841-1908), a powerful journalist of republican beliefs.

Simarro: Luis Simarro (b. 1851), republican, physician, professor at University of Madrid, director of the insane asylum at Leganés.

Notes

Besteiro: Julián Besteiro (1870-1940), socialist leader and professor of philosophy at Madrid.

Morente: Manuel García Morente (1888-1944), disciple of Ortega, professor of philosophy at Madrid, translator of Kant, and author of books on philosophy. In later life he converted to Roman Catholicism and became a priest.

Maura: see above, note to p. 182.

La Cierva: Juan de la Cierva y Peñafiel (1869-1938), conservative politician who occupied several high governmental posts. During the "tragic week" in 1909 in Barcelona, he was Ministro de Gobernación (Interior) under Maura.

"*mancomunidades*": the Catalans' long struggle for more autonomy.

206. *La Fuente de San Esteban*: a town near Salamanca.

Elorrieta: Tomás Elorrieta, a professor at the University of Salamanca.

Costa: Joaquín Costa (1844-1911), outstanding Spanish reformer and author of books on law, economics, history.

Herrmann's "Ethics": Wilhelm Herrmann (1848-1922), liberal Protestant theologian at Marburg who assimilated religion to ethics.

Cohen's "Logik": Herrmann Cohen (1842-1918), Neo-Kantian professor at Marburg with whom Ortega studied.

Croce: Benedetto Croce (1866-1952), Italian idealistic philosopher.

208. *Vitoria*: Francisco de Vitoria (1486-1546), Spanish theologian and theoretician on the conduct of international affairs.

Soto: Domingo de Soto (1494-1560), Spanish theologian and jurist.

Notes

Melchor Cano: (1509-1560), Spanish theologian.

208. TO PEDRO DE MUGICA 21 JAN. 1914: From Fernández Larraín, pp. 356-358.

209. *Intelligenti pauca*: a word to the wise is sufficient.

210. TO JOSÉ ORTEGA Y GASSET, 3 SEPT. 1914: From Ortega, pp. 22-23.

my dismissal: When Unamuno returned from vacation in Portugal on 30 Aug. 1914, he read in the newspapers that the Minister of Public Education, Francisco Bergamín, had dismissed him as rector of the University of Salamanca. Even today, the exact reasons for the dismissal, which aroused widespread furor among intellectuals, remain obscure, although Unamuno's anti-German public pronouncements may have had something to do with the matter. On 2 Sept. 1914 Ortega wrote Unamuno from Victoria:

> Friend Don Miguel,
> On the road, I learn from the press of Bergamín's blast. If his move involves the least injustice or even disdain or odium for *Kultur*, I ask you to count on me unconditionally—on me, my pen, and my bad temper.
> I shall be in Victoria, Sur 5, until the 7th.
> Yours, ORTEGA

211. *Meditations on Quixote*: *Meditaciones del Quijote*, Ortega's first book, published in 1914 and one of his most important; English translation by Evelyn Rugg and Diego Marín, New York, 1961.

211. TO GIOVANNI PAPINI, 15 JULY 1915: From Vicente González Martín, ed., *Miguel de Unamuno: crónica política española (1915-1923)* (Salamanca, 1977), pp. 88-92. Papini (1881-1956) was a journalist, critic, polemicist; a leader of Italian Futurism, he returned to Roman Catholicism in 1920.

212. *two Spains*: metaphor, in long use, denoting

the continuing struggle between conservative and liberal Spaniards.

Salandra: Antonio Salandra (1853-1931), Italian premier at outbreak of WW I, who brought Italy into the war in 1915 on the Allied side, despite the Triple Alliance (1882) of Germany, Austria-Hungary, and Italy; forced to resign in 1916 because of military difficulties; after the war he was briefly a moderate supporter of Mussolini.

213. *Vázquez de Mella*: Juan Vázquez de Mella (1861-1928), outstanding orator who represented the Carlists in Parliament.

Gott mit uns: God with us; *Wir mit Gott*; We with God.

214. *Schadenfreude*: joy in someone else's suffering.

Werther: the hero of *The Sorrows of Young Werther* (1774), a novel in diary and epistolary form by Johann Wolfgang von Goethe (1749-1843). Werther, whose love for Charlotte S., who is engaged and then married to another man, drives him to excessively poetic agony and then to suicide, was widely admired by a whole generation of young European readers who emulated his style of dress—and, in some cases, his act of self-destruction.

Leopardi: Giacomo Leopardi (1798-1837), greatest modern poet of Italy; Unamuno's admiration for his work was constant throughout his career, and he translated his "La Ginestra" ("The Broom Plant") into Spanish as "La Retama." When exiled in 1924 by Primo de Rivera he carried with him Leopardi's *Canti*, along with the New Testament and *The Divine Comedy*.

215. *Treitschke*: Heinrich von Treitschke (1834-1896), German historian and political writer whose advocacy of power politics was influential at home and

caused distrust of Germany abroad. A vociferous herald of German unity through Prussian might, he opposed socialism, despised Metternich and the English, supported German colonialism, believed that Germany was the true heir of the Holy Roman Empire, and espoused the State as the center of life, not to be inhibited by the check of a parliament.

216. TO PEDRO JIMÉNEZ ILUNDAIN, 26 SEPT. 1915: From Benítez, p. 449. See also in Benítez, p. 447, another short letter to Ilundain, dated Salamanca, 30 Sept. 1914, in which Unamuno broods over his dismissal as rector, muses about his fiftieth birthday and the ten years of active life he believes remain to him, and ventilates his distaste for Germany: "Now what has me preoccupied is the war. I will write a book about it, a book against Germanic pedantry. (Even German brutality is unnatural and carried out in a pedantic way.) It will, of course, probably be studied as a text in Germany ten or twenty years from now."

217. TO MATILDE BRANDAU DE ROSS, 7 JAN. 1916: From Fernández Larraín, pp. 398-401. For Matilde Brandau de Ross and the circumstances surrounding her husband's death and his friendship with Unamuno, see above, note to p. 191.

220. *Iquique*: small city on the Pacific coast at the northern extreme of Chile.

220. TO ELVIRA REZZO, 28 JUNE 1919: From *Sur*, 117 (July 1944), pp. 7-9. In a preamble Juan Arzadun writes that "Señora Elvira Rezzo de Henriksen was kind enough to give us the two letters from Unamuno which we publish here. While still unmarried, she studied drawing and poetry in the Academy of Genoa. Attracted by Unamuno's work, she wrote him from Genoa, and he answered. [. . .] Later while she was studying French and Italian literature at the University

of Genoa with Professor Antonio Restori, a famous Hispanist, at his direction she wrote for the review *Nuovo Convito* an article called 'Don Miguel de Unamuno ed il suo pensiero filosofico religioso,' which appeared in 1920. Her brother, Luigi Enrico Rezzo, editor of the *Revista di Roma*, [. . .] published in the 1 Jan. 1924 issue a short story by Unamuno, translated into Italian, and accompanied by an enthusiastic introductory note."

221. *to whose masters . . . much*: Unamuno was especially devoted to Dante, Leopardi, Mazzini, and Carducci.

223. TO PEDRO JIMÉNEZ ILUNDAIN, 6 JUNE 1920: From Benítez, pp. 453-455. Ilundain was then in Paris.

legal prosecutions: From 1914 on, Unamuno's attitude toward King Alfonso XIII changed for the worse. His dismissal as rector, his objection to the pro-German sympathies of the royal family, and the severe economic difficulties within Spain, all contributed to his predictions of impending cataclysm, which the king and his advisers insisted on ignoring. His article "Antes del diluvio" ("Before the Flood") in a newspaper in Valencia seems to be the immediate cause of his indictment. The court sentenced him to sixteen years in prison for offences against the king.

Unamuno refused to request a pardon and was left at liberty temporarily. In response to a message of support from the Argentine Federación Universitaria, he answered on 28 Oct. 1920, attributing the wrong done him to the Queen Mother, María Cristina, who had favored the German cause on several occasions during the war, despite official Spanish neutrality. (Unamuno also blamed her for his dismissal as rector.) The Spanish Supreme Court upheld the decision of the court in Valencia, but the sentence was never car-

Notes

ried out. Unamuno was elected dean of the Faculty of Philosophy and Letters in September 1921, and vice-rector early the next year.

224. *Romanones*: Álvaro de Figueroa y de Torres, Conde de Romanones (1863-1950), eminent Spanish politician who was several times prime minister.

Marcelino Domingo . . . 1917 strike: Marcelino Domingo (1884-1939), republican politician and strike leader. The high cost of living, the Russian Revolution, war profits, and the clash between pro-German and pro-Allies sympathizers were the background of the strike. The army officers organized juntas. Reformist movements promoted strikes in Valencia, Santiago, and Bilbao in late July. On August 13 there was a general strike, on August 15 shootings and killings in Madrid, in Catalonia, and in the mining regions of the north. The strikes were put down by the government. Some leaders were arrested, others fled. The disturbances continued until September 1923 when Primo de Rivera made his coup d'état. Marcelino Domingo was the first Minister of Public Education in the Spanish Republic after the fall of the dictatorship of Primo de Rivera.

225. *Barbusse*: Henri Barbusse (1873-1935), French radical writer and novelist.

Clarté manifesto: Cf. Unamuno's article of 23 Nov. 1919 in *La Nación*, in *OC*, VIII, 983-988.

In Prison under the Russian terror: En prison sous la terreur russe.

225. TO AN UNKNOWN PROFESSOR, DEC. 1923: From Francisco Madrid, *Genio e ingenio de Don Miguel de Unamuno* (Buenos Aires, 1943), pp. 70-71. This letter was written privately to a professor from Spain, whose identity is a matter of dispute, who while on a visit to Argentina unthinkingly gave it to the magazine

Nosotros in Buenos Aires, which published it in Dec. 1923. Martin Nozick points out in his *Miguel de Unamuno: The Agony of Belief* (2nd edn., Princeton, 1982) that it was "the immediate cause of Unamuno's banishment" by the dictator Miguel Primo de Rivera on 21 Feb. 1924. Primo de Rivera (1870-1930) made his coup d'état on 13 Sept. 1923. A royal decree suspended all constitutional rights during the period that the dictator declared would be a temporary "parenthesis" in Spanish history. Unamuno attacked Primo de Rivera openly from the very outset of his dictatorship, but it was the publication of this letter, inadvertently, for a South American audience, that resulted in his exile.

barbarians of the Suspensory: bárbaros del suspensorio: wordplay linking the dictator's suspension of civil rights with a male truss.

226. *the Royal Gander: el ganso real*, King Alfonso XIII.

Martínez Anido: General Severiano Martínez Anido (1862-1938), appointed "captain-general" to control Barcelona after the 1917 strike, member of Primo de Rivera's cabinet, and Minister of Public Order for Franco's Nationalists at the outset of the Spanish Civil War. Of him, Gerald Brenan writes in *The Spanish Labyrinth* (2d edn., Cambridge, 1950), p. 73n., that his "character was well-known and his appointment to put down the 1917 disturbances in Barcelona was an act of defiance to all moderate and humane opinion in the country. . . . Unamuno describes him as follows: 'The man is a pure brute—he can't even talk, he can only roar and bray, though his roars and brays always mean something.' "

Santiago Alba: (1872-1946), leader of liberal left, strong pro-Allies sympathizer in World War II, several times a minister and deputy.

Menéndez Pelayo: see above, note to p. 119.

the Carlist leprosy: The Carlists were conservative supporters of two pretenders to the Spanish throne who brought civil war to Spain in the nineteenth century.

227. *Maeztu*: see above, note to p. 134.

Silvela: Francisco Silvela (1845-1905), conservative lawyer and writer who in the mid-1890s exposed corrupt practices in municipal cement and gas contracts much like those of Boss Tweed and the Tammany Hall gang in the U.S.A.

Arlegui: José Arlegui, chief of police in Barcelona under Martínez Anido; killed by anarchists.

Marañón: Gregorio Marañón (1887-1960), famous physician, professor of endocrinology, and literary essayist.

228. TO ELVIRA REZZO, 2 FEB. 1924: From *Sur*, 117 (July 1944).

the political campaign: against Primo de Rivera and the suspension of all constitutional rights. Very shortly after writing this letter, Unamuno was exiled to the Canary Islands (owned by Spain); he extended his exile voluntarily to the beginning of 1930, when the dictatorship fell.

Rivista di Roma . . . "L'assalto dellamore" . . . your brother: see above, note to p. 220. The story is "El amor que asalta" in Spanish.

229. *Don Juan Chabás y Martí*: (1898-1954), writer and professor, born in province of Alicante, best known for his *Historia de la literatura española* (1932).

Professor Restori: see above, note to p. 220.

230. TO CARLOS VAZ FERREIRA, 11 MAY 1924: From Vaz Ferreira, *Tres filósofos de la vida: Nietzsche, James, Unamuno* (Buenos Aires, 1965), p. 224-226; partially reproduced in García Blanco, *America y Unamuno*

(Madrid, 1964). Vaz Ferreira (1873-1958), of Montevideo, was an eminent Uruguayan intellectual, educator, and author.

the manifesto of the intellectuals of Uruguay: published in the daily *El Diá* of Montevideo, 12 March 1924, it reproduced the telegram sent to Primo de Rivera by Vaz Ferreira, which read: "To exile Unamuno is deplorable . . . All the writers of America will speak for him. We, the American descendants of Spain, who love her so much, exhort you to reconsider or resign, not for the sake of Spain, which shall always be able to save herself, but for your own sake, for at this moment history will work its revenge and you shall have no other salvation."

the Samson Carrascos: those who sought Don Quixote back to his senses.

Maese Pedro: the puppeteer in *Don Quixote*.

232. TO JORGE LUIS BORGES, 26 MAR. 1927: This letter was found in the Unamuno archives in Salamanca. Borges (b. 1899), the world-renowned Argentine poet, short-story writer, and essayist, is often referred to as the father of contemporary Spanish-American literature.

La Prensa: Starting in 1926, Borges wrote for the literary supplement of the Buenos Aires newspaper, *La Prensa*.

"Quevedo Humorista": to be found in Borges, *Inquisiciones* (Buenos Aires, 1925). In a later essay, "Quevedo," included in *Otras Inquisiciones*, Borges says of Quevedo, "he is less a man than a vast and complex literature": p. 42 of *Other Inquisitions*, tr. Ruth L.C. Simms (New York, 1969).

Francisco Gómez de Quevedo y Villegas (1580-1645), poet, scholar, novelist, wit, is one of the great names of Spanish literature. Employed as counselor in

Italy by the Spanish viceroy, the Duke of Osuna, he became involved in intrigue and disgrace and was confined in 1620 to his estate in Torre de Juan Abad. He was again imprisoned for four years (1639-1643) after being suspected as the author of some verses on corruption at court. During his exile, Unamuno came to feel a special kinship with Quevedo, and called the verses of his *De Fuerteventura a París* (1925) "Quevedian sonnets."

Cervantes . . . Lepanto: Cervantes (1547-1616) was permanently crippled in his left hand as a result of wounds sustained in the battle of Lepanto (1571).

Loyola: Ignatius of Loyola or Iñigo de Loyola (1491-1556), founder of the Society of Jesus, the youngest son of a Basque nobleman, was wounded during the French siege of Pamplona. During his convalescence he read much in the lives of Christ and the saints and determined to dedicate his life to the service of Christ.

233. "*Is there not to be one brave soul?*": a line from Quevedo's famous "Epístola satírica y censoria contra las costumbres presentes de los castellanos escrita a Don Gaspar de Guzmán, Conde de Olivares" ("A Satirical Epistle, Critical of the Present Customs of the Castilians, written to Don Gaspar de Guzmán, Count of Olivares.")

envy . . . only bites and never eats: Unamuno saw envy as the cancer of the Spanish soul. See "La envidia hispánica" (1909), *OC*, IV, 417-435. Here he is quoting from Quevedo: "La envidia está flaca porque muerde y no come," in *Virtud miltante contra las cuatro pestes del mundo y cuatro fantasmas de la vida* (written ca. 1634-1636, published posthumously in 1651; in the 1966 edn. of his *Obras Completas*, I, 1228).

the House of Austria: refers to the Spanish Hapsburgs, descendants of Joan the Mad (Juana la loca) and her husband, Philip, starting with Charles V. It was under Philip III and Philip IV that Quevedo suffered imprisonment.

Domine Cabra: the emaciated, miserly schoolmaster pitilessly caricatured in Quevedo's masterly picaresque novel *La vida del Buscón*, first published in 1626.

Just listen to this: The poem that follows is Unamuno's not Quevedo's.

234. *gravely and ascetically . . . Christ's regime*: Some of Quevedo's finest verse is of an intense religious nature. In *La cuna y la sepultura* (1633) he demonstrated the vanity of the world, and he wrote about God and His providence in *Providencia de Dios* (1621). In *Política de Dios, Gobierno de Cristo Nuestro Señor* (1621), he depicts the Christian ruler whose actions are modeled after those of Christ.

Praetorian tyranny: one of Unamuno's favorite derogatory epithets for the regime of Primo de Rivera.

General Severiano Martínez Anido: See above, note to p. 226.

the politics of the rear guard . . . avant-garde: Unamuno disapproved sharply of the younger generation of poets—commonly known as the Generation of 1927 or the Generation of the Dictatorship—who in 1927, at the height of Primo de Rivera's power, celebrated the tercentenary of the death of the great Baroque poet Luis de Góngora (1561-1627), whose work Unamuno never liked.

Hendaye hotel: From Aug. 1925 until he returned to Spain, at the fall of the dictatorship in 1930, Unamuno spent his exile in Hendaye, a small French town in the Basque country of the Pyrenees, just over the border from Spain. During this time he lived in the Hotel Broca, facing the railway station.

the bells of Fuenterrabía, resounding off the stark, na-

ked Jaizquíbel: Fuenterrabía, a Spanish town just across the international bridge from Hendaye; Jaizquíbel, a high peak near the coast.

235. TO MATILDE BRANDAU DE ROSS, 15 NOV. 1927: From Fernández Larraín, pp. 401-402. Brandau de Ross was in Paris.

236. TO MANUEL GÁLVEZ, 15 APR. 1928: From Manuel García Blanco, *America y Unamuno* (Madrid, 1964), pp. 46-49. Gálvez (1882-1962) was an Argentine writer and novelist. His early book *El solar de la raza* (1911) recounts his travels in Spain. *La maestra normal* (1914) is a realistic novel portraying life in a small Argentine town. Unamuno mentioned the first book in the essay "España en moda," *La Nación* (Buenos Aires), 15 Feb. 1914, and the second in "La plaga del normalismo," ibid., 8 June 1915.

Síntesis: The first number of this review (Madrid) is dated June 1927. No. 10 (Mar. 1928) contains Gálvez's study "La filosofía de Unamuno." The issue containing Unamuno's article "Hispanidad," which he had not seen when he wrote this letter, is No. 6.

Bóveda: Xavier Bóveda was the first editor of *Síntesis*.

237. *our school text . . . González*: The book is still in the Unamuno library: *Filosofía elemental*, 2 vols. (Madrid, 1876). It was written when the author (1831-1894) was still bishop of Córdoba. Unamuno unfailingly referred to it with contempt.

Maritain: Jacques Maritain (1882-1973), eminent Neo-Thomist philosopher; reared a Protestant, converted to Catholicism in 1906.

P.E.N.: international organization of poets, essayists, and novelists.

L'agonie du christianisme: cf. vol. 5 of this series, *The Agony of Christianity and Essays on Faith*. In a prologue to the 1931 Spanish edn. of *La agonía del cristianismo*, Unamuno tells us that he wrote the book in Paris at the end of 1924 and turned it over to Jean Cassou, who translated it into French for publication. It has been translated into German and Italian and three times into English. Only in 1931 did it appear for the first time in Spanish.

Warner Fite: See note to Unamuno's letter to him of 19 Nov. 1928, following.

Don Juan: Shortly after this letter, in 1929, Unamuno wrote his Don Juan play, *El hermano Juan o El mundo es teatro* (Brother Juan, or The World Is a Stage), in which he develops the concept of Don Juan adumbrated in these lines.

238. *Erwin Rohde*: (1845-1898), German classicist; his *Psyche, Seelencult und Unsterblichkeit der Griechen* (Tübingen, 1907), was quoted in *Tragic Sense*. It was translated by W. B. Hillis as *Psyche, The Cult of Souls and Belief in Immortality among the Greeks* (London, 1900).

Spencer: Herbert Spencer (1820-1903). Unamuno was fascinated by Spencer in the 1880s and then rejected his influence. Although he translated many of the Englishman's essays, he later found him a *bête noire*.

239. TO WARNER FITE, 19 NOV. 1928: From *De la correspondencia de Miguel de Unamuno*, ed. Manuel García Blanco (New York, 1957), pp. 53-54. This monograph contains a number of letters to Unamuno from Antonio Machado and both sides of the Unamuno-Fite correspondence.

Warner Fite (1867-1955) was professor of philosophy at Princeton University, a strong admirer of Unamuno, and the translater of his *Niebla* (1914) as *Mist, A Tragicomic Novel* (New York, 1928). Fite was the author of several books, including *Moral Philosophy: The Critical View of Life* (New York, 1925), *The Living Mind* (New York, 1930), and *The Platonic Legend* (London, 1934), all in Unamuno's library in Salamanca.

The correspondence between the two men began on 26 Nov. 1925 when Fite wrote Unamuno in Salamanca, sending him reviews of the English translation of the latter's *Essays and Soliloquies* and enclosing a copy of his own *Moral Philosophy*, which on p. 234 contained this footnote: "The reader who is reminded here of the *Quixotic* philosophy of the Spanish writer, Miguel de Unamuno, may be interested to learn that this and the following chapters . . . were completed, nearly as they now stand, before I had heard of Unamuno. Since then I have read nearly all of Unamuno with immense appreciation and delight. Besides *Del sentimiento trágico de la vida* and *Vida de Don Quixote y Sancho* he has published several volumes of essays, also novels, short stories, poems, memoirs of travel in Portugal and Spain, and of his childhood and youth in the Basque provinces. To the English reader who would make the acquaintance of this remarkable man— a *passionate* writer who never loses his critical sense— I recommend the two volumes of admirable translation by Mr. J. F. Crawford Flitch, *The Tragic Sense of Life* [. . .] and *Essays and Soliloquies*. . . ." As Unamuno was in exile in Hendaye, the book and reviews Fite sent him were not received in Salamanca. In 1927 Fite began his translation of *Niebla*, published by Knopf in the following year.

Fite's fascinating and admirable letters to Unamuno reveal Fite to be a man of broad culture and deep learning, with more than a touch of the iconoclast in his nature—as in his argument in his last letter to

Unamuno, written from Princeton on 30 May 1929, that "Platonic piety works like Christian piety: it makes any critical treatment of Plato or of Socrates impossible" and that, in his conviction of impiety and of corrupting the youth of Athens, Socrates "got what was coming to him." Furthermore, of all of Unamuno's translators, Fite had perhaps the most able grasp of the theoretical basis of the art of translation.

your translation of my "Mist" . . . the Dana book and the Dewey. . . Charnwood's "Abraham Lincoln": In August 1928, after the two men had met in Hendaye, Fite wrote Unamuno from Segovia: "I will send you a copy of the translation of *Niebla* as soon as it appears, and also a copy of *Two Years Before the Mast* (by Richard Henry Dana), and I will see if I can find something good on Abraham Lincoln." On 29 Sept. 1928 Fite wrote that he was sending the translation of *Niebla* and also *The Philosophy of John Dewey* (New York, 1928), an anthology of Dewey's writings. Of Dewey, Fite wrote that although his "philosophy has at bottom what I take to be a 'vulgar' point of view (an imputation that he resents), that does not mean that Dewey is vulgar. He is distinctively a man of brains. He is expressing the 'vulgar' point of view resolutely, deliberately, and in spite of the vagueness of his writing he is a man of much critical sense. Of all the men I know in philosophy just now he is the least to be despised." On 4 Oct., Fite sent Unamuno a copy of *Two Years Before the Mast* ("an important item of American, and genuinely American, literature" by a "fine type of New England gentleman"), and on 16 Oct. he sent Lord Charnwood's biography of Lincoln (New York, 1928). According to Manuel García Blanco, *De la correspondencia de Miguel de Unamuno*, pp. 48n. and 52n., the copies of the books by Dana, Dewey, and Lord Charnwood in the Unamuno library are all profusely annotated in the hand of Don Miguel.

240. *I am delighted . . . Pérez Galdós*: In his letter of 4 Oct. Fite wrote Unamuno, "In Madrid José Balseiro . . . (a most delightful fellow) told me that the writing of Pérez Galdós was not 'art' but simply a case of writing down what was in his mind. If so, I am afraid I am not interested in 'art.' I enjoy every page of Pérez Galdós, I get a sense of companionship, and I enjoy seeing the world through his eyes. And it is the same pleasure that I get out of this book of Dana" (From *De la correspondencia*, p. 51).

241. TO JORGE GUILLÉN, 3 JAN. 1929: From *OC*, XV, 877-882. Jorge Guillén (b. 1893), then living in Valladolid, is one of the greatest Spanish poets of the twentieth century; his *Cántico* (definitive edition, 1950) is his most important work. The first *Cántico*, referred to here by Unamuno, had just been published (Madrid, 1928).

my Father Astete: the catechism of Fr. Gasper Astete, S.J. (1537-1601), was widely used in Spain; Unamuno pointed out very often that it fostered passive acceptance of dogma and narrowness of thought.

João de Deus: João de Deus Ramos (1830-1896), Catholic traditionalist, love poet, and satirist.

Don Antonio Sánchez Moguel (1838-1913), Unamuno's professor at the University of Madrid who directed his doctoral thesis.

Camões: Luis de Camões (1524?-1580), Portugal's greatest lyric poet and author of the epic *Os Lusiadas* (*The Lusiads*).

the Andalusian: Sánchez Moguel.

242. *não o conheço*: I don't know him.

when you visited me here, my canciones . . . five hundred and eighty: Guillén visited Unamuno in Hendaye in the summer of 1928. The complete *Cancionero* was published posthumously (New York, 1953) under the editorship of Federico de Onís. The *Cancionero* (*Book of Songs*) contains 1,755 compositions written from 16 Feb. 1928 to 28 Dec. 1936, three days before Don Miguel's death.

242. TO THE EDITOR OF SÍNTESIS, 13 NOV. 1929: From *OC*, XV, 919-923. For the Argentine review *Síntesis*, see above, n. to p. 237.

243. *Guillermo de Torre*: (1900-1973), eminent Spanish critic; married to Borges' sister Norah.

Keyserling: Count Herman Keyserling (1880-1946), German philosopher who wrote in both French and German.

Cassou: Jean Cassou (b. 1897), French Hispanist born in Bilbao, poet, biographer, and translator of Unamuno's *La agonie du christianisme* (1925).

245. TO BOGDAN RADITSA, 16 APR. 1930: From *OC*, XV, 910-912. *Raditsa*: (b. 1904), a Yugoslav writer who had met Unamuno in Hendaye and who was in Athens when this letter was written. Cf. his "Mis encuentros con Unamuno," in *Cuadernos* (Paris), No. 34 (Jan.-Feb. 1959), 45-50.

once the main obstacle was overcome: Primo de Rivera, dictator of Spain, resigned on 28 Jan. 1930. On 9 February, Unamuno crossed the border into Spain, where huge ovations greeted him at every railway station en route home to Salamanca.

246. *Kostis Palamás*: (1859-1943), national Greek poet, twice proposed for the Nobel Prize. Several of his books (in modern Greek) are in Unamuno's library, of which his favorite seems to have been one whose title translates as "The Dodecalogue of the Gypsy" (1907), which he received from Palamás in 1929 with a warm dedication.

Elefteron Vema: (*To eleutheron bima*, or The Free Tribune), Athenian periodical.

the desolation of Karst: an allusion to Unamuno's visit, along with other notables, to the Austro-Italian front in 1917. Cf. "De vuelta de Italia en guerra," *OC*, X, 388. The region (Ital. Carso, Serb. Kras), north of Trieste, is now part of Yugoslavia.

247. TO JACQUES CHEVALIER, 28 APR. 1934: from *OC*, XV, 864-866; *Jacques Chevalier*: (1882-1958), professor of philosophy at the University of Grenoble; minister in the Vichy government (1940-1941).

249. TO TEIXEIRA DE PASCOAES, 24 MAY 1934: From *Epistolario Iberico, Cartas de Pascoaes e Unamuno* (Nova Lisboa [Angola], 1957), p. 56. For Teixeira, see note above, to p. 197.

250. TO MATILDA BRANDAU DE ROSS, 22 DEC. 1934: From Fernandez Larraín, pp. 402-403.

251. *first my sister died*: María Unamuno, Unamuno's older sister, went to live with him and his family upon the death of their mother in 1908. She died in 1932.

My widowed son-in-law is going to marry my other daughter: this marriage of Unamuno's son-in-law, José María Quiroga Plá, never took place.

the poor little thing: Salomé, Unamuno's fourth child and first daughter, was slightly crippled from childhood on; she died on 14 July 1933.

the national tribute paid to me: Spanish law provided that Unamuno had to resign from the University of Salamanca in 1934, at seventy years of age. The academic year opened on 30 Sept. with ceremonies in his honor, attended by governmental officials, former students, and representatives of universities from many countries. Alcalá Zamora, the president of the Spanish Republic, issued proclamations naming Unamuno

Lifetime Rector of the University (an honorary title) and establishing a Chair in his name.

Gabriela Mistral: (1889-1956), pseudonym of Lucila Gody Alcayaga, outstanding Chilean poet and teacher; Nobel Prize in Literature, 1945.

252. TO RAMÓN PÉREZ DE AYALA, 17 DEC. 1935: From *OC*, XV, 892-895. *Pérez de Ayala* (1881-1962), famous novelist, essayist, poet, was ambassador of the Spanish Republic to England at the time of this letter's writing.

accepting the offer: The offer was to come to England to give lectures and to receive a doctoral degree *honoris causa* from Oxford. Unamuno went in Feb. of 1936, accompanied by his eldest son, Fernando.

253. *Duhamel [et al.]*: Georges Duhamel (1884-1966), French novelist; Maurice Maeterlinck (1862-1949), Belgian-French playwright, Nobel Prize 1911; François Mauriac (1885-1970), French Catholic novelist and essayist, Nobel Prize 1952; Ernst Robert Curtius (1886-1956), German essayist, scholar, critic; Ramiro de Maeztu (1875-1936), journalist, essayist; Wenceslao Fernández Flórez (1885-1964), essayist, novelist, humorist.

254. *keeps me . . . Spanish Academy*: On 15 Dec. 1932 Unamuno was elected to the Royal Spanish Academy, but never took his seat, which requires an inaugural address.

Baroja: Pío Baroja (1872-1956), one of the most important novelists of the twentieth century. He entered the Spanish Academy in 1935.

255. *Crawford Flitch*: J. E. Crawford Flitch, pioneering English translator of Unamuno, whose translations have guided others in their craft. See translator's foreword to vol. 4 of the present edn., p. xxv.

255. TO GUILLERNO DE TORRE, 7 JAN. 1936: From *OC*, XV, 924-926. *Guillermo de Torre* (1900-1973),

born in Madrid, resided in Argentina from 1927 to 1932, and married Borges' sister Norah in 1937. Famous critic.

cor-dial: coming from the heart.

Ahora: a Madrid newspaper to which Unamuno contributed.

Sur: a highly regarded review founded in Buenos Aires by the Argentine writer and publisher Victoria Ocampo (1891-1979).

256. *my son-in-law*: José María Quiroga Plá, married Unamuno's daughter Salomé (1897-1933), who gave him his first grandchild, Miguelito, born in 1929.

Norah: Norah Borges de Torre, sister of Jorge Luis Borges, wife of the recipient of this letter.

256. TO ENRIQUE DÍEZ-CANEDO, 10 APR. 1936: From *OC*, XV, 867-869. Díez-Canedo (1879-1944), a poet, translator, and critic, was Spanish ambassador to the Republic of Argentina.

doctorate . . . from Oxford: cf. above, n. to p. 252.

257. *Raquel Encadenada* (1921): a play.

258. TO RAMÓN CASTAÑEYRA SCHAMAN, 22 APR. 1936: From Sebastián de la Nuez, *Unamuno en Canarias* (Santa Cruz de Tenerife, 1964), pp. 289-291. Nothing is known about Castañeyra Schaman, the recipient of this letter, who was then in Fuerteventura.

259. *C.N.T.*: Confederacion Nacional de Trabajo, an anarchist labor union.

260. *Soriano*: Rodrigo Soriano (1871-1944), Republican politician and writer, also deported by Primo de Rivera, was with Unamuno in Fuerteventura. They had a serious falling-out; cf. *Unamuno en Canarias*, p. 285.

EPILOGUE: UNAMUNO'S LAST LECTURE

From *Horizon* (London), Vol. IV, no. 24 (Dec. 1941), 394-400; reprinted in Robert Payne, ed., *The Civil*

War in Spain (New York, 1962). Luis Portillo, the author of "Unamuno's Last Lecture," was a young professor of civil law at the University of Salamanca at the time of Unamuno's open defiance of the Spanish Nationalists in 1936. Soon afterward he left Spain and found refuge in England. He remained there, working as a translator and information officer for the BBC, until the passing of Franco. He now divides his time between Salamanca and London. His essay on Unamuno's last lecture was brought to the attention of Cyril Connolly for publication in *Horizon* by Ilsa Barea, who translated it into English. Mrs. Barea also translated her husband Arturo Barea's famous autobiographical novel, *The Forging of a Rebel* (London, 1943, 1946; new edn., New York, 1972).

263. *Spanish Fascism . . . in its first triumphant stage*: The Civil War had begun in July 1936, when General Francisco Franco led an army revolt in Morocco. By October, the Insurgents controlled a large part of Spain, including the province of Salamanca.

265. *Millán Astray*: General José Millán Astray (1879-1954), founder in 1920 of the Spanish Foreign Legion, or "El Tercio."

267. *"Spain! . . . One!"*: *"España Una, Grande, y Libre*—'Spain One, Great, and Free'—is the obligatory Falangist slogan, which is converted on all solemn occasions into chorused responses to a leading voice, as in the following scene" (footnote in *Horizon*).

270. *"Muera la Inteligencia!"*: The Spanish is ambiguous, meaning both "Death to intellectuals" and "Death to the intellect."

Index

341

Index

Index

101, 214
Calvin, John, 159
Calzada, 54 & *n*
Camöens, Luis de, 241 & *n*
Campión, Federico Balart, 134
  & *n*, 141*n*; writing, 145
Campoamor, Ramón de, 146
  & *n*
Canalejas, José, 204*f* & *n*, 206
Cancionero (M. de U.), 242 & *n*
Canillas, 53 & *n*
Cañizo, Augustín del, 203
Cano, Melchor, 208 & *n*
Cántico (Guillén), 241 & *n*
capitalism, 114, 116
Caras y Caretas, 192
cardiac writers, 3*n*
Carducci, Giosuè, 221*n*
Carlist War, 40*n*, 87*f* & *n*
Carlists, 40 & *n*, 89, 112, 213*n*,
  226 & *n*
Carlyle, Thomas, xi, 76 & *n*,
  157*f* & *n*, 164*f*
Carret, Juan, *see* Urales, Fede-
  rico
Cassou, Jean, 237*n*, 243 & *n*
Castañeyra Schaman, Ramón,
  258*ff* & *n*
Castejon sisters, 97
Catalan separatism, xxvi, 103
  137, 161*f* & *n*, 205, 266;
  Unamuno's attitude towards,
  182*n*, 183*f*
Catecheses (St. Cyril), 79 & *n*
Catherine of Siena, St., 73
Catholicism: ascetism in, 162*f*;
  communion, 119; de-Christianization of, 130, 172*f*,
  182*n*; mass in, 119; national
  aspects, 186*f*, 207; Protestantism and, 25*f*; rationalism, 53;
  salvation in, 70*f*; vanities of, 5
celibacy, 95
Cervantes, Miguel de, 214, 232
  & *n*
Chabásy Martí, Don Juan, 229
  & *n*

charity: acts of, 8; salvation and,
  47; self-love and, 22
Charles V, 233*n*
chastity as virtue, 32
Chávarri, (?), 111
Chevalier, Jacques, 247*ff* & *n*
*Chief Works of Benedict de Spi-
  noza*, 4*n*
childhood: development in,
  112*f*; habits of, 7, 63; remembrance of, 60*ff*
children: Unamuno and, 93*f*;
  work and, 95
children's literature, 93*f*
Chile, 191*n*, 218, 236
Christ: divinity of, 149*ff*; hope
  of, 41; humanity of, 61*f*, 72*f*;
  pain of, 71; passion of, 71, 79;
  perfection of, 131; resurrection of, 58*f*; Samaritans and,
  74*f*; teachings of, 73; in temple, 29
Christ of Velázquez, The (M. de
  U.), xxi, 219
Christianity: ascetism in, 162;
  civilization and, 129*f*; forms
  of, 121; Hellenic philosophy
  and, 76*f*; immortality and, 59;
  Kierkegaard on, xxii; purity
  of, 32; society, 129*ff*; women
  in, 221
Church: attendance in, 35*f*;
  Christ in, 61*f*; life of, 11;
  meaning of salvation in, 70;
  ministers, 62; rituals in, 62*f*;
  tradition in, 25
Ciencia Social, La (M. de U.),
  166 & *n*
Cierva y Peñafiel, Juan de la,
  205 & *n*, 253
civilization, Christianity and,
  130
Clarín, *see* Alas, Leopoldo
Clarté manifesto (Barbusse), 225
  & *n*
class struggle, 116*ff*
Cohen, Hermann, 206 & *n*

343

Index

Index

Index

Index

history, 74; philosophy of, 15*f*
History of Dogma (Harnack), 58
& *n*, 149
History of Materialism (Lange),
109 & *n*
History of the French Revolution
(Carlyle), 76*n*, 157*f*
Hölderlin, Friedrich, 109 & *n*
Hölle, Dr., 209
Holtzmann, (?), 80
Homer, 4, 43 & *n*
Horizontes (Campión), 141 & *n*
How a Novel Is Made (Zubiza-
rreta), xxiv
How to Make a Novel (M. de
U.), 243
House of Austria (Spanish
Hapsburgs), 233 & *n*
Hugo, Victor, 152
Huguenots, 186
humanity: charity to, 47*ff*; so-
cialism and, 120
humiliation, 66
humility, 61; birth and, 78; of
Christ, 72*f*; purification of,
73*f*; wisdom of simple, 5
hypochondria, 185

I: concept of, 23; nihilism and,
26; nothingness of, 55; slavery
to, 45; universality of, 81
I-ism, 64*f*
Ibsen, Henrik, 109*f*, 165 & *n*
idealism, 42
Idearium español (Ganivet),
133*n*, 187*n*
ideas versus existence, ix*f*
ideocracy, 147
ideophobia, 147*n*
Ignatius of Loyola, St., 161 &
n, 232 & *n*
Il corriere della sera, 229
illness, as escape, 36. *See also*
hyponchondria
*Illustración española y ameri-
cana, La*, 154

Illustration français, L', 245
imagination, deception of, 67*f*
Imitation of Christ, 7 & *n*, 16,
28 & *n*, 33*n*, 38 & *n*; Gardiner edition, 76 & *n*; Granada
translation, 35*n*
immortality: Christianity and,
xix, 59; consolidation of, 67;
death and, xvii*ff*; faith and, 9;
happiness and, 48; of heroes,
35; intensity of, 33; letters
and, 65*f*; material, socialism
and, 123; Unamuno obsession
with, 8 & *n*
*Imparcial, El, see Lunes de El
Imparcial, Los*
indecision, 37*f*
individualism, 115
infinità vanità del tutto, L',
(Leopardi), 183 & *n*
in-me-myself-ism, 65 & *n*
*In Prison under the Russian Ter-
ror* (Nadeau), 225 & *n*
Integralists, 40 & *n*
intellectualism, 42, 57*f* & *n*,
122, 137*ff*, 155, 270; blindness and, 39; faith and, 52;
feeling and, 13; goals of, 71;
lust for, 75*f*; science and, 49;
socialism and, 116; terrible-
ness of, 36; versus faith, 69;
versus meditation, 104; versus
spirituality, 127
Intelligenti pauca, 209 & *n*
interconnectedness of life, 17
internal life, 41
intrahistoria, 6*f* & *n*
Irurac-bat, 86 & *n*
Iquique, 220 & *n*
Isabella II, 96*n*
Italy, 193, 196*f*, 212*ff* & *n*,
222, 228*f*

Jacobinism, 150, 201
Jaizquíbel, 234 & *n*
James, William, 146, 164 & *n*

Index

349

Index

Lloyd George, David, 204, 206
logic, slavery to, 51
Logic (Croce), 206 & *n*
Logic (Hegel), 103
Logic of Pure Knowledge
    (Cohen), 206 & *n*
love: illusion of, 94, 97; mystery
    of, 27
Loyola, *see* Ignatius of Loyola,
    St.
Lucha de Clases, La, 65 & *n*,
    113*f* & *n*
Luchana (Galdós), 145 & *n*
Lunes de El Imparcial, Los, 132*f*
    & *n*, 145*f* & *n*, 154, 179*ff*,
    182*n* 183
Lusitania (ship), 213
Luque, Augustín (General), 177
    & *n*

Machado, Manuel, 168 & *n*
Machado y Ruiz, Antonio, xxv,
    168*ff* & *n*
madness, 35
Madruga, Don Esteban, 270*f*
Maese Pedro (*Don Quixote* char-
    acter), 157*f* & *n*, 230
maestra normal, La (Gálvez),
    236 & *n*
Maeterlinck, Maurice, 166 & *n*,
    253 & *n*
Maeztu, Ramiro de, 134 & *n*,
    145, 158 & *n*, 227, 253 & *n*
Magnificat, 24
Malaga, 161
Maldonado, Don Francisco, 264
mankind: cultural progress, 47;
    defined, 46
Maragall, Juan, 182*ff* & *n*,
    184*ff*
Marañón, Gregorio, 227*f* & *n*
Maria Cristina (Queen Mother),
    96*n*, 224 & *n*
Marillier, Henry Currie, 146
Maritain, Jacques, 237 & *n*
marriage: purpose of, 94*f*; work

and, 94*f*
Martín Fierro (Hernández), 108
Martínez Anido, General Severi-
    ano, 226*f* & *n*, 230, 234
Martínez Ruiz, José, 141 & *n*
Marua, 201*f*
Marx, Karl, 110, 114
Mary Magdalen, 24
Mary, Virgin: ascent to God,
    24; cult of, 11*f*; focus of faith,
    28; grace in, 27
Mass, attraction of, 63
mathematics, 100, 127, 244
matter, perpetual change of, 55
Maura, Antonio, 182*n*, 184,
    200*n*, 205
Mauriac, François, 253 & *n*
Mazzini, 221*n*
mechanics, 100
meditation, versus intellectual-
    ism, 71*f*, 104
Meditations on Quixote (Ortega y
    Gasset), 211 & *n*
Melilla, 200*n*
Memoirs of Childhood and Youth
    (*Recuerdos de niñez y de moce-
    dad*) (M. de U.), xi, 7*n*,
    102*n*, 191*f* & *n*, 195, 209
memory: death and, 39; immor-
    tality and, 9; loss of, 69
Mendine, F., 103
Menegoz, Eugène, 165 & *n*
Menéndez y Pelayo, Marcelino,
    119 & *n*, 136, 142 & *n*, 218,
    226 & *n*
Mercier, Abbé, 146
Mercure de France, 141 & *n*,
    155 & *n*
Messianic currents, 77
Mestizos, 40 & *n*
method versus solution, 100*f*
Metternich, Clemens Lothar
    Wenzel, Furst von, 215*n*
*Miguel de Unamuno: The Rheto-
    ric of Existence* (Lacy), ix*n*
militarism, 177

Index

Index

352

Index

Index

Romanones, Alvaro de Figueroa y de Torres, Conde de, 224 & *n*

Ross, Luis, xxvi, 191 & *n*, 193*f*, 218*f*, 236

Rousseau, Jean-Jacques, 186

Royal Gander, *see* Alphonso XIII

Royal Spanish Academy, 254 & *n*

Ruiz, José Martínez, 57 & *n*

Sabatier, Auguste, 149 & *n*, 165 & *n*, 186

Sabatier, Paul, 165 & *n*, 186

Sacchi, Filippo, 229

"Saint Manuel Bueno, Martyr, and Three More Stories" (M. de U.), 250

saintliness, versus wisdom, 59

"St. Paul on the Areopagus" (M. de U.), xx, 129*n*, 131

saints, recognition of, 62

Salamanca, Unamuno description of, 117

Salamanca University: M. de U. appointed professor, xiii*f*; M. de U. as professor of Greek, xiii*f*, 98*ff*, 118*n*; M. de U. as rector, 153*ff*; M. de U. dismissal as rector, 210*f* & *n*, 216*ff* & *n*; M. de U. lifetime rectorship, 251*f* & *n*; M. de U. reinstatement, 246

Salandra, Antonio, 212 & *n*

Salcedo, Emilio, xxvi & *n*

salvation, 123; charity and, 47; in Church, 70; versus health, 157 & *n*; salvation, 123

Samaritans, 74*f*

Samson Carrascos, 230 & *n*

Sánchez Barbudo, Antonio, xxiii

Sánchez Moguel, Don Antonio, 241 & *n*

Santiago Alba, 226 & *n*

"São Paulo" (Teixeiro de Pas-

coaes), 249*f*

Schadenfreude, 214 & *n*

Schiller, Johann Christoph Friedrich, 125

Schleiermacher, Friedrich, 125, 160, 165 & *n*

Schmidt, Johan Kaspar, 26 & *n*

Scholasticism, 99, 215

Schopenhauer, Arthur, xii, 47, 77, 103, 123, 125, 146*f*, 164*f*, 214; M. de U. translation of, 138 & *n*

science, xiii, 99*f*, 151, 179, 182, 200, 216; art of, 104; intellectualism and, 49; religion and, 155*f*

sectarianism, 5*f*, 165*f*

sects, 70*f*

Sein-zum-Tode (being-towards-death), xvii

self: awareness of, 21*f*; fleeing from, 21*ff*; internal versus external, 128; knowledge of, 3*f*, 22*f*; love of, 22; reality of, 41

self-centeredness, 36; conversation and, 14

self-indulgence, 65

self-knowledge, 76

self-love, 65

self-satisfaction, 3

"semana tragica, la," 200*n*

Sénancour, Etiennne Pivert de, 3*n*

Senhora da Noite (Teixeira de Pascoaes), 197*f* & *n*

sentimentalism, 42, 78

Sermon on the Mount, 129

Shakespeare, William, 140

Shelley, Percy Bysshe, 109

Sienkiewicz, Petronius, 156 & *n*

Silvela, Francisco, 227 & *n*

Simarro, Luis, 205 & *n*

simplicity, 10, 30; of time, 53

sin: faith and, 13; infinitude of, 17*f*; retroactive action of, 29

354

Index

Index

Index

Index

Library of Congress Cataloging in Publication Data

Unamuno, Miguel de, 1864-1936.
  The private world.

  (Bollingen series ; 85) (Selected works of
Miguel de Unamuno ; v. 2)
  Includes bibliographical references and index.
  1. Unamuno, Miguel de, 1864-1936—Diaries.
  2. Unamuno, Miguel de, 1864-1936—Religion and ethics.
  3. Unamuno, Miguel de, 1864-1936—Correspondence.
  4. Authors, Spanish—20th century—Biography. I. Title.
  II. Series. III. Series: Unamuno, Miguel de, 1864-1936.
  Selections. English. 1967 ; v. 2.
  PQ6639.N3A25 vol. 2   868'.6209 s   83-43054
  ISBN 0-691-09927-8   [868'.6209]